Practising Critical Reflection
A Resource Handbook

Practising Critical Reflection
A Resource Handbook

Jan Fook and Fiona Gardner

 Open University Press

Open University Press
McGraw-Hill Education
McGraw-Hill House
Shoppenhangers Road
Maidenhead
Berkshire
England
SL6 2QL

email: enquiries@openup.co.uk
world wide web: www.openup.co.uk

and Two Penn Plaza, New York, NY 10121-2289, USA

First published 2007

A catalogue record of this book is available from the British Library

ISBN-13 978 0335 221707 (pb)   978 0335 221714 (hb)

Library of Congress Cataloging-in-Publication Data
CIP data applied for

Typeset by RefineCatch Limited, Bungay, Suffolk
Printed in Poland by OZGraf S.A.
www.polskabook.pl

The *McGraw·Hill* Companies

Contents

Preface

You might say that we came to critical reflection in a relatively 'natural' way, perhaps the way it should be approached. Our practise of it largely preceded our theorizing of it. Once we had become familiar with the initial idea, in some ways it felt much easier to do it and use it, than it was to read, write, research and think about it. And in some ways this felt 'natural'. It offered us a fresh way of engaging students at all levels. It was also a process that, in many ways, felt like it 'took over', rapidly developing into a complex and uncertain, but strangely satisfying, dialogue between collegiate learning professionals. Classes and groups engaging in critical reflection took us on exciting walks, full of dark alleys, bright lights, shadowy mazes, enticing doorways and thorny bushes. It was a welcome challenge to constantly renegotiate our roles as teachers, facilitators and fellow learners, not always knowing whether the dark alleys or the bright lights would induce better learning, and not always being sure of our responsibilities to guide learners through the maze or open doors, or confront them with the thorny bush.

One thing however has been clear from our experience in teaching critical reflection: the majority of students love the process. They seem to learn about relatively fundamental perspectives in a very contracted period of time, and speak of feeling 'liberated', despite the uncertainties. These of course are very welcome responses for us as teachers, and it is tempting to attribute these positive outcomes to our own skill as teachers. However, we are sceptical enough to believe that there are too many factors operating to be so smug about our own abilities. In all honesty we are highly aware that we cannot be certain what it is about the critical reflection process that induces positive changes, or indeed what it is that does not work for some people. Yet if the process does work, it is vital that there be an attempt to document what happens, in order to expose it to further scrutiny and development. Above all we would like to hope that we can replicate the process and positive outcomes with some degree of certainty. The time has obviously come for us to more clearly theorize the process. This book is therefore our attempt to contribute to some of the systematic documentation that is needed to better understand the learning and changes involved in critical reflection.

We are of course well aware that many other people have documented some highly engaging and thoughtful models of critical reflection, and we will of course be referring to these throughout our book. We are highly indebted to our colleagues, from across the globe and from various professional backgrounds, who have contributed a wealth of fascinating literature in this equally fascinating field. What we found, however, in perusing this extensive body of material, was that there did not appear to be any other models that are similar enough to our own to allow us to use this material to better theorize our own model in a way we found meaningful. This is not meant as a criticism of existing literature and practice in critical reflection; on the contrary, we have learnt much about different ways to practise critical reflection, and much about some of the complexities involved. What it does indicate, we believe, is that there is room and need for many different ways of understanding, theorizing and practising critical reflection. This book is our attempt to document our particular model.

Since those early days of teaching critical reflection in social work courses, we have spent the last few years developing a model for interdisciplinary use in continuing professional education. Our participants have mostly included people from the health and human services sectors, who have come from a variety of professional backgrounds and worked in a variety of roles as educators, managers, direct service workers, policy makers and researchers. We have conducted short courses in critical reflection both at our specialized Centre for Professional Development (at La Trobe University, Victoria, Australia) and also at the request of particular organizations throughout the world, as part of their staff development programmes. We have used the process for professional supervision, programme review and practice research. We estimate that over 500 people have undertaken our critical reflection training in the last few years, and this is continuing as we write this. We have increasingly been asked to train educators as facilitators in the use of the model, and have found that other than having people participate in a full training programme whereby they themselves learn to critically reflect, it is extraordinarily difficult to represent what it is we do, and what happens, in the process. This book is therefore an attempt to document the process in some detail for colleagues who may wish to use it.

When we speak of colleagues we mean this in the broadest sense possible. We regard as our colleagues anyone who is interested in the learning or teaching of critical reflection. These may be people who are totally new to the idea and process, or they may be people who are long experienced, and have developed their own models and processes. While this may seem like a tall order, we believe that the process, and the educational philosophy that underpins it, lends itself so well to such a diversity of learning situations that it would be selling it short to confine its application. We also firmly believe that one of the ways forward in further development of critical reflection is to contribute to cross-disciplinary dialogue and fertilization.

In this spirit we have tried to present the content in a way that is cross-disciplinary and accessible, but theorized in relative depth. Our intention is to describe very basic and concrete practices, but also to include the reasoning and appropriate theorization of these where possible. Not only should this satisfy a range of audiences, but also it will assist readers in thinking through their own rationales for particular practices. In this sense we intend what we present to be illustrative of our thinking and practices, rather than an argument or prescription about the way critical reflection ought to be practised. Contrary to this view, our firm belief is that critical reflection is something that must, and can, be practised in a variety of ways, to suit the social setting, purpose and characteristics of learners and facilitators. To this end we have decided that the best way to present our model is to do so in some detail, so that readers will be able to think through these intricacies for themselves, and make their own choices about how they will apply the material. We have tried to assist in this by presenting the model in a relatively generic form, and also discussing ways in which it might be modified to suit different circumstances.

We have also decided on this approach as, in our experience, we have found it extraordinarily difficult to represent the process faithfully without resorting to extensive detail, description and examples. These are the sorts of very concrete details that have been requested from colleagues in wanting to know more of our model. We have decided to take this approach – of presenting one model in some detail, as opposed to presenting a broad theoretical approach and suggesting particular tools that might be used – for the following reasons.

- Presenting the one model in some depth should provide a better understanding of the complexities of the learning process.
- This depth should allow for more complex application of the model in different settings.
- We have found that one of the major difficulties of critical reflection is not so much the understanding of the approach, but the facilitation of it in practice: the juggling of different issues that arise; the handling of complex emotions and experiences; the balancing of challenge with support; the multiple roles of teacher, colleague and fellow learner. From this point of view, our understanding of critical reflection feels like it has to start with the practise of it, and only in that way will there be some appreciation of the totality of the experience.

To these ends we have also supplied extensive web-based resources on the website that accompanies the book – www.openup.co.uk/fook&gardner – which illustrate the learning process in a variety of ways. We have also included examples of different exercises and questions, as well as examples of key pieces of literature. In short, the book should provide all the material a person might need to present and facilitate a programme of critical reflection. Details, of course, may need to be modified or added according to the particular setting in which it is undertaken.

Overview of the book

The book is divided into three main sections: the theory and contexts of critical reflection; the process; and applications. In the first section we overview the current social and political contexts that give rise to the need for critical reflection in professional learning, and review the major historical theoretical roots of critical reflection. From this we draw up our own theoretical framework for critical reflection, which provides the framework on which we base our model.

In the second section we focus in detail on the model itself. This includes a description of the process from the very first decision to set up a critical reflection group, an overview of the broad structure and process, and then details of the three specific stages involved.

The last section focuses on applications of the model. This includes a discussion of the issues and themes that are likely to arise as well as benefits and outcomes that are evident from more systematic study of participants' responses. The book concludes with three chapters that outline specific uses of the model in organizations, for research purposes and for direct service work.

We provide illustrative examples throughout from our own groups, refer to relevant literature, provide annotated bibliographies, and note where resource materials provide further illustration. Further DVD material is available by contacting the authors. The DVD material referred to on the accompanying website is particularly useful in getting a feel for the interactive dialogue involved in the critical reflection process.

Acknowledgements

There are many people we wish to thank, not only for assistance in writing this book, but for their own participation in our learning.

Geraldene Mackay has acted as research assistant throughout the last few years and is responsible for keeping us in touch with the huge array of literature necessary. Mundy Fox has been administrative officer at the Centre for Professional Development at La Trobe University, where our experience over the last few years has taken place. Our postgraduate students – Helen Hickson, Belinda Hearne and Lynne Allan – have patiently helped *us* learn by responding to our repeated inquiries about what helped *them* learn! They have all generously allowed their assignments to be reproduced in the resource materials, and for us to analyse them in an effort to understand the change process. Our colleagues, Rikki Savaya and Julie Cwikel, more than generously agreed to let us film a workshop with them. Finally, there are numerous colleagues who have participated in our workshops and who have consented for quotes of theirs to be used. We thank you all warmly, not only for what we have learnt from you, but also for modelling that risk of vulnerability and trust upon which the success of critical reflection depends.

PART I

The Theory and Contexts of Critical Reflection

1 The context for professionals

This chapter provides the context for using critical reflection in organizations through identifying the:

- common issues faced by those working in human service organizations, including
  - a sense of powerlessness linked to uncertainty
  - fear of risk
  - increased complexity
- organizational responses to these, which create further stress, including
  - pressure to work to rules and procedures
  - generating paperwork
  - focus on the parts rather than the whole
  - focus on outcomes.

It also identifies the resulting issues for practitioners:

- the tensions between value-based professional practice and economically and technically focused organizations, and
- the need to find ways to continually develop knowledge and practice that fit with this changing and complex context.

Finally, it begins to explore how critical reflection is relevant and helpful in managing these issues, and the implications for practice.

Why are participants interested in critical reflection? Often, they say that they are wrestling with how to manage the experience of working in human service organizations. Many find their direct work relatively manageable, but struggle more with the nature of the organization they work in. Some say they need new ways of making sense of practice; their current theory base is not adequate for processing the dilemmas and issues they face. In critical reflection workshops, we begin by setting the context for critical reflection with a brief exploration of current issues for workers and human service organizations. Participants generally contribute specific examples from their own practice, which deepens this exploration.

This chapter reflects this beginning and provides a more detailed outline of what participants perceive as current issues. Some of these reflect broader social issues, particularly a pervading sense of uncertainty and concern about risk, which is manifested in specific ways in organizations. Some issues identified by participants are about how human service organizations respond to these – by, for example, generating rules and procedures to minimize or contain risk or a focus on narrow service delivery. These issues can be expressed in various ways and we have used the language of workshop participants to name them here.

A sense of powerlessness: uncertainty and human service organizations

Feeling powerless is one of the issues most frequently mentioned by participants. This often seems to connect with a sense of uncertainty and unpredictability. A common example from participants is 'managers make decisions on your behalf that you haven't been consulted about and aren't happy with'. Beck (1992: 33) talks about uncertainty generating a sense of powerlessness combined with a lack of personal responsibility. Participants identify with this, suggesting that a sense of uncertainty permeates practice so that they assume change is not possible even within their sphere of influence. For some workers, this view is strengthened by the political nature of working in human services organizations: a change in policy or a restructure is likely to be dictated by political change rather than client-centred initiatives. This feels too distant for workers to influence and they can then feel they are passive recipients of new directions.

To some extent, participants see a degree of uncertainty as desirable, they affirm this as part of their work; they have often chosen to work in people-related jobs because they can expect unpredictability. However, this was previously within a context of greater certainty: professionals had a greater sense of confidence about their professional status, had long-term job stability and expected to be supported in decisions they had made (Beck 1992). They felt more able to influence what was happening around them.

Perhaps more importantly, participants suggest there was more shared understanding of 'how things worked' or what was important. Pellizoni (2003) uses the term 'radical uncertainty' to identify situations where knowledge may be interpreted in different ways in relation to problems whose underlying premises are not clearly identified. Participants say they may perceive what is important in a situation in fundamentally different ways from a colleague or manager. Related to this, Barnett uses the term 'supercomplexity', where workers and organizations have to deal with what they experience as conflicting frameworks – for example, a counsellor might also be a coordinator of services, a doctor expected to offer counselling (Barnett 1999). Again this contributes a sense of uncertainty: what will I be expected to do next? Who will be directing me and will I be able to influence them?

Myra had been working as a child protection worker for 12 months. Somewhat to her surprise, she found her work with clients very satisfying. However, she described herself as increasingly disillusioned with the organization and its lack of responsiveness to clients and to herself as a worker. She and her partner were on a tight budget and it took six months before she was being paid the level agreed at her interview. This fitted with her experience of seeking resources for clients, and trying to assert the need for change meant she was seen as a troublemaker. She had decided that she was powerless in the organization; she would just focus on her work with clients and survive as best she could. The critical reflection process enabled her to affirm her values of high-quality services for clients and to start to seek ways she could bring about change.

Fear of risk

How risk is experienced varies for participants, but again is a major theme. This is often related to fear of the consequences of making the 'wrong' decision (Banks 2002; Gibbs 2002) or of allowing something to 'go wrong'. There is a 'ubiquity of risk awareness and risk management in the life of modern organizations and in the consciousness of workers and managers alike' (Cooper and Darlington 2004). Workers talk about risk assessment in relation to client work, supervisors about risk in terms of workers' actions; the organization is likely to have a risk management plan aimed at preventing anything going wrong. This partly comes from fear of negative media coverage (Taylor and White 2000: 3); as one participant said, 'How do you stop yourself from feeling guilty at not doing something because of fear of negative publicity?'

The pressure – both internal and external – to be a perfect worker is another aspect participants identify as part of risk. Participants often have high expectations, matching those of the organization. They are reluctant to risk 'failure'. This focus on risk and expectations of perfection creates particular problems for them in their organization. This desire to always have things go well is an unrealistic expectation in what Schon (1983) called the 'messy swamps' of practice. This is partly about looking for the 'right answer' rather than acknowledging that in professional work there are no absolutely right answers.

It also results from a sense of confusion between what Banks calls the 'technical rational' and 'moral' realms; for example, when an action is seen as right when the outcome is right – which can be clear only in hindsight (Banks 2001). For workers this creates a sense of incongruence between their core values and their actions. Are they judged to be 'good' practitioners only when their actions fit desired outcomes in spite of working in a complex and highly uncertain environment? This links to another question often raised by participants: Will I be supported? What will happen to me if things do go wrong?

Mark talked about an incident where he had visited a client for the first time after a worker left. On the way, he thought about how the previous worker described the client: her aggressive, possibly dangerous, attitude; her resentment of social workers and unwillingness to cooperate. When he arrived, Mark was alarmed by his cold and formal approach to the client, who did react negatively. He tried to retrieve the situation by explaining more about what the organization could offer but, in the end, it was clear that it was too late. Mark was concerned that he had created the situation he wanted to avoid because of his fear of what might happen.

Increased complexity

Participants often talk about the increasingly complex work they are expected to undertake. This is often for structural rather than organizational reasons:

- family structures are now more complicated, with blended families of many different kinds
- more individuals with disabilities are now supported in families and/ or communities
- greater migration and movement of refugees means greater variety of cultural backgrounds
- clients more often express anger and a sense of alienation from society in reaction to social exclusion
- complex and rapidly changing service systems are often challenging for workers and clients alike to understand.

While complexity and diversity can be, and generally are, also perceived positively, they present challenges to organizations and to workers. Participants say they do not always feel adequately trained to deal with this, particularly in a context of uncertainty and fear of risk.

Organizational responses to uncertainty, risk and complexity

How, then, do organizations and individuals respond to this context? Participants suggest that organizational responses fall into four categories, as described below.

Working to rules and procedures

Participants suggest that their organizations often respond to issues of uncertainty and risk by trying to create certainty in the form of rules and procedures. The current focus on managerialism requires this to some degree: workers are expected to work in regulated ways in order to maximize efficiency and ensure uniform and measurable outcomes, to manage the 'messy and complicated business' of practice (Taylor and White 2000). Participants have mixed feelings about this: some, particularly new workers, seek clear answers and direction, they would prefer to be told what to do; others see increased numbers of policy and procedure manuals as a way of managing the anxiety generated by human service work, a way of trying to increase predictability in a situation where this is not really possible. The response to child deaths, for example, is often to develop more policies and guidelines to control worker behaviour and so reduce risk (Gibbs 2002). Participants more often say, however, that this reinforces their feeling devalued, and their professional judgement or discretion is lessened, some would say minimized.

Generating paperwork

Another example of organizational response that affects participants is the amount of paperwork generated. In some organizations, they suggest, it can feel as if the focus is on getting the paperwork done rather than focusing on the clients. Jones (2001: 553), for example, in talking about social workers employed by government departments in Britain, says that 'the contact [with clients] is more fleeting, more regulated and governed by the demands of the forms which now shape much of the intervention'. One of the main reasons people gave for leaving the public service in Britain was the 'sense of being overwhelmed by bureaucracy and paperwork' (Firth 2005). Participants confirm that this again reinforces their feeling devalued as professionals, and contributes to a sense of powerlessness.

Focus on the parts rather than the whole: narrowing or limiting service delivery

Participants suggest that organizations and their funding bodies also aim to control work and increase accountability by breaking it into what are seen as defined and manageable work areas. Participants experience this as frustrating; there is pressure to work in narrowly focused service delivery – working with an aspect of a person and their situation rather than being able to work in a more holistic way (Gardner 2006). Workers often comment on the impact of 'silos': government departments, each concentrating on its mandated area rather than having a broader awareness and ability to work with the interaction between departments. Within organizations, services are often delivered according to narrow funding guidelines so that the focus is on a target problem, rather than an individual or family as a whole. Examples participants give are prolific: a practitioner might be frustrated by the standardized and limited number of sessions allowed for a client with major sexual abuse issues; a policy maker at having to focus on funding support packages for people with disabilities when housing is clearly a major issue. This connects with the fourth response, a focus on outcomes.

Focus on outcomes

The focus on outcomes at the expense of processes is also a current issue for participants. Their organizations generally talk about this in terms of accountability: demonstrating to funding bodies that the work they have contracted for has been done. One of the issues that participants have with this is that it is easier for organizations to measure quantity rather than quality – how many families have been seen, rather than exploring the quality and complexity of the interaction. It also does not take into account some of the less definable aspects of work in human service organizations or whether the organization is working in the most effective way. For example, it may be relatively slow to build a working relationship with a sexually abused adolescent new to counselling compared with an older woman who has previously experienced counselling and is clear about what she wants to work on. The expectations in terms of time allowed and outcomes may be the same.

A typical dilemma for organizations was experienced at Agency X, which provided alcohol and drug counselling services. Agency workers had identified a lack of housing services in their area, which had a major impact on their clients' ability to remain in control of their alcohol and drug use. Two of the workers wanted to have time allocated to them to carry out a research project to demonstrate the need for housing, which could be used to lobby for funding. The manager and management committee refused the request on the basis that the funding agreement required the agency to see a certain number of clients a year, so all workers needed to remain casework focused.

Where does this leave professionals in organizations?

Participants find these organizational responses often create other tensions for them. The rules and procedures simply don't work for all clients; given the complexity of work, participants need to be able to generate creative possibilities not encouraged in their workplace. Past training has not necessarily provided participants with the processes to recognize and value their own knowledge-making and to generate other ways of operating.

Participants see two main issues for themselves in managing these issues as professionals in their organizations.

1. There is a tension between value-based professional practice and economically and technically focused organizations. Participants see a major dilemma in their ability to express their values as professionals in organizations, saying, for example, 'What do I believe is the right way to go here? If the decision was mine what would I do?' Often, it feels as if their own and their organization's priorities are different, and this creates conflict for them.
2. There is a need for ways to continually develop knowledge and practice that fit with this changing and complex context. Participants have often found that past formal or informal training has not helped them manage the uncertainty and complexity of their current work environment. As Jones (2001) found, the sense of constant change can in turn be stressful and contribute to high turnover. Participants suggest a need for processes that enable them to engage with and manage these issues constructively.

The place of critical reflection

Much has been written about uncertainty and risk in our current culture as well as in organizational life. This suggests workers have to constantly adapt to changing conditions, developing knowledge that is seen as useful and relevant, making and remaking themselves in response to uncertainty (Giddens 1991; Ferguson 2001). The sense of dealing with uncertainty, risk and complexity also permeates recent writing about organizations. The development of the notion of 'the learning organization' or 'organizational learning' is one response to this (Gould and Baldwin 2004). This approach emphasizes the need for workers and organizations to be learning continuously in order to manage change effectively. The learning organization can also provide opportunities for workers to name current stresses, to explore how they fit with core values and the implications for practice.

Critical reflection provides both theory and processes to enable this making and remaking of knowledge to happen. Participants acknowledge that critical reflection provides a framework that enables them to manage these issues more effectively. How this happens will be covered in more detail in the rest of the book, but we will look at it, in brief, now.

First, participants find that critical reflection provides a way of 'standing back' and seeing the issues from a different perspective. They say the theory of critical reflection as well as the process, makes it possible for them to articulate and analyse these issues, particularly identifying what they have assumed about how things are and how they could be. For example, the process encourages participants to name the influence of uncertainty and the complexities of power, including their own assumptions about the place of power, and to see other possible perspectives.

Second, participants articulate the value of knowledge generated from their own experience as practitioners, as well as knowledge from formal or informal training, and how either or both can help generate new knowledge or theory. This validates practitioners' theory-building and provides a process that can be used in practice.

Third, as a result of this exploration, participants are able to be more active in their organizations, expressing their values and challenging organizational expectations with a view to more creative, satisfying and effective practice.

Chapter summary

Professionals currently work in a social environment that is preoccupied with uncertainty, risk and complexity. These permeate human service organizations and are expressed in how professionals relate both to the internal world of the organization and the external world of clients and communities. Organizations often seek to contain uncertainty and risk, and manage complexity by emphasizing rules, increasing paperwork, narrowing service delivery and focusing on outcomes. As a result, practitioners can feel their professional practice is compromised: they are less able to express their professional values. They may also feel that they lack the capacity to manage these challenges and need new frameworks and processes that develop their ability to work creatively with these issues. The chapters that follow explore how critical reflection can provide a way of recognizing and engaging with these issues.

2 Clarifying our approach to critical reflection

The purpose of this chapter is to outline our own approach in broad and preliminary terms. (In this book's accompanying website – www.openup.co.uk/ fook&gardner – we have included more detail about how our approach fits within other disciplines, uses and models of critical reflection; this material will be of particular interest to educators and researchers who wish to develop their own models further.) We hope that readers will be able to fully understand our perspective, but also take their own discerning stance on it, depending on their own perspectives, needs and contexts.

Why do we need to spend substantial time clarifying our approach to critical reflection? Let's begin to answer that by asking another question: is there anyone who isn't critically reflective? At the beginning of our critical reflection programmes we often ask whether there is anyone present who doesn't critically reflect. Funnily enough, we have yet to see a hand go up in answer to this question! Yet we don't seem to have any trouble attracting people to participate in critical reflection training, wanting to find out more about it. It seems that the conundrum of critical reflection is that everyone thinks it should be done, but when it comes down to the detail, many people are not sure specifically what is involved. There is a worrying gap between our theory and practice if you like: in theory we think critical reflection is a good idea, but we do not always support this with the necessary practices. We have indeed heard it said that, although many professional courses require students to be reflective, there is often no literature provided on the topic, or no specific segment of the course that focuses on what is involved. In addition, specific assessment criteria are not always spelt out (Fisher 2003). This can lead to an understandable scepticism about whether reflection actually exists (Ixer 1999). This sort of situation is supported by Issit (1999), who noted that people who say they are critically reflective often haven't read anything recently about it.

On another note, there also seems to be a strong belief that there is no need to spell out the detail of the theory, since everyone knows that critical reflection is just a practice! Another comment we have heard is that everyone knows how to critically reflect, and we all do it, so why do we need to provide specific programmes in it?

These sorts of comments set the scene for what is both so simple and yet so complex about critical reflection. It is bound up in our very assumptions about who we are, and how we ought to be as intelligent human beings. And of course there is a range of perspectives on these issues, including a huge array of 'common sense' and popular views (Moon 1999). On one level, of course, reflection may simply be seen as 'thinking', and may be something that most people feel they do naturally. Yet there are so many different perspectives often assumed in our understanding of what 'thinking' and 'natural' is, that it makes it difficult to sort through what it is, how it might be used and how it is understood. Our own experience, which largely involved developing a practical model for critical reflection before reading and researching in great detail, is also an example of some of the culture that perhaps surrounds critical reflection. There is perhaps a certain safety and comfort in the focus on doing.

In some ways the literature on critical reflection does not help. There is a huge range of literature. It spans many broad fields that do and don't overlap, such as education, professional learning and organizational learning. It also spans different disciplines, which again may or may not overlap, such as social theory (Giddens 1992), management, health professions, social work, allied health, law (Fook *et al.* 2006), economics (Fisher 2003) and industrial relations (Cressey 2006). In addition, to complicate matters, there is a host of related ideas, such as reflective practice (Argyris and Schon 1974; Schon 1983), reflexivity (Taylor and White 2000), action research/learning, experiential learning (Kolb 1974), transformational learning (Mezirow and associates 1990), notions of criticality, critical/emancipatory education and productive reflection (Boud *et al.* 2006). There are also varying views on the origin of the idea, some going back as far as early educationalists such as Socrates and Dewey (1933) and others emphasizing more recent professional learning traditions (Argyris and Schon 1974). Still others are more founded on critical theorists such as Habermas (1984, 1987). Although speaking about 'productive reflection', Cressey (2006: 54) sums up the complexity of the situation, which can also be applied to critical reflection nicely:

> the notion of productive reflection has no central academic core in a singular disciplinary approach but takes a position which crosses accepted academic boundaries. Because of this it is an unsettling concept and the journey leads writers into unfamiliar territories whose correspondence may not at first glance seem obvious. However the growing importance of the issue does seem to be manifest and comes from an observation that similar long term trends or phenomena are being observed from the very different areas . . .

It is this capacity to unsettle, to challenge taken-for-granted disciplinary boundaries, however, that is also the gift of critical reflection. It is potentially an inclusive idea, able to be understood and applied flexibly to suit differing situations, purposes and learners. It is adaptable to different teaching styles and cultural perspectives, and can assist in pointing up alternative meanings not readily apparent through more conventional thinking processes. There is mileage therefore in detailing what is involved, while recognizing that any one representation of critical reflection will represent only one perspective on it.

Developing our approach to critical reflection

We start with a broad-brushstroke picture of our approach to critical reflection, and in subsequent sections of the chapter will provide more detail. Overall our approach is founded on an understanding of the individual in society, and how the surfacing of assumptions held by individual people about their social worlds may ultimately lead to a capacity to change the ways people act in relation to their social contexts. Critical reflection, from our perspective, is therefore a process (and theory) for unearthing individually held social assumptions in order to make changes in the social world. In our approach, then, reflection is more than simply thinking about experience. It involves a deeper look at the premises on which thinking, actions and emotions are based. It is critical when connections are made between these assumptions and the social world as a basis for changed actions.

Let us look at the three main features of this approach:

1. the understanding of the individual in a social context
2. the linking of the theory and practice of critical reflection in the model
3. the importance of linking changed awareness with changed actions.

The individual in their social context: linking individual and society

Our approach is grounded first and foremost in the idea that individual people are social beings whose personal characteristics are formed and reformed in interaction with (and within) different aspects and layers of their social worlds. In this sense, individual people are microcosms of their social environments. Very often, however, these social influences are masked as purely personal features of individual people. This means that people's understanding of themselves as social beings, made in relation to social contexts, is therefore hidden. Critical reflection as we understand it is therefore a process for unearthing these social aspects of individual lives. In order to do this effectively, the process needs to include an appreciation of social influences on personal experiences, and how and why these may become and remain hidden. We will discuss the theory of this in much more detail in the next chapter.

A critical reflection process in the main, then, focuses on the sorts of assumptions people make that reflect their social worlds – that is, its primary focus is on the level at which the individual and society interact (as evidenced in the sorts of assumptions people make). The process is designed to create an environment in which people are enabled to unsettle the major assumptions on which their practice is based, making connections between these assumptions and their beliefs about their social world. Obviously there may be many different sorts of assumptions that fit these categories, so the ways in which the connections between the individual and their social environments are understood and theorized is crucial. Again, we will detail this further on.

Both a theory and a practice process

The second major feature of our approach is that we have developed both a theoretical approach to critical reflection and a practical process for how it may be done. This is important to us, given that many of the criticisms of critical reflection centre on the idea that it does not necessarily lead to any practical changes, or that it is easy to support in theory, but much harder to do. In our approach we very much try to model the idea that if there is a clear theoretical framework, there should also be some clear indications for changed practices that logically follow. Our model therefore consists of some relatively complex theory around different understandings of the ways in which individuals interact with their social worlds, which we then develop into specific methods for reflecting upon the concrete practice experiences of individual professionals.

Linking awareness and action

The last major characteristic of our approach is that we emphasize the immediate connections between the changed awarenesses of assumptions unearthed through the reflective process, and the changed practices that suggest themselves on the basis of these changed awarenesses. In other words, our model is very much one of learning how to develop actions from awareness, and to keep dynamically connecting them. In our experience it is this aspect that participants often find most difficult, and it is often all too easy to find the experience of reflecting so emotionally and intellectually satisfying that it is tempting to leave the process on that high note. Although these changed practices cannot all necessarily be trialled within our formal programmes, in our model we try to set up as many of the other necessary conditions as possible, to enable the indicated changes to be practised in the relevant context.

In summarized terms, then, critical reflection for us is a process of unsettling individual assumptions to bring about social changes. The assumptions may be individually held (and of course may be collectively common as well) but will involve some assumptions about social influences on personal lives. When these are shaken up and examined, they may be remade in ways that lead to changes in the way the individual person practises in, and in relation to, their social contexts.

Summary: critical reflection

'unsettling individual assumptions to bring about social changes'

Emphasizes that:

- reflection is deeper than popular notions of 'thinking'
- critical reflection is based on an understanding of the individual in social context and links between individual and society
- critical reflection is both a *theory* and a *practice*
- critical reflection links changed awareness with changed action.

Unsettling individual assumptions to bring about social changes: details of the approach

In this section we describe in more detail what is involved with different aspects of the critical reflection process. We cover:

- details of the process
- the broad theoretical framework for understanding the individual in their social context
- the purposes of critical reflection
- the professional settings of our model of critical reflection.

The process: unsettling assumptions

What does 'unsettling individual assumptions' mean?

We have chosen the term 'unsettle' deliberately as it implies a 'shaking up' of assumptions. The image that comes to mind is of dice being thrown, with little ability to predict how and even when they will fall, and what face will show. The process is one of shaking up assumptions in order to deliberately surface those that may be hidden for a variety of reasons. The term 'unsettle' is also deliberate as it does not necessarily imply a predetermined framework for evaluating or even placing in a hierarchy the more hidden assumptions that emerge. In this sense, it is important that the assumptions be unsettled in a way that is in fact experienced as unsettling for the individual participant involved. In other words, there needs to be a degree of discomfort or unease in order to motivate learning. *How the process is facilitated, and the learning environment created, are therefore both crucial.* These aspects are vital to our model of critical reflection, and indeed incorporate the important values dimension of our model. We will spend a great deal of the later part of this book discussing the process of critical reflection, the facilitation involved, and the learning culture that is created.

When we speak of individual assumptions, we are referring primarily to assumptions that are held, in the first instance, by individual participants in our programmes. This does not mean that other people in the group may not also hold these assumptions (in fact, in our experience, this is more likely than not). However, our initial focus is on individual practice experience and the assumptions embedded in that. Our beginning point is deliberately the individual, since we are trying to draw out connections between individual experience and social life. Often it becomes apparent of course how these are social, when it is easy to see parallels between the assumptions of different individual participants. At later points in our programme we draw connections between individually held assumptions that may be common to the group or the broader context.

When we speak of assumptions, we are also referring to what we regard as the more fundamental assumptions. These often remain hidden since they are taken for granted, assumed to hold either within a broader social or national culture, or within a more specific professional or organizational subculture. The process of facilitation, the learning environment (and of course the theoretical framework) are also vital in influencing how, and what type of, fundamental assumptions are unearthed. We understand that fundamental assumptions may express themselves in a variety of forms: as beliefs, ideas, values and even theories, which may be explicit (or implicit) to varying degrees.

The theoretical framework: the individual in their social context

When we speak of the theoretical framework here, we mean the framework of beliefs and ideas that underpins our understanding of the links between individually held assumptions and the social world. We are not in the main referring to the wealth of literature and research around learning, or group facilitation for learning. We will refer to aspects of these latter practical theories when we discuss details of the process in later chapters of the book.

Our primary theoretical framework is made up of different types of theories, which seek to explain the various cultural, economic, interactional, structural, historical and political influences in individual lives. Our framework draws primarily on critical social science perspectives, in that we believe the relationship between individual and society to be essentially political – that is, to do with the operation of power in creating and recreating social beings, and in resisting (and transforming) this process. From this point of view, fundamental assumptions tend to be those that are socially dominant – that is, they function to maintain existing power arrangements, and this function may or may not be masked. Nevertheless, we also believe that experience must be approached holistically, and from the perspective of the person whose experience it is. Therefore, we recognize that we need to draw on a range of frameworks that might make this experience meaningful for different individuals in different and similar social contexts. These theories might therefore include:

- theories that focus on the connections between power and knowledge
- an understanding of emotions, and how they are created in social and political contexts
- an appreciation of how the social structure and hierarchy is internalized through ideology and discourse
- a focus on how individuals make meaning of their social worlds
- theories of how specific work cultures are interpreted and maintained by individuals.

In short, our interest is in how individuals participate in their social worlds. Our focus is the intersection of the macro and micro worlds, and in particular how these are played out at micro level. We are therefore interested in the person as individual social agent, both influenced by, but also with the capacity to influence, their social environment.

We therefore incorporate specific concepts like:

- power and its various theorizations
- different ways of knowing
- the self, identity and how difference is created
- the role of language and discourse
- how different cultures and subcultures are made and maintained
- the making of meaning.

In the next chapter we will discuss these in more detail through reference to the relevant literature, and later in the book we will also present this material in the way we would present it to a group of interprofessional participants in one of our critical reflection programmes.

The purpose: bringing about social changes

The idea of 'change' here is both broad and specific. We are specifically using our model of critical reflection to make changes in professional practice, so it is primarily a model for professional learning and development. However, the idea of change is broad in that we are open to what the changes might entail. We are assuming that an initial unearthing of hidden assumptions will provide the opportunity to scrutinize them. This evaluation can lead in many ways: from a simple reaffirmation of them, through a modification, reframing, improvement or drastic reworking. All are changes in one sense. In our experience, since the assumptions unearthed are generally fundamentally important ones, then even a reaffirmation of them can be experienced as a significant change for some participants. Sometimes the change may not be a change of assumption so much as a change in the way it is seen (perhaps a reaffirmation or a different perspective). This, however, often leads to changes in the options for enacting this assumption in practice.

For example, when I [Jan] critically reflect on my experience in a programme, I unearth 'social justice' as a prime value of mine. I choose not to change this, as it is a fundamental value I like. However, what changes for me is that I realize I tend to see it in very dichotomous terms (people are either 'for' or 'against' social justice, there is no middle ground – colleagues are either 'enemies' or 'allies' (Fook 2000)). This often means that when I 'practise' social justice, I tend to polarize everyone else involved, and take the moral high ground. This does not give me many options for action, and tends to end in stalemate.

    The above mentioned article (Fook 2000) is included on this book's accompanying website (www.openup.co.uk/fook&gardner).

Broadly, the change process, in critical terms, is often experienced as 'liberating' in the words of some participants. They are referring here to the experience of being freed from socially restricting beliefs, beliefs that often in turn restricted their ways of being and acting. In critical social science terms, the change is therefore one that involves more individual choice because they are freed from the hidden power of socially imposed views (Fook and Askeland, in press). Later in the book we will describe and analyse in more detail some of the changes participants claim they have made.

    The purpose of our critical reflection model is primarily to lead to changed (improved) professional practice by allowing scrutiny of assumptions and improved capacity to enact desired assumptions. The process may of course be used in many different ways, however, since this specific type of change may be associated with other types of changes as well. For instance, aside from experiencing a type of social liberation, many participants report a great sense of personal development, and are keen to enact changes in their personal lives. Similar outcomes are an important part of other research processes, in that it is the underlying practice theory (assumptions) that are often being unearthed and articulated. Similarly, the change process can also involve a type of ethnography, an unearthing of professional or work cultural beliefs and practices, which might hitherto have remained hidden.

The settings: professional development

As we have made clear, our perspective is that of professional educators; the main purpose of our critical reflection programmes is therefore professional development. However, this may take a wide variety of forms. We work primarily as educators of individual learners who seek development on a voluntary basis. Our model has therefore primarily been used in universities as part of formal undergraduate or postgraduate professional education award programmes or in short continuing education courses. However, we find that there is a call to undertake and use our programme in a variety of other ways. Sometimes the model requires modification to suit these different settings, sometimes it does not. Our model has been used in many specific workplaces at the request of both managers and employees in the following ways: for professional supervision; practice research; practice review; organizational review; team building; learning from error; as part of a broader package to stimulate organizational learning.

Now that we have developed our approach in more detail, it can be summarized in the following way: critical reflection involves the unsettling and examination of fundamental (socially dominant and hidden) individually held assumptions about the social world, in order to enable a reworking of these, and associated actions, for changed professional practice.

On the website that accompanies this book – www.openup.co.uk/fook-&gardner – (in the section entitled 'How does our approach relate to other perspectives on critical reflection?') we discuss in more detail:

- the different fields and disciplines involved (ranging from education and adult education, through management and workplace learning, to professional development); while many interests in the different fields overlap, each also has its particular focus
- related areas and associated terms, including
    - reflection and reflective practice
    - other areas of research and education, like action learning and discourse analysis
    - other terms, like criticality and consciousness-raising

- other models and theories, including
    - reflective practice and the work of Schon
    - learning from experience models
    - transformative learning
    - the work of Brookfield.

Chapter summary

Critical reflection involves the unsettling and examination of fundamental (socially dominant and often hidden) individually held assumptions about the social world, in order to enable a reworking of these, and associated actions, for changed professional practice.

There are four aspects to this:

1. the process – unsettling and examining fundamental assumptions using a facilitated process in a safe learning environment
2. the theoretical framework – the individual in their social context
3. the purpose – bringing about social changes
4. the settings – professional development.

---

3 The theoretical frameworks underlying critical reflection

This chapter covers the theoretical traditions that inform our model:

- reflective practice
- the concept of reflexivity
- postmodernism and deconstruction
- critical social theory.

In order to:

- appreciate the contribution of different theoretical traditions
- equip readers with the tools to further develop their own theoretical understandings
- develop a further appreciation of how theory links with practice.

In Chapter 2, we presented the broad framework of our model of critical reflection. In this chapter we flesh out in more detail the theoretical traditions that underlie and help to frame our model. These frameworks relate both to the learning process involved in the unsettling of assumptions to change practice, as well as to an understanding of the connections between individual lives and social worlds. They include: the reflective approach to theory and practice; the concept of reflexivity; postmodernism and deconstruction; and critical social theory. These frameworks overlap on certain key points, yet they also each make a unique contribution to our understanding of critical reflection. We have therefore chosen to deal with each in some detail, as we believe it is important for people undertaking critical reflection to have an appreciation of the different theoretical traditions. With a reasonable understanding of the differences, similarities and complementarities of these traditions, we are partly hoping to equip critical reflective learners with some of the tools to develop their own theoretical understandings, and partly also to develop an appreciation of how theory links with practice.

Since our perspective is primarily one of educators for professional practice development, we take as our starting point for the process the reflective approach to theory and practice, partly based on the reflective practice framework of Argyris and Schon (1974) and Schon (1983, 1987). This provides a clear framework for understanding the links between theory and practice in professional work, as well as a framework for reworking these links.

We use the concept of reflexivity for two reasons. First, it is often inter-twined in the literature with the notions of reflection, self-reflection and critical reflection (D'Cruz *et al.* 2007). Second, it provides an excellent framework for understanding the influences of the self in social context, especially the links between the different types of knowledge-making and 'research' needed for everyday practice.

Postmodernism and deconstruction are included for several reasons. First, they provide a very useful link between our understandings of power and language, and their operations in everyday experience. Second, they provide a useful perspective for looking again at our assumptions about knowledge and how it is made. This is especially useful in critiquing professional knowledge and its epistemological bases.

Finally, we discuss critical social theory and the basic premises of these approaches, which have a bearing on our beliefs about how individuals are socially created, particularly through the internalization of socially dominant thinking. These approaches also hold valuable ideals regarding the importance of the dynamic interaction between social and individual lives, as well as values regarding communication and dialogue, and how individual and social actions might be linked.

Summary: the four theoretical traditions underpinning critical reflection

1. The reflective approach to theory and practice
2. Reflexivity
3. Postmodernism and deconstruction
4. Critical social theory

The reflective approach to theory and practice

Reflective practice as an idea builds on the notion of reflection on experience, and applies it specifically to learning in the field of professional practice. As such it is specifically a model for reflecting on practice experience in a way that allows its examination and improvement. Not all reflection therefore takes a reflective practice framework. In the professions, the idea of reflective practice is often credited initially to Argyris and Schon (1974), and later to Donald Schon (1983, 1987). These works form much of the initial basis for subsequent later writings in the professional learning traditions, such as nursing (e.g. Taylor 2000, Rolfe *et al.* 2001).

The starting point for reflective practice for Schon (1987) is the crisis in confidence in professional knowledge. This crisis results from the idea that the 'high ground' of theorizing about professionalism does not always match the 'swampy lowlands' of actual practice. The problem is that professional knowledge on the high ground can be researched and taught more easily, but it is the messy work in the swamps that defies easy solution. Schon's model is therefore based on an alternative understanding of professional knowledge. It acknowledges that there are different types of professional knowledge. 'Knowing that', or what we might normally understand as 'facts' or general theories, is what conventionally has been taught to qualifying professionals. However, the 'knowing how', or the application of 'knowing that', is much more difficult to teach outside the actual contexts where the 'knowing how' is practised. Reflection in action is needed in order to convert 'facts' into useable knowledge. Schon therefore posited that what is needed in professional knowledge are both 'technical rationality' (rules) and professional artistry (reflection in action). Part of the crisis for professionals arises from the fact that, very often, the 'theory' or rules espoused ('espoused theory') by practitioners are quite different from the 'theory' or assumptions ('theory in use') embedded in the actual practices of professionals. This is often because the 'rules' are limited in their applicability to specific situations, and because individual practitioners are not always aware of the myriad of different rules that might be needed to inform any one set of actions in a changing situation. They therefore need to reflect on the general rules in order to practise relevantly in any specific context. These general rules can be unearthed through a process of 'reflection on action'.

Reflective practice therefore is an approach designed to assist professionals to become aware of the 'theory' or assumptions involved in their practice, with the purpose of closing the gap between what is espoused and what is enacted. Ultimately this should contribute to improving both, as it may be used to scrutinize both practices and embedded theories. However, a process of reflective practice may also serve to help improve practice, by helping to develop practice theory, through a process of articulating the underlying principles upon which practice is based. In this sense, too, reflective practice can be seen as a process of researching practice theory, by developing it directly from concrete practice.

Because this reflective type of approach to practice recognizes the importance of mining the theory implicit in actual actions, it represents a rather non-traditional view of the relationship between theory and practice. There are several key features of the reflective approach (Fook 1996). First, in traditional views, we tend to apply generalized theory to specific practices in a rather top-down, *deductive*, sort of manner. The reflective approach places equal importance on knowledge formed in an *inductive* manner, in which a broader theory might in fact be developed from specific experiences, allowing for theory development and creation. This might be seen as a more 'bottom-up' approach, in which existing theories are modified, and in which new theories may also be devised.

Second, what thus becomes important in a reflective approach are aspects of practice that may not formerly have been valued in more traditional views. Phenomena like *intuition* and *artistry* become a logical focus for better understanding how professionals operate, and as a site for the enactment of practice theory. Intuition may be important in recognizing important factors and prioritizing them, or in making connections between seemingly unrelated phenomena. It becomes important to value intuitive moments in order to pinpoint the assumptions that may be involved and to subject them to scrutiny (Adams 2002). Artistry may be involved in the creative way different elements of professional knowledge may be combined to suit a unique situation, or in the way new methods may be created to address a new problem or context (Higgs and Titchen 2001; Froggett 2006).

This points to the third characteristic of a reflective approach, which is the importance of *context*. Given that professional artistry involves the application of prior knowledge and skills in particular contexts, there needs to be a readiness to respond to what might be new or different about these contexts. Not only might this involve the creation of new knowledge, but also an openness to new contexts, and the new and different perspectives that might be operating in those contexts. An emphasis on context therefore also includes a recognition of the importance of different perspectives in that context.

Lastly, an awareness of different perspectives carries with it an emphasis on a *holistic* approach. If different perspectives are taken into account, then there needs to be an appreciation of how these different perspectives interplay and relate. Situations and experiences need also to be understood as a whole. This particularly includes the role of emotions as a point of learning in experience (Fook 1999a). In this sense, the reflective approach tends to focus on the whole experience and the many dimensions involved: cognitive elements; feeling elements; meanings and interpretations from different perspectives. We will discuss this aspect in some detail later in the book.

A reflective approach therefore questions some of the taken-for-granted assumptions about knowledge that we might associate with more 'scientific', 'positivist' or 'technical-rational' paradigms. Such paradigms tend to break professional knowledge into specialist domains, and to produce generalizable knowledge based on empirically observable phenomena only. This tends to legitimize only knowledge created through empirically researched means, and therefore, by association, only the knowledge of researchers who use these methods. A reflective approach, however, affirms the importance of other ways of knowing, particularly personal experience and the interpretations this might entail. Experiential and participatory research methods are therefore also important. The traditional distinctions between 'knowing and doing', 'values and facts', 'subjectivity and objectivity', 'art and science' are blurred. What becomes more important is a holistic understanding of the complexity of experience, and the sorts of knowledge that support relevant practice in complex and unpredictable situations.

How is this approach relevant to critical reflection?

The reflective approach, most importantly, supplies the framework for a basic way of understanding the process of critical reflection – as searching for the assumptions implicit in actual practice. This then enables a clear comparison with the more stated or explicit assumptions that practitioners often believe themselves to be enacting, prior to a process of reflection. The comparison of implicit and explicit assumptions provides a crucial starting point from which to examine both sets of assumptions further, and of course some sets of options about how the discrepancies might be addressed. In this way the reflective approach provides a framework for practice evaluation, by examining it for contradictions and discrepancies. We see this understanding of the process as only a starting point, however, since it is preliminary to assume that the gap might be addressed only through the changing of the theory or the practice. In fact, discrepancies can be addressed in a myriad of ways, and not necessarily only through a resolution of the discrepancy. For instance, it may also be a viable option to live with and accept the discrepancy; and of course discrepancies are only one of the features that might contribute to ineffective or undesirable practices. This outline of the process therefore needs to be built upon through the use of other frameworks (which we will discuss further on).

A second way in which the reflective approach informs critical reflection is related to the value placed on holistic practitioner experience, especially the more hidden aspects, which are difficult to articulate and measure. Critical reflection in this sense may be seen as a way of researching these more complex aspects of experience, which are difficult to access in other ways.

Third, because the knowledge created by practitioners in the actual process of practice is valued, this effectively provides another way of creating practice theory. The critical reflection process, from this point of view, may be seen as a way of researching and developing practice theory. In this sense practitioners become researchers of their own practice, and creators of practice theory, when they engage in critical reflection. This effectively blurs the boundaries between practitioners and researchers, and accords some responsibility directly to practitioners for more systematic and transparent research of their practice.

Summary: the reflective approach

A model for improving practice by reflecting directly on experience, it involves:

- a 'bottom-up' understanding of theory and practice – theory as also embedded in practice
- exposing problematic gaps between espoused and enacted theory
- closing the gap, which may improve practice
- placing a value on intuition, artistry and creativity
- a contextual, holistic and experiential approach.

It is useful:

- in searching for discrepancies between implicit and explicit assumptions
- as a starting point for evaluating practice
- for articulating the holistic and complex nature of practice
- for researching the unarticulatable – hidden and difficult to measure practice
- in developing practice theory and creating practice knowledge.

Reflexivity

The idea of reflexivity comes from different traditions again, and is often associated with social science research (Marcus 1994) in fields like anthropology (for example, Rosaldo 1993). In these fields it was especially important to recognize the influence of self on research, as the anthropologist was often a participant-observer in trying to document the culture (often foreign to the researcher) of a particular group. It has been developed more recently in the health and human service professions (e.g. Taylor and White 2000), presumably because of the concern with managing 'objectivity', and the recognition that, in many of these occupations, use of self is integral to practice (Kondrat 1999; Ruch 2002).

Reflexivity – a 'turning back on itself' (Steier 1991) – has been defined in various ways. White (2002: 10) emphasizes the ability to look both inwards and outwards to recognize the connections with social and cultural understandings.

Our understanding is a little broader in that we see it as involving the ability to recognize that *all* aspects of ourselves (including physical and bodily aspects) and our contexts influence the way we research (or create knowledge) (Fook 1999b). When we refer to 'research' here, our understanding is also broad. We are referring to all the different ways in which we create knowledge – this occurs in more or less formal and systematic ways (depending on the situation), yet is used daily, and often in unarticulated ways, to make sense of immediate surroundings. In this sense, research, or knowledge creation, is integral to the daily business of living, and therefore to the daily business of professional practice.

Therefore, in order to be reflexive, we need to be aware of the many and varied ways in which we might create, or at least influence, the type of knowledge we use. How do we actually participate in the creation of our own knowledge? In this sense, the idea of reflexivity alerts us to the fact that knowledge does not necessarily exist in some independent form, separate from our experiences and own sense of who we are. We are often responsible for interpreting, selecting, prioritizing, sometimes seeing and not seeing, and using knowledge in particular ways that are to do with a myriad of things about ourselves and our social and historical situations.

There are four important aspects of knowledge that point to ways in which we might participate in its creation:

1. knowledge is both embodied and social (as well as emotionally and intellectually influenced)
2. knowledge is subjectively mediated
3. there is a reactivity element (the tools used to discover knowledge influence what is found)
4. knowledge is created interactively (influenced by the specific situation).

First, knowledge is *embodied and social in nature* – it is mediated by who we are physically and socially, and by the consequent lenses through which we experience our world. So our physical and bodily state of being, and our social positions, will influence how we interpret and select information, and indeed how we are socially interpreted and interacted with by others. Often whether we are tired, or ill, will make a difference to our temperament, of course, but also to what we see as important at the time, and what we therefore factor in, or out, about our situation. Not only will I have more patience if I am not tired, but also this may mean I will listen more intently to what a complainant has to say, and perhaps interpret it less negatively. Our age makes a difference to our perspectives, both for physical and social reasons. Not only am I a different person (bodily) at a different age, but I also have different social statuses at different ages. Also I may see situations differently depending on the amount of experience I have had with those situations, and obviously this will vary according to my social status and age. These factors work on social levels as well, of course. Social cultures and groups are also embodied – that is, they have a physical presence, context and manifestation that influences the ways knowledge is made and communicated. Being reflexive from this point of view will involve an understanding of how physical and social contexts influence what knowledge is created and how.

In broad terms, this leads to the second major way in which reflexivity is important. If knowledge is both embodied and social in nature, this means that knowledge is also mediated by our own *subjectivity* – our particular being, embodiment, experience and social position will influence what phenomena we see and how we see them. The point being made here is that, while knowledge may have an objective aspect (i.e. have some existence outside our individual perceptions), it may at the same time be subjectively created or modified. Knowledge of ourselves as particular individuals, as social, cultural, psychological and embodied beings, therefore, is important in understanding and evaluating the sorts of knowledge we use and hold. For example, if a family member of mine dies, I will most likely experience some type of bereavement. There will be some knowledge about this that has some credence outside my own experience – for example, the legal requirements for inter-ment, social expectations of relatives, financial arrangements for the deceased, and professional knowledge about grief. Nevertheless, my own experience of the death will be determined by my interpretation of, and reaction to, all of the above. And my own interpretations and reactions may lead me to create my own set of knowledges about the death. These will in part depend on my previous experiences of death, my experience and relationship with the deceased, my professional background and expertise, my social and financial position, and so on. Being reflexive by taking into account subjectivity will involve a knowledge of who I am as a whole being (social, emotional, physical, cultural, economic, political) and understanding the effects this has on the knowledge I perceive and create.

Third, there is a *reactivity* element in reflexivity. This involves understanding that the knowledge or information we obtain or take in about a particular situation is at least partly determined by the kinds of tools and process we use to determine it. This is often a clearer issue for those of us engaged in formal and systematic research, but much harder to see of course in the kinds of everyday research we engage in, in order to make meaning of current contexts as a guide to action. Consider, for example, what different kinds of informa-tion you might elicit from someone if you met them at a party, as opposed to interviewed them for a job. Or what you might find out if you simply observed someone while they were unaware of your observation, as opposed to watching them on television as part of a *Big Brother*-type programme. The setting, and the method we use for gaining information, will have a direct effect on what we find out, and of course ultimately on the assessment we make of that person. So our own beliefs about what constitutes legitimate knowledge and its legitimate creation, and the types of methods we should and do use, will influence what we find out. Being reflexive from this perspective therefore means being aware of what methods we are using, the setting and purpose of the information being gathered, the effects this has on the information obtained, and, of course, making an assessment about whether they are mutually appropriate.

Lastly, knowledge is also *interactional* – it is shaped by historical and structural contexts, and is made in a dynamic and political process. In this sense, what counts as knowledge is not a purely objective phenomenon, but is a result of a number of factors. It is normally forged through the broader social processes at play. For example, what items make it onto the evening television news provides a good illustration of the dynamics of how knowledge becomes recognized as important, and moreover is recorded as historically important. There is presumably an interplay of perspectives operating, such as what is deemed newsworthy (sensational; backing up popular trends; fitting with a current political struggle; potentially attracts dollars; is of interest to the station owner). As another example, our views about particular wars (who were victims and who were perpetrators; what acts are deemed justifiable) are irrevocably shaped by the information that is available to us at the time. Being reflexive from this perspective means understanding how any knowledge may in fact represent only limited perspectives, from a particular point in time or a particular standpoint. This means being open to the possibility of other perspectives.

How does the idea of reflexivity apply directly to our understanding of critical reflection?

We might see reflexivity as one way of being critically reflective. Being aware of ourselves as researchers who participate in the selecting and creating of our own knowledge means that we can become aware of the tools we might use to create that knowledge, the assumptions that underlie our choice of tools, and how who we are as tools ourselves (as social, cultural, physical, emotional and political beings) mediates what we see or remember. This in turn helps us directly connect who we are as individuals with our social and historical contexts. In this sense, critical reflection becomes a way of researching the knowledge inherent in our practice, and connecting this knowledge (and ourselves) with our broader social contexts. With an understanding of reflexivity, we become more aware of ourselves as researchers, creating knowledge directly from practice experience. We focus particularly therefore on our assumptions about knowledge, its different forms, its role, what is important and how it is created.

Summary: reflexivity

Reflexivity is the ability to recognize that *all* aspects of ourselves and our contexts influence the way we research (or create knowledge).
Knowledge creation is embodied, social, reactive and interactional.
Reflexivity is useful in critical reflection for:

- awareness of ourselves as researchers creating knowledge directly from practice experience
- focus on assumptions about knowledge and its creation.

Postmodernism and deconstruction

The influence of postmodern thinking brings with it particular ways of thinking that to some degree transcend yet complement those associated with reflexivity. For the purposes of this chapter we also include poststructural thinking, in that there are common threads that are useful to our understanding of critical reflection (Fook 1999a).

By postmodern thinking we are referring simply to the questioning of 'modernist' (or linear and unified) thinking (Parton 1994). In modernist thinking, the 'linear' idea is that knowledge must be arrived at in a progressive way, with the successive accumulation of better knowledge through subsequent research efforts. It is 'unified' in that it is assumed to be non-conflictual, in the sense that all later versions of knowledge are by definition better, merely a clearer and better representation of the one 'truth'. Thus it is assumed that there is only one right way of seeing, which can be arrived at in a progressive and cumulative way (that is, later knowledge builds on earlier knowledge).

In this way, postmodern thinking alerts us to the relationship between knowledge and power (an analysis useful in critical reflection), for in order to arrive at the 'one truth', many conflicting perspectives may need to be ignored. Focusing on what is accepted as the 'one truth', or dominant discourse or perspective, is useful as a concept for understanding the operation of power through the language we use, and what we accept as truth. By pointing up the role of dominant discourses in creating what is perceived as legitimate knowledge (and therefore highlighting the operation of power) postmodern thinking sheds light on where power rests and how it is maintained by focusing on how certain thinking, and its association with certain groups, might function to strengthen the position of those groups in relation to others (Healy 2000; Fook 2002).

Poststructuralists alert us to the role of language in forming our knowledge and therefore dominant discourses (Weedon 1987). The way we speak about things, what we choose to label or name (and what is not labelled as a corollary), and the relationships we imply through the language we use, all have a role in marking what is legitimate and what is thus powerful. The language we use, and the discourse we imply or support, therefore become useful pointers in tracing the influences of power in our own practice and experience (White 2006).

In particular, the tendency to construct binary opposites is an important element in language-making (Berlin 1990). A binary opposite is a paired category of phenomena that is: total (encompasses all of the population); mutually exclusive (involves forced choice categories – an element can be a member of only one or other category, not both or neither); binary (only two); and oppositional (usually conceptualized as contradictory or opposite to each other, and the second part of the binary is usually defined in terms of the other, so is by definition inferior). It often underlies how we make difference, and is therefore a crucial part of identity-making and, by implication, inclusion and exclusion. A basic example to which postmodern feminists alerted us long ago is the splitting of the whole human population into 'male' and 'female' categories. For instance, we often attribute inferiority to the second part of a binary category (e.g. 'female' is inferior to 'male' by definition) and indeed the second part of the binary is often defined in terms of the first (e.g. females are defined as 'not male'). Thereby the first category in the binary opposite retains primacy, and is regarded as the norm.

The idea of deconstruction is important in relation to postmodern and poststructural thinking, as both focus on the ways in which knowledge (and power) is constructed through language: the specific terminology we use, the categories we create; and the patterns and ways of talking (discourses) we support. This gives us a framework for deconstructing our thinking – that is, it gives us a framework for unpicking the ways in which power operates through our language use and the way we frame our meanings (and by implication our practices based on it).

It is useful to discuss the concept of power here, and to analyse it as a dominant discourse. In modernist ways of thinking, power is seen as a commodity, a type of material entity that can be traded or given. It is seen as structural, as owned by someone (usually a person with a higher position in the social structure). This means that it is easy to create any two binary categories: those who are power*ful*, as opposed to those who are power*less*. Yet ironically, empowerment, taken from this perspective, may often be experienced as disempowering (Fook 2002: 51). This is because it is usually the dominant group 'doing' the empowering to a more disadvantaged group. This is empowerment from the perspective of the dominant group, perpetuating the dominant discourse of power, and empowering others in its likeness. This type of understanding of power of course appears to privilege structural power, and ignores the other perspectives, especially the perspectives of those who lack structural power. In fact these groups may have different types of power, and may pride themselves on this. For example, non-Anglo people may not necessarily wish to be regarded as 'white'. Their 'non-white' identity may be important to them – an important source of power, in fact. This is one of the issues involved of course in identity politics – the battle over the right to construct one's own identity (Fook 2002).

Deconstructing the modernist idea of power is useful in critical reflection, as it directly addresses one of the main sets of assumptions that underpins the way power is currently maintained. Many postmodern writers (e.g. Brookfield 2001) use the work of Foucault to rework the idea of power. In this view power is exercised, rather than possessed, and can take many forms. It is not finite, but can be created. The focus is on how it operates, rather than its static existence. It may operate in many different ways – positively, negatively and in contradictory ways at the same time (depending on the perspectives involved). For example, a professional counsellor seeking to empower a client may try to involve them in making decisions about the sort of therapy they would like, and resist giving direct advice. The counsellor may view this as giving the client some of her power. However, the client may feel that she has paid a substantial fee for the therapist's services, and therefore that she is not 'getting her money's worth' because she is not getting direct and clear advice. She may also feel the counsellor is patronizing, because the counsellor is maintaining her own superior position by not committing to her own opinion on the client's situation. What is intended as empowering is not experienced in this way because of the differing sets of assumptions about the counselling.

In broad terms, then, both postmodern and poststructural thinking recognize that knowledge (and power) can be socially constructed. By assuming that any particular knowledge is linear and unified, we can unwittingly support a dominant power base, and unwittingly participate in preserving these power relations through the very language we use to speak about our world. Thus postmodern thinking opens up an awareness of the possibilities for contradiction, change and conflict in thinking, by recognizing that many different experiences can be legitimate, and providing the basis from which to question accepted dominant ways of thinking. Deconstruction, then, simply involves using this type of analysis to become aware of the discourses that unwittingly shape our thinking and actions. Thus the idea of deconstruction provides a useful framework for uncovering the more hidden assumptions we ascribe to, and the powerful ways in which they operate.

From a postmodern and poststructural angle, then, critical reflection can be aided by deconstructing our thinking in order to expose how we participate in constructing power. This opens the way for us to explore conflicts and contradictions that may previously have been silenced, and to question how that silencing has operated in a powerful way. For example, often asking why a particular way of seeing is dominant in our practice, or why we have ignored or not even been aware of other perspectives, is useful in pointing out which dominant discourses we might unwittingly have subscribed to.

Another way in which deconstruction is useful is in helping to explore difficulties in practice that are brought about because of perceived (binary) dilemmas or tensions, such as where we have reached an impasse in practice because we believe there is a fundamental dilemma or conflict involved. For example, professionals often conceptualize a basic dilemma in their work as being between 'care' and 'control', or about 'values-based practice' versus 'outcome-driven practice', as if the two categories are mutually exclusive. Postmodern thinking can lead us to question these divisions, to formulate perhaps more complex ways of working, which may include third or fourth options beyond the binary categorization.

The deconstruction of binaries is also useful in analysing the construction of identities. It can assist us in pinpointing how and why we categorize, particularly the way we categorize ourselves in relation to others. This type of awareness is pertinent in the fields of international and cross-cultural work (Fook 2004b) and of course in race relations and disability (Fook 2004c) – in short, in any area where our understanding of the work involves categorizing the populations we work with as in some way different to a more mainstream 'norm'. However, more generally, it is useful in understanding the construction of professional identities, and relating these to discourses in relation to one's biography, the workplace and the broader culture. (Please refer at this point to the book's accompanying website – www.openup.co.uk/fook& gardner – and to Lynne Allan's student assignment, included in the resource materials, where Lynne very usefully discusses questions about her own professional identity and its impact on her practice. The paper by Jan Fook, entitled 'The lone crusader: constructing enemies and allies in the workplace', also available on the website, illustrates this issue too.)

Deconstruction and related discourse analysis (Ellerman 1998) are therefore useful to our model of critical reflection in that they provide a framework for unearthing how our particular assumptions underpin particular constructions (of ourselves, of others, of knowledge, of power, of practice), which in turn help construct or maintain particular power relations in particular situations. In this way they provide a means of analysis that connects us directly as individuals with prevailing power situations.

However, what postmodern and poststructural thinking lack in their contribution to critical reflection is details about the evaluative aspects – how do we determine which forms of power actually preserve or challenge domination, and how we might change this, need further explication. For this we need to turn to critical social theory.

Summary: postmodernism and deconstruction

Postmodern thinking is a questioning of linear (progressive) and unified ('one truth') thinking.

Deconstruction involves understanding:

- the role of dominant discourses in connecting power and knowledge
- the role of binary thinking in constructing difference
- the silencing of multiple and marginal perspectives.

Deconstruction is useful in critical reflection in helping unearth how we participate in constructing power by participating in dominant discourses:

- constructions (and categorizations) of our own identities and how we make difference in others
- constructions of binary 'dilemmas' in practice
- what perspectives we leave out.

Critical social theory

There are aspects of the work of many different theorists that share some commonalities with this category (e.g. Marx, Marcuse and Habermas (see Agger 1998)). For our purposes here, we focus on the five common themes of critical social theory; these have been paraphrased and summarized from Fook (2002) and Agger (1998) as follows: first, the recognition that power is both personal and structural; second, that individuals can participate in their own domination; third, social change is both personal and collective; fourth, knowledge is both empirical and constructed; and last, the importance of communication and dialogue.

First, critical social theory recognizes that power, or domination, is both personally experienced and structurally created. Therefore any understanding of the operation of power in critical reflection needs to incorporate an understanding of how the personal and structural levels of power interact. For example, how do individuals interpret structural power and how it operates in their lives? How have individuals acted upon the operation of structural power? What is the person's structural position and how has this influenced their view of themselves? In a sense this point also involves recognizing that structural and personal levels interact in any one person's experience of power.

Second, therefore, individuals can participate in their own domination, by holding self-defeating beliefs about their place in the social structure, their own power and possibilities for change. The concepts of ideology and false consciousness are important here. Ideology is a term that refers to an idea that has political or social functions, aside from whether or not it is valid. In other words, its truth or falsity is less an issue than the effects it produces. Sometimes these may appear to have little directly to do with the content of the idea itself. For example, many of us like to believe that we work from a participatory framework, and hence often dislike colleagues who we perceive to be unlike us, as undemocratic. (Refer at this point to the paper 'The lone crusader: constructing enemies and allies in the workplace', which is included on the website that accompanies this book: www.openup.co.uk/fook&gardner.) This belief in ourselves may or may not be true (depending of course on what circumstances we are talking about and what colleagues we are talking about). However, that is not the main issue. What is important is that this belief in ourselves might mask a need to see ourselves as participatory, which might then blind us to recognizing instances in which our behaviour is not experienced as democratic by others. This belief in ourselves as participatory therefore has ideological functions.

Alternatively, we may subscribe to the view that professionals are ethical and objective, which of course may or may not be true. Holding this view, however, makes us feel that whatever we do is right, and in the best interests of our clients (which may or may not be true!). This masks the possibility that sometimes we may act for our own gain, or out of our own interests, and may unwittingly disadvantage service users as a result. Holding this particular ideology of professionalism can in fact work against the very view it appears to uphold. From an ideological standpoint, critical reflection involves understanding the ideological functions of personally held beliefs, in order to assess whether these functions run counter to the fundamental intentions or values of the person.

Third, if effective social change is to be achieved it must occur on both personal and collective levels. One does not preclude the other, but the two are intertwined. Social changes involve personal changes, and vice versa. In this sense, then, it becomes important for the individual person to be able to recognize how their own personal changes are linked with changes on broader levels. This may be important in providing a sense of agency (a sense of the ability to actually effect direct change) and also an accessible site for change. One of the difficulties for many people in making a structural analysis is that it then seems that, logically, the site for change becomes something much bigger than themselves, the implication being that acting alone is not feasible. However, if we see the two levels as intertwined, this also means that individual people themselves can become a site for social change. (Please refer at this point to the film, mentioned on the book's accompanying website – www.openup.co.uk/fook&gardner, of a discussion between Jan Fook, Gail Baikie and Caroline Campbell, where we talk about the individual as a site for social change.) It also means that social changes need to be experienced at personal levels in order to be meaningful. The concept of ideology above provides a useful starting point for making social changes at individual levels.

Fourth, recognizing the interplay of social and personal realms involves a recognition that knowledge often has an empirical reality, but the way that knowledge is used and interpreted may be constructed (socially and personally). In this sense, critical social theorists differ from pure constructivists in that they do not solely emphasize the socially constructed nature of knowledge. Instead they emphasize the interaction between empirical reality and members of society. What therefore becomes important is not whether or not knowledge has an empirical reality, but how this reality is interpreted and used in the social world. This view effectively leaves room for different views of 'reality', and therefore is important to critical reflection in that it is inclusive of different perspectives.

Finally, therefore, in bringing about social and personal changes, communication and dialogue are important so that new shared understandings can be created. In this sense critical social theorists place importance on the way different meanings and practices are created in social relationships, since there needs to be some dynamic negotiation of mutual understandings in order for effective practices to be carried out. Therefore the environments in which mutual dialogue can be fostered become important (Habermas 1984, 1987).

What is the contribution of critical social theory to our model of critical reflection?

First, there is a direct analytical and dynamic link between the individual and society, both in the experience of power and domination, but also in the need for change at both levels. This provides a theoretical framework for understanding how individuals can both influence, and be influenced by, their social contexts, and can participate in the changes that should result from this understanding.

Second, the concept of ideology provides an invaluable framework for focusing on individually held assumptions that may work in powerful ways on a personal and social level. The operation of ideology in everyday experience provides a clear site for critical reflection (Brookfield 2000).

Third, critical social theory alerts us to the sorts of conditions that are needed in order to foster environments that are conducive to critical awareness and dialogue.

In broad terms, then, critical social theory provides a broader framework for understanding what critical reflection can and should help achieve. In this sense also, critical social theory provides an important values dimension to critical reflection. From this point of view, an overarching purpose of critical reflection is to create a socially just environment that is both equitable and democratic. By making connections between the personal and structural, and emphasizing the importance of communication, critical social theory points to how a critical reflection process might help us build bridges between our own experience and that of others to bring about desired social changes. As Mezirow points out: 'precipitating and fostering critically self-reflective learning means a deliberate effort to foster resistance to technicist assumptions, to thoughtlessness, to conformity, to impermeable meaning perspectives, to fear of change, to ethnocentric and class bias, and to egocentric values' (1991: 360).

In broad practical terms, a critical perspective on critical reflection simply involves the idea that when dominant social understandings or assumptions are exposed (through a reflective process) for the political (or ideological) functions that they perform (i.e. that they exist for political reasons in supporting the status quo, apart from whatever inherent truth they might have), the individual who holds those assumptions is given a choice. Once these hidden ideas are exposed people who hold them are thus given the power to change them (Fook and Askeland, in press) and the guidance to change them in ways that may overturn previous inequitable arrangements.

Summary: critical social theory

Five key points:

1. domination is both personal and structural
2. individuals participate in their own domination
3. emphasizes both personal and collective social change
4. knowledge is empirical and constructed
5. the importance of communication.

Useful for critical reflection:

- provides a framework for understanding links between the individual and society
- shows how dominant power works in individual lives
- links personal and collective processes
- provides a framework for unsettling dominant assumptions and their operation in everyday practice
- provides a framework to free individuals from the restrictions of dominant thinking, providing choice of thinking and actions.

Chapter summary

In this chapter we have outlined four different theoretical frameworks that underlie critical reflection and help us understand the relationship between individual practices and social contexts. These understandings help us more effectively unsettle the dominant assumptions involved in connecting individual experiences with the major beliefs that are behind many social arrangements. It is important to appreciate these theoretical frameworks in some depth, as they alert us to the many different ways our fundamental assumptions can remain hidden, and can function in social ways, despite our awareness or intentions. In Chapter 6 we will 'translate' these frameworks into more specific questions and ways of interrogating our practices in order to reveal these hidden assumptions.

PART II
The Process of Critical Reflection

4 The critical reflection model and process

This chapter aims to:

- provide a broad overview of the design of our critical reflection model, including
  - the design of the model
  - the specific principles that inform it
  - the features of the design that are based on these principles (i.e. the specific purpose, structure, content and process)
- explore what you need to consider in starting critical reflection, particularly using this model; more specifically
  - the influence of organizational context
  - how to promote critical reflection
  - participation issues – voluntary or involuntary
  - composition of critical reflection groups
  - practical issues in planning workshops.

Introduction

In the foregoing chapters we have outlined the broad theory behind our model of critical reflection, and the issues that need to be considered and addressed before establishing a critical reflection programme. This chapter divides into two sections: first we present a broad overview of the design of our model, and second we explore what you need to consider in introducing critical reflection into your organization. In subsequent chapters we describe the detail of specific aspects of the design. This chapter also serves to outline the 'blueprint' of the model, if you like. Understanding the blueprint and the thinking behind it will allow readers to modify or change the blueprint in particular ways, which we will also discuss in this chapter. The blueprint model we present here ideally involves a small group of voluntary participants, who either all come from the organization that has sponsored the programme, or are individuals from various organizations who have chosen to participate in the programme, which is being run independently of their employing organization. There may of course be many variations on these two options and these will be considered here and in subsequent chapters.

Overview of the model

What is the broad design for our model of critical reflection?

In concrete terms the model involves small groups of critical reflective learners, in which group members assist each individual participant in turn to reflect on specific examples of their practice experiences. This process is structured in two main stages. The first focuses on unsettling the fundamental assumptions that are implicit in their account of their practice experience; the second focuses on how their practice (and the way they understand or conceptualize it) might change as a result of the new awarenesses they have arrived at from the first stage of reflections. The process is managed by a group facilitator, who also introduces the model before the first stage begins. The whole process is undertaken within a trusting and collegiate climate.

The membership of the small groups is ideally voluntary, and members have chosen to participate on some kind of informed basis (see below). The ideal maximum is around eight participants, but of course numbers can be varied. Although there are two main stages of reflection, the first is normally preceded by an introductory session, which aims to introduce the model and establish the appropriate group culture. There are, then, usually three sessions in total: an introductory session, followed by stages 1 and 2 of the model. The sessions are normally held about one week apart. In most of the groups we have run, we allow about three hours for the introductory session, and approximately six hours for each of the subsequent sessions. This means that, in a group with eight participants, each will have approximately 30 minutes to present their material for reflection. Each reflection presentation is therefore quite brief, so the process needs to be facilitated in a focused way in order to create an open climate, but at the same time to develop alternative perspectives that are meaningful for each participant. While there is a basic structure, the process is open-ended, the guiding principle being to unearth assumptions that are meaningful to the participant.

The main principles of the model and their rationale

Small facilitated groups are our preferred way of working because:

- they allow learning through dialogue and some focus on the

communicative process, which is a key principle underlying the idea of critical reflection
- they allow enough space for individual reflection, but also provide for the input of multiple perspectives and, additionally, the opportunity for further identification of collective and social thinking, and the links between this and individual experience
- the size of the groups can vary – we find that the model may be conducted with as few as three group members (including the facilitator) up to as many as twelve; normally, however, each participant needs at least 20–30 minutes to present and reflect on their critical incident, so this factor will guide the size of the group and available time; the model can also be used between two people in supervision, for example, or critical friends (see Chapter 9), or by individuals on their own as part of self-reflection.

The direct involvement of each individual participant is important. In our model our preferred option is that each group member (including the facilitator) actually presents some concrete practice experience for reflection. There are several reasons for this.

- We find that the learning that can be gained from actually undertaking a reflection on one's own experience is different from (and additional to) the learning gained from assisting in reflecting on other people's experience. In order for people to maximize their learning about critical reflection it is important for them to learn from both perspectives, as both a reflector on their own and other people's experiences.
- This is also an important aspect of establishing the appropriate group climate. The culture is usually more participatory if everyone has a similar role. If everyone knows they will be having a turn in exposing their practice and becoming vulnerable to the group, this sets up a more democratic climate. For example, we often find that people who are aware that they will also be in the 'hot seat' will take more care to temper their questions, and will be more sensitive to different perspectives, and the perspectives of the person currently in the hot seat.
- The facilitator modelling the process with their own material at the beginning of the programme contributes to this participatory climate by modelling participation. This also allows modelling of the appropriate types of responses to critical reflective questioning.
- We would suggest varying this only if just a short training programme is possible, so that a selected proportion of participants can present their material. These are usually 'volunteers', who have been approached beforehand to agree to present their material, although

often we have called for volunteers on the day. The advantage is that more people may be exposed to the process, but the disadvantages are many: the risk that the model will not be understood or experienced in depth; the associated risk that the model or process will be misunderstood; the risk of not creating the necessary trusting environment; the added anxiety for those presenting. All in all, a shortened model is probably recommended only when the advantages of including a larger number of participants outweigh the risks involved.

Using critical reflective questioning is important. By critical reflective questions, we mean questions that are clearly derived from our specific ways of theorizing critical reflection. We deliberately devise sets of example questions from the different theoretical traditions of critical reflection and model these to participants (there are examples in Chapter 5). The aim here is twofold:

1. to model the direct connections between the theory of critical reflection and the practice of it
2. to assist participants to experience the direct links between the theory and practice of critical reflection.

What is critical here is to use language, and word questions, according to the group and individual participants involved. The main principle at work here is to find a language for wording the questions that is meaningful to the person reflecting. In this sense, the facilitator (and group members with the facilitator's assistance) is trying to communicate the questions in ways that help the person reflecting to see other perspectives in looking for assumptions.

Unsettling the fundamental assumptions that are implicit: we deliberately choose terms like 'unsettle' for the following reasons.

- We are emphasizing that the process aims primarily to 'shake up' thinking, but that this does not necessarily provide ready-made solutions. In fact we emphasize that the process is not about finding a solution; primarily we are aiming to create a climate (and process) that might assist a person to be open about exposing their fundamental assumptions, and then open to finding new ways of thinking and acting that incorporate whatever changes are brought about through the process.
- The model is process focused, with the outcome being open. In this sense it is not more process than outcome focused, but the outcome desired is open-ended. The model is therefore deliberately designed as a particular communicative process without foreclosing on what the particular outcomes might be for each participant. It is important that

the process instead creates an open climate so that possible changes might be as open, flexible and non-predetermined as possible. This principle is important if participants are to be as creative as possible in finding new ways of working.

- We are focusing directly on assumptions that are fundamental and implicit. What these are must necessarily be open, since their relative meaning will depend on what theoretical perspective is taken. And since, ultimately, we are trying to develop an understanding of fundamental assumptions that will be useful to the person in question, then it is important that the process we construct is able to be inclusive of many different perspectives. The assumptions unearthed do need to be implicit, rather than those that are within easy reach of the current explicit awareness of the presenter. In our experience, not a great deal that is new is learnt if easily stated assumptions are focused on. In some ways this can be an inhibitor to learning, as the learner is often motivated to defend assumptions that are more explicit. In a sense these are often the more desired assumptions, so the person may have a vested interest in preserving them. Our focus therefore is deliberately on that which is implied rather than stated. It is the focus on the taken for granted that contributes to the power of the learning in critical reflection.

- The degree to which the thinking is hidden will vary, as of course will what participants choose to focus on as fundamental to them. This may vary from thinking that is hidden because it is part of the taken-for-granted cultural and social environment, to thinking that is hidden because it is associated with past, often painful, personal experiences. Of course the two are not necessarily mutually exclusive, but some participants may feel more comfortable about discussing different things in a group environment. Each facilitator (and group and individual participant) will to some extent need to make their own decisions.

The use of examples of specific and concrete practice experience. We insist on using practice experience that is described in both concrete and specific terms. This material can be accessed, through observation, case files, reports, and so on. However, for the purposes of focused small group dialogue, we find that the more concrete and brief the account of practice is, the better we are able to focus and delve into it in some depth. Therefore usually we ask people to bring a written description of a critical incident – that is, of something that happened that was important to them (see Chapter 5). For our purposes here, what we are emphasizing is the need for some raw material for reflection. A description of a concrete critical incident is useful as this raw material for the following reasons.

- It is grounded directly in practice, and therefore provides a concrete example that is also able to be readily used in group discussion. This is easier for the group to access than, for example, direct observations of practice, case files, and so on.
- Because it is concrete, it is easier for people to imagine how they might change concrete practices on the basis of their reflection.
- The more 'raw' it is – that is, the closer it is to the person's own version of the experience – the better. The less the person has theorized, analysed or reflected upon the material, the easier it is to pinpoint assumptions that are more specific to the individual. With material that has already been analysed, often the assumptions that are implicit are those the person believes are the 'right' ones, so that what then becomes unearthed in the process is simply the person's view of what is 'right'. This can mean that a more limited analysis of assumptions is unearthed.
- Focusing as directly as possible on 'raw' experience also allows people to engage with the process of learning directly from their own experience. In this sense we are trying to create a model of learning that can easily be replicated by individual practitioners in everyday situations. However, it is useful to note that, often, material that is less directly related to personal practice experience can also be used well for self-reflection. For example, Lehmann (2003) uses fictional stories for reflection. The advantage of using material that is slightly removed from personal experience is that it is less threatening, so may be more relevant in groups where there has been less voluntary choice about participation, or where less prior information has been available to participants. Alternatively, this may be relevant as an approach for people who are less used to reflecting.
- The critical incident format can also be used quite flexibly to fit the interests of a particular group as discussed in the case below.

I [Jan] was once asked to conduct a critical reflection workshop for social workers in a large, very bureaucratic government organization. Although they wanted to learn about critical reflection, they also wanted to think through one of the dilemmas they experienced as professionals: how to maintain a professional role under pressure to act merely as bureaucrats. Since this was their own stated issue, we used the normal critical reflection model, but participants brought to the workshop specific critical incidents that encapsulated this dilemma for them. This meant we could draw out both personal and common assumptions, which gave a basis from which to draw up alternative ways of thinking and acting for both individuals and the whole group.

Devising new practices and approaches to practice. We have deliberately separated the first stage of 'unsettling assumptions' from the second stage of developing changed practices for several pertinent reasons.

- We find that many professional practice cultures tend to value finding solutions, rather than necessarily focusing on developing new analyses (Fook and Askeland, in press). A clear distinction between the two stages allows practitioners to develop a clearer sense of how analysis and action might be linked, and also how they might learn to develop action directly from their own analysis.
- We deliberately speak about changing practices or approaches to practice, as it is an important part of our model that participants recognize that a middle stage of reflection may involve changing assumptions about practice, as well as changing the actual practices themselves.

A trusting and collegiate climate: the climate and culture of the critical reflection process are probably as important as the techniques and tools used. We will write at some length about the details of this culture later, but it is an important part of the design of our model that the culture that encourages reflection is articulated and agreed to by all participants. This culture shares elements of the communicative spaces spoken about by Habermas (1984, 1987), but also includes important elements that acknowledge the experience of reflecting, and the potential pain, risk and vulnerability involved. Clearly this is easier to achieve in some settings than others. However, at this point, the most important issue to bear in mind is deciding how much the climate can be established and maintained as a microclimate, within a broader macroclimate, which may or may not be supportive. We will discuss this in more detail in subsequent chapters.

Facilitated by a group facilitator. The actual facilitation of critical reflection is integral to the process. While this obviously includes the expertise (skills and knowledge) of the facilitator, the broader role of the facilitator in establishing and maintaining the critical reflection culture is in some ways more important. Again this is an aspect we will discuss in some detail in later sections, but we emphasize here the need for facilitation by someone who understands the group culture that needs to be created and can model this well themselves. While all group members participate as equals, the facilitator has particular responsibility for ensuring that the appropriate culture is maintained and that the critical reflection process stays focused and works well for each individual. The facilitator must possess skills but also a particular value system, and be able to enact this in order for the process to work effectively. Having a facilitator also ensures that there is input independent of the specific workplaces of the participants. (Refer to the article

'Facilitator in focus' in the online resource materials at www.openup.co.uk/
fook&gardner.)

However, if these above principles can be ensured in the group without
the presence of an independent facilitator, then there is no reason it cannot be
conducted without one. For instance, following the process of critical reflec-

---

Summary: the design of the critical reflection model

- Small groups
- Focus on each individual participant in turn
- Using critical reflective questioning
- To unsettle the fundamental assumptions that are implicit
- Using examples of specific and concrete practice experiences
- To devise new practices and approaches to practice
- In a trusting and collegiate climate
- Facilitated by a group facilitator

The main principles of the model

- The importance of dialogue and a communicative process for learning
- Participatory and democratic values
- A focus on the interactions between individual and society – individual
  reflection in the social context, as well as reflection that includes both
  individual and social responsibility
- The importance of context, culture and climate in supporting reflection
  – tools and techniques are seen as a way to create the appropriate
  cultures, not necessarily as the main defining features of critical reflection
- Process and outcome are intertwined
- The importance of developing a culture that supports a process that
  allows open-ended outcomes
- The importance of making and maintaining direct connections between
  theory and practice
- An inclusive approach to outcomes and theories – a recognition of the
  importance of multiple and diverse perspectives
- A commitment to focusing on the hidden and the taken for granted
- The importance in learning of personal experience – direct, specific and
  concrete – taken from one's own perspective
- The importance of the individual participant's perspective – in presenting
  the initial account of practice, in focusing on meaningful assumptions
  and changed practices and approaches

tion, especially using the critical reflective questions, the session should have an inbuilt mechanism to enable independent and new perspectives. If the model is understood properly, then it should be relatively easy to stay focused on the process. For instance, group members might take it in turns to act in the role of facilitator, or choose as a facilitator one of their members who is more experienced with the model.

The main features of the model and process

The purpose of critical reflection

The broad purpose of the model is broadly to unsettle the fundamental (and dominant) thinking implicit in professional practices, in order to see other ways of practising. The thinking that is unearthed and the other ways of practising that might be developed are open-ended; they must simply be meaningful or significant to the participant. This model may be used in a number of specific ways, which may or may not be combined.

- To develop professional practice theory: in the process of unsettling thinking, the fundamental assumptions about practice are unearthed. This practice theory is then able to be reworked once it becomes available for scrutiny.
- To research professional practice: the process of unsettling thinking unearths fundamental assumptions about practice and how these are linked with actual practices. This effectively yields data about practice that were formerly hidden, so enabling practice theory and models to be better articulated. In this sense, the critical reflection process might be seen as a type of deconstructive research conducted on accounts of practice.
- To evaluate professional practice: the process of unearthing implicit assumptions allows a comparison with desired thinking and actions, so pinpointing changes that may need to be made.
- To change professional practice: from a critical perspective the process of unsettling assumptions reveals those that are socially dominant, and may in fact function to be restrictive of practice. The critical reflection process therefore allows practitioners to remake their practice in more freeing ways.
- To learn directly from professional practice experience: the process models a method that individual practitioners may replicate in their daily practice. By developing the habit of regularly unsettling the assumptions involved in significant experiences, practitioners can actually become involved on a regular basis in better articulating, developing and researching their own practice.

The structure and content of the process

The process is broadly divided into three sessions each separated by about a week.

1. Introductory session (half a day): includes an introduction to the theory and process (includes culture) of critical reflection, and a modelling of the process by the facilitator.
2. Stage 1 critical reflection: unsettling the assumptions of each participant in turn, through reflection on a specific critical incident presented by each.
3. Stage 2 reflection: presentations by each participant in turn, which focus on changed thinking (from stage 1), and the implications for practice.

The process is focused but open. It is facilitated in small groups in which all members assist each other to reflect. The culture of the group is important in sustaining the appropriate process. The process is structured (i.e. it follows the above structure and purpose) but is open-ended in that the main focus is to be open about what assumptions are unearthed and what practices may result. The main principle here is that whatever is focused on is of meaning to the individual participant.

Starting the critical reflection process

Depending on what you want to do, and your own knowledge and experience of critical reflection, there are a range of questions to consider. How will you negotiate having critical reflection? What form will it take? Are others already interested in critical reflection or do you need to convince them that it will be a valuable activity, worth allocating time, funding and energy to? If you are planning a workshop, will you be running it yourself or finding a facilitator? Do you want to have a critical reflection workshop in your organization or across organizations? Who will be involved? Is this for a group of practitioners or for people training in a particular field? A range of questions needs to be considered about participation and practical issues: there are questions about who will attend; will workers at different levels of organizations or training be able to participate in the same group, for example; will attendance be mandatory or voluntary?

The contexts of critical reflection

Before we consider these questions it is important to think about the organizational context. The culture of some organizations is more encouraging of practising reflectively than others (Reynolds and Vince 2004). Some organizations expect a certain level of openness, willingness to share values and assumptions and in-depth discussion about practice; others focus more on achieving tasks and outcomes and expect adherence to established procedures. Some organizations already use the language of some form of reflective practice and build reflection into supervision; others are not familiar with the language or concepts, and may not initially see how these are relevant. Critical reflection can work effectively across a wide range of organizations, but it is important to think about how best to 'promote' it for a particular context or across several contexts.

Before you start suggesting critical reflection, then, it is useful to think about the organizations that might be involved. How do they operate? What are the norms and expectations about how practice is explored? What experience have workers had with critical reflection? How would workers react to the idea of using critical reflection in supervision? How might managers react to the implications of a critical reflection framework for analysing practice? We are suggesting here that it is helpful to start with experiencing critical reflection in a group setting such as a workshop. What, then, might be the reactions to suggesting a critical reflection workshop? What is possible in terms of funding? How are resources allocated for training?

Promoting critical reflection

Probably the most effective way of promoting critical reflection is having workers who have experienced it generate enthusiasm. It may be that you or someone in your organization has been to a workshop or has explored critical reflection as part of undergraduate or postgraduate study. Our experience has been that having someone able to speak from direct experience of critical reflection is often more powerful than providing information in other ways. However, it is important to think about who speaks and how. Is the person who can talk from their own experience someone who is respected in their own and other organizations, or is their support likely to be counterproductive? Participants say that if they are aiming to convince managers and those who control the training budget they need to think about strategies like providing information about outcomes for participants (see Chapter 8 and the online resources at www.openup.co.uk/fook&gardner), or at least illuminating examples about how critical reflection works in practice.

Having a critical reflection workshop is often an effective way to introduce this subject. This might be, to give some examples:

- within an organization
- offered to a set of organizations in a particular geographic area

- for a number of organizations with a shared field or practice or interest
- for interested individuals within many organizations.

Running a workshop means that there are a number of people who have experienced critical reflection at the same time. Participants say that this can create momentum to implement critical reflection in other ways; participants support each other to maintain the learning from the workshops and to implement this either in their own organization or across organizations, through supervision (see Chapter 9), research and evaluation (Chapter 10) or direct practice (Chapter 11).

Generally, we have found that the next most usual and effective way to promote critical reflection workshops is to make information available, so that all staff and/or possible participants are clear about:

- the purpose of the workshop
- how it operates
- what will be covered
- what is expected of participants
- the usual outcomes for the participants
- what previous participants have seen as the benefits and uses of critical reflection.

Ideally, this information is provided at a briefing session where the facilitator of critical reflection workshops presents the information to all potential participants. This means that possible participants can also gain a sense of the facilitator and how they operate. For some people this is important; they can see from the briefing session that critical reflection can be challenging and they want to feel that they can trust the facilitator to maintain a positive culture in the workshop.

Where this is not possible, it is helpful to think about other ways the information can be distributed. Sometimes, the facilitator might meet with a small group or the staff member organizing the workshop and they will then pass the information on to possible participants. Alternatively, written information can be sent out to all possible participants either directly from the facilitator or from the person within the organization who is arranging the process. Articles about critical reflection can be made available to give a clear idea of the process.

Participation issues: voluntary and involuntary

This is one of the contentious issues in setting up critical reflection: should participation be voluntary and, if so, how do you ensure that it is? In many ways, our preference is for voluntary participation. Critical reflection, as we are outlining it here, does require at least a minimum amount of self-disclosure. There are questions about how ethical it is to expect this if people have no choice about participating (Brookfield 1995). There is no choice, for example, about sharing an incident from practice and engaging in discussion with a workshop group. This expectation is clearly stated from the beginning and demonstrated in the first session. Although participants can decide not to answer specific questions about their incident, there is a group expectation that everyone will share to a reasonable degree. Because of this, the group process is likely to be more effective with willing participants. Critical reflection can also be at least unsettling, 'as troubling and unrestful as unquestioning lack of change can be boring' (Bolton 2001: 51). For some people, it can raise painful issues (Brookfield 1994; Duke and Copp 1994) as we will discuss later, and this also supports critical reflection being voluntary.

However, this issue is more complex than it might appear. The apparently clear binary between voluntary and involuntary is not always so in practice. Workers may come to a workshop, for example, partly because they were told it was compulsory, but become interested in and committed to the process after the first session. For some, even though they resent the involuntary expectation, they may also have become interested because of feedback from other workers. In some pressured work environments, workers have said they were pleased the workshops were involuntary: they were able to come only because the workshop had been deemed compulsory by senior management and was therefore given priority reluctantly by middle managers. In other situations, a team may decide, it seems voluntarily, to have a workshop together, but some team members may feel somewhat pressured by others to agree.

In agency Y, all staff had been told that they would be expected to attend a critical reflection workshop over the next six months. When the facilitator arrived for the fourth set of workshops, the first two participants (who were early) were discussing this and expressing their frustration about it. As the other participants arrived, this issue continued to be explored. It soon became clear that there were mixed views: two people were angry on principle – they didn't think this training should be compulsory; another pointed out that other training was and nobody objected; a fourth said she would never get to training unless it was compulsory and a fifth that the issue was about confidentiality more than choice. Finally, I [Fiona] as the facilitator asked what the group wanted to do, did they want to proceed with this training or not? All then agreed that they had heard about the training from other people and thought it sounded great, so the workshop got under way.

Suppose a team decides that as a group they would like to participate in a critical reflection workshop partly as a team-building exercise and partly because they think it would give them a shared language and understanding of useful theory, and as a way of moving to group supervision using critical reflection. However, one of the team members may feel less comfortable about the expectations of the group, but not feel able to say so and simply not arrive on the first day. What does the team and the facilitator then do? Do they respect the right of the person not to participate or do they require that they attend the next session. What does this mean for other participants and the group dynamic?

It can be more helpful to think about this issue as a continuum of voluntary–involuntary. There is more choice than there may initially appear. Obviously, participants decide on their own incident, for example, which means that they can choose what at least appears to be a relatively 'safe' incident if they want to, an incident from a past workplace or with colleagues who are no longer part of the work environment. They can also choose how to respond, how open to be and what questions they will respond to. Ultimately, and this is made clear in discussion about the group climate (see Chapter 5), they can choose to end the process. Our experience is that for the majority of participants the process is positive and so even involuntary participation becomes increasingly voluntary.

Group composition

The question of choice is further complicated by the question of who is in the group. Some participants would say that they will accept an involuntary group if they like all the people in it! The question of group composition needs to be thought about in terms of organizational and inter-organizational contexts. In organizations where there is a lot of conflict between individuals and/or teams there are more likely to be issues about who is in the same critical reflection group. This raises the issue of whether people need to know beforehand who else will be in the group and what this means in terms of confidentiality. Part of the question here is about how participants can feel free to explore; Brookfield (2005: 354) talks about the need for people to have 'momentary separation from the demands and patterns of everyday life [that] allows them to view society in a newly critical way'. For some people, this is better achieved by being separate from supervisors, for others by mixing with those from other organizations.

A mix of levels?

This raises the question of whether participants should be from the same level if they are all from the same organization or whether there will be a mix of team leaders/managers and workers on the ground. Again, there are no definitive answers. On the one hand, we have had experience with some workshops where the issue of who is in the group does not seem to matter. For example, one group had three people from the same organization at different levels of the hierarchy – a base-grade worker, her supervisor and then her supervisor's supervisor. All three agreed that being in the same workshop helped deepen their understanding of each other's perspective. On the other hand, and probably more frequently, workers and supervisors are reluctant to be in the same group, feeling that they will not be able to speak as openly. There are issues of power and control here: workers may fear that, consciously or unconsciously, their supervisors will be negatively influenced by what they say. Supervisors may fear their authority will be eroded if they are perceived as less than perfect. Some of the underlying assumptions here can usefully be challenged in workshops, provided participants feel safe to do so. Often it is helpful to ask organizations to think this through for themselves beforehand, and to help them by providing guidelines for doing so.

Jacquie, a supervisor of a residential care team, went to a critical reflection workshop with her team. She chose an incident from a previous position where she had felt undermined as a supervisor because she hadn't prevented a traumatic incident for a worker. As the group helped her look at her underlying assumptions, she realized that she took for granted that supervisors should be perfect, never make mistakes, and always be available and supportive to staff. She could see how unhelpful this was and started to explore new assumptions: supervisors are also human, can learn from mistakes, and need to be realistic about what they can and can't do. One of her team members commented: 'I know you are still talking about that other job, but it would be great if you could bring those new assumptions here too – we would feel like we were relating to a real person, not a perfectionist.'

Should there be a mix of professional background or practice focus?

In some ways it can seem easier to use critical reflection with people from similar professional backgrounds. They will be more likely to have a common language and theory base, and will be familiar with the kind of work each other is likely to do, especially if they come from the same organization. Similarly, having a mix of workers from the same organization can provide a common starting point: a policy development worker and a residential care worker may choose to present very similar incidents in terms of working in a large bureaucratic organization.

However, there are also advantages to having mixed professional groups; participants are more likely to question each other's assumptions about how things are done because they come from a different perspective. This can also demonstrate how critical reflection can be used across different professional work areas as well as different work domains. Some writers would suggest that there are many similarities between professionals anyway – for example, that professionals are aiming to translate a body of theory into practice in a service-orientated way (Higgs and Titchen 2001). Looking at key assumptions and values in critical reflection workshops certainly seems to elicit common themes across professional groups. Such groups are also likely to come from a mixture of organizational backgrounds. This can also provide different perspectives to prompt useful questioning of assumptions.

Mike, a social worker, and Dave, a teacher, were intrigued by each other's assumptions about what was important about their work. Mike assumed that he needed to understand each person's individual perspective in a given situation; Dave assumed that his first priority needed to be establishing discipline in a class. As they each explored their incident it became clear that they had more in common than first appeared: both saw their work as a balancing act between the needs of individuals and their context – whether that was a family, class or community. What was stressful about their work was recognizing different needs and not being able to fulfil them.

Inside or outside organizations?

Workshops can be run inside organizations – with teams or a mix of participants from across the organizations – or from outside organizations, probably with a mixture of people who don't know each other. Again there are advantages and disadvantages in each case. Feedback about running workshops with a mixture of participants from different organizations is often positive: participants say they feel more able to speak freely about their incident, their reactions and their organization to 'outsiders'. This is partly because there is no history, no other agendas, no need to think about the impact on current relationships. Hearing about how other organizations are both similar to and different from their own gives new perspectives on organizational life and possible reactions to it.

Kate and Jennifer work in different organizations. Kate was surprised to hear how similar Jennifer's incident was to her own; when she heard it she commented, 'You could have written that incident for me.' Both talked about how a specific inflexible organizational policy had unexpected and negative consequences for them. Realizing that this was not something that happened only in her own organization changed Kate's feelings about working there; she had been thinking about leaving, but decided that she should stay and work on changing the policy.

Other participants, though, have valued having the workshop in their organization. They felt that there was much of the culture of organizational life that was understood that would have needed more explanation for people outside the organization. In some groups in large organizations, participants have come from many different sections and didn't know each other beforehand. The workshops then provided a way of networking, forging new links, and some people continued to meet afterwards. Some preferred knowing other participants, felt safer with people they had already established relationships with and so more able to speak honestly about their incident. They also felt that as a group exploring the same organization as the context for their incidents they were building a common picture about what needed to change and how they could support each other to do that.

Practical issues in planning workshops

Facilitation

Who will facilitate the workshop is a central question. As we identified earlier in the chapter, having good facilitation is central to the success of workshops. Related to this is having someone who is seen as a 'safe' facilitator, who can be trusted by the group. In some ways having an outside facilitator is easier: there are no complications about lines of authority; facilitation is perceived in a more neutral way. On the other hand, an inside facilitator understands how the organization operates and is likely to be familiar to participants (Askeland 2003).

How much funding you need will depend on how you are planning to run the workshop. Outside facilitators may charge a fee for running workshops, which may or may not be negotiable; and of course services may be negotiated in kind. Particularly in rural areas, there may be extra charges for travel and/or accommodation. Alternatively, if staff are travelling to the facilitator, there will be costs for them of travel and/or accommodation, and these may be a major factor in the financial viability of conducting the workshop.

Think creatively about cost

Having an outside facilitator may seem expensive, but if you divide the amount charged by the number of staff at the workshop it is likely to be reasonable. This is especially so if the facilitator travels to the staff rather than the other way round. If you are in a small organization and can't afford the cost, think about sharing the workshop with another organization. Alternatively, see the workshop as a community development initiative and offer places to a number of organizations.

Other costs are those that would need to be considered for any workshop: catering, venue, advertising, and printing of resource materials.

Group size

As suggested earlier in the chapter, our preference is for a group of about eight participants; the maximum group size should be ten, and our ideal would be between six and eight. This is small enough for the group to develop a sense of trust and 'knowing' each other relatively quickly (Brown 1994). It also allows enough time for each person to explore their incident. The group is big enough for diversity; participants hear a range of incidents and see how the process can be applied to each one. This also means participants have enough experience or practice working with the process to develop confidence in being able to use the process on their own, in supervision or in teams.

However, this also depends on the organization and the needs of the participants. Some organizations want a workshop for a particular team, which could be as small as three participants. While three may seem very small, participants say that the relative lack of variety is balanced with intensity: time to explore each incident in more depth. The issue of size relates very much to time.

Time and timing

Organizational context is critical here too in considering the timing of workshops; there is no point, for example, planning to run groups in a child protection setting on court days. Most organizations seem to have particular days when staff are more likely to be able to attend workshops. Some have times of year that are better than others: school holidays, for example, tend not to work as well because more people are on leave and those left have to cover for them.

We have tried various ways of structuring workshops. Our preferred way was outlined earlier – three sessions over three weeks. Having said that, we have also had positive feedback on quite different timings, including the following.

- Having the three sessions a month instead of a week apart: for some workplaces a weekly workshop is seen as impossible given workloads, and monthly is more realistic. In such cases, it helps to start the workshops by checking where people are, what they remember, what feels distant, reminding participants about the purpose of this particular workshop.
- Running the three sessions together in a two-day workshop with a very long first day: again this was done to fit a particular organizational context. It did mean that participants were asked to read material beforehand and to come with an incident already prepared. Some people commented that they might have chosen a different incident if they had seen how the process worked first. Some commented that they liked the intensity of the process; others would have liked more time for reflection.

- Having five half-day sessions over two to three months: this means that contact is being maintained reasonably frequently. The participants' presentations are spread over two sessions rather than one. This is easier to fit in for busy organizations – half a day in training feels more manageable.

> David's incident focused on an argument with a colleague who David thought wasn't advocating sufficiently for clients needing services. The group had asked him whether he had an assumption that his way was always right and so didn't ask his colleague why he was acting as he was. David reacted angrily, disagreeing with this, but arrived at the second session saying that he had realized that he did operate like that and it caused problems in many areas of his life. Having the time between sessions helped him calm down and think more about his reaction. He had also talked to the colleague in question and found that the colleague's assumption was that being less pushy got better results. David wanted to use the workshop to look at his own assumptions more and to think about his actions.

Venue

One of the main questions here is where to locate workshops: in the organization requesting the workshop or at a separate venue? There are advantages in having a neutral venue: workers comment that this helps them leave work behind and concentrate on the workshop. Some organizations can find a relatively neutral venue that is still part of their own facilities, such as a conference room at a different location, for example, or a training room in a residential facility.

Organizations often prefer to have the workshops in their workplace because of cost – not having to pay for another venue and because the perception is that it is easier for workers to go to their usual workplace. Depending on the organizational context, there may also be a feeling that it is useful to be able to access workers. This, of course, is one of the disadvantages of running workshops in organizations. Workers can easily return to their desks during a tea break or lunch and get distracted from the workshop, possibly even getting caught up in a crisis and not returning.

> A child protection team decided to hold a critical reflection workshop on a Friday in the conference room, located next door to their offices. During the lunch break, several of the team members discovered that their colleagues were feeling very pressured about placing several children in care for the weekend. One

decided to stay and help, the other two returned to the workshop but were clearly distracted. This was raised and the workers articulated their assumptions: first, that training was a luxury compared to dealing with the important work on the ground and, second, that a good worker would put supporting stressed colleagues first. The group worked together to critically reflect on these issues, and decided they needed new assumptions, but found it hard to let go of their immediate concern about their colleagues.

We have facilitated workshops next to a pool at a conference, in a small windowless room in the middle of a four-storey building, in conference rooms and tea rooms. Clearly, critical reflection workshops can be run almost anywhere. Ideally, though, such workshops need the same basic conditions that any group work requires; given that the sessions may last a whole day and can be relatively intense, it is more important than with usual learning groups that the environment be comfortable (with access to refreshments and facilities), well ventilated and pleasant, allowing enough room for participants to sit in a circle or to see each other easily and thus encourage equal participation.

Chapter summary

This chapter provides a broad overview of the design of the model. The essential aim of the model is to unsettle the fundamental (and dominant) thinking implicit in professional practices, in order to see other ways of practising. What is unearthed and the other ways of practising will vary depending on what is meaningful or significant to the participants.

Generally the process in this model is to work in facilitated small groups of up to eight members in three sessions separated by roughly a week.

1. Introductory session (half a day): includes an introduction to the theory and process (including culture) of critical reflection, and a modelling of the process by the facilitator.
2. Stage 1 critical reflection: unsettling the assumptions of each participant in turn, through reflection on a specific critical incident presented by each.
3. Stage 2 reflection: presentations by each participant in turn, which focus on changed thinking (from stage 1) and the implications for practice.

The culture of the group is vital in sustaining a focused but open process, where all members assist each other to reflect. Because of this, context is important in setting up training in critical reflection. In thinking about initiating a critical reflection process, it is useful to explore the advantages and disadvantages of working within an organization, across organizations or outside organizations. Group composition and choice about attending, for example, are important issues to consider. Planning carefully, taking into account the dynamics of power and relationships, makes for more effective workshops. The venue, timing, times of workshops and choice of facilitator will all impact on workshops.

5 The introductory session

In this chapter we aim to describe in detail the content covered in the introductory session, as well as relevant issues that may need to be addressed. We follow the structure in which the topics would normally be covered in the session. We begin with group introductions; this is followed by the introduction to the critical reflection model (definitions, purposes, theory, process and culture); next we discuss the facilitator's modelling of the process and handling of issues that arise; and we finish with suggestions for how to link this session with the next one.

Sample programmes for the introductory session are included in the online resource materials on the website that accompanies this book (www.openup.co.uk/fook&gardner).

Group introductions

It may seem self-evident, even banal, to point out that good groups begin with adequate introductions (Brown 1994; Northen and Kurland 2001) but we find it is particularly important with critical reflection groups to ensure that introductions of members are done in a way that is relevant to the purpose and culture of the group. We usually allow a couple of minutes' self-introduction by each participant (including the facilitator). In general, we like to offer an opportunity for people to introduce themselves in the terms of their own choosing – this helps to establish a culture that values and legitimates people's own perspectives. However, we have found that, for a group like this it is also helpful to include something more specific regarding critical reflection. The introduction of each person therefore usually includes:

- name, organization, description of position or work role, profession or discipline background
- why they want to participate in a critical reflection group

• their prior experience or understanding of critical reflection.

Obviously the introductions may vary a little depending on whether or not members come from the same organization, but it is usually worthwhile to have some reasonably extensive formal introduction period, whether or not members already know each other. This acts as a way of establishing a relatively equal and neutral footing for the new group.

The input about why people want to participate in the group offers useful stimulus material that the facilitator can pick up on to address issues around the purposes of the specific group, and how people's expectations may or may not be addressed. For example, group members will sometimes say they do not know what to expect or are apprehensive, or, as has happened to us often enough, that they are here because they were told they had to come! These introductions provide an excellent and focused opportunity to set a climate of openness, to address anxieties or misapprehensions, and to maximize the participatory input of group members. For example, for people who feel they are involuntary members, it might be useful to focus on what they think they might get out of the group despite this, or how any defensive or negative attitudes as a result of this might be addressed – for example, 'What would be your preferred way of learning?', 'How might you gain some of those benefits from this group?'

The input regarding prior experience provides a platform from which to address people's prior conceptions of critical reflection, and to undertake some preliminary discussion of how the model being presented may or may not differ from it. For example, we often find that many social workers and nurses have been taught reflective practice approaches, and say that they are therefore familiar with critical reflection. We might then point out that, while there are some important similarities between critical reflection and reflective practice, there are also some important differences. What we are trying to do here is lay the groundwork for all participants to be open to some new learning, whether or not they have prior experience of critical reflection. We might also invite those who have had prior experience to comment in an ongoing way on how that experience compares with the model we'll be using in the group, so that we might all learn from the comparisons. In this sense we are trying to value prior experience, but also carve out a legitimate place for new learning as well.

Obviously, in addition to the above, the points raised by participants in introducing themselves provide good reference points for later discussion, and enable the facilitator to draw individual participants directly into more generalized discussion. For instance, we may often refer to earlier comments made by participants as a way of comparing a later point with earlier thinking. For example, if someone had stated at the beginning of the group that they felt anxious, we might refer back to this later on when discussing feelings that have arisen during the process. We might further discuss what the anxiety is about, what it meant in the process and how it related to learning.

Introducing the critical reflection model

Why critically reflect? The broader context of critical reflection

We often begin the session by asking why we need critical reflection in an age when there seems to be more certainty (in some quarters of the world and in some organizations) about right and wrong ways to act, and about what are good and bad outcomes. Our argument is that, in the face of increasing uncertainty, some people's reactions are to try to assert more certainty. Critical reflection can be a way of acknowledging, and in fact managing, uncertainty in the contexts and work of professionals.

In this section therefore we begin with the current challenges to professional knowledge as being the key reason for the need for critical reflection (as discussed in Chapter 1) (see also Schon's Chapter 1, 1983; Fook *et al.* 2000; Fook 2002, 2004d, 2007). (A reading pack for postgraduate students is included in the online resource materials at www.openup.co.uk/fook&gardner. These are articles that we usually provide copies of for workshop participants.) This analysis provides an important legitimizing framework for critical reflection in professional practice. We emphasize the following points:

- current contexts of practice are characterized by risk, uncertainty, changeability and complexity
- practice must rise above the routine in order to be effective in unpredictable environments
- abstract theories learnt at university or from textbooks are often inadequate as a basis for professional practice knowledge in situations that are so new or so complex that they are under-researched or even unresearchable
- in addition, much professional practice is values-based, seemingly at odds within a context that is increasingly technological or economically driven
- practice knowledge must constantly be remade in relation to context, since contexts are so changeable.

In discussing these points it is useful to ask for participants to volunteer examples of instances where they have felt their professional knowledge is inadequate, or where they have felt they have had to 'make it up' on the spot, or draw on personal resources or intuition.

The above points are also useful to participants if they wish to make an argument for incorporating critical reflection more formally in their workplaces.

What is critical reflection and what is involved?

We cover the following points, presented here in order of importance.

Critical reflection is both a theory and a practice

The basic point we are emphasizing here is that critical reflection is a method or process for thinking in a particular way. It is not necessarily just done naturally by people, but is in fact based on an identifiable framework, which informs the way it is practised, and assists in enabling it to be practised better.

Critical reflection involves both analysis and action – changed awareness that leads to changed practices

The point we are making here is that critical reflection is not just 'navel-gazing' or 'armchair thinking' (although there is nothing necessarily inherently wrong with these activities), nor is it primarily about just finding better ways to practise. It is about both – about finding better ways to practise based clearly on different ways of thinking. What is as important about both aspects of analysis and action is the ability to link them.

What is primarily involved is the unsettling and examination of assumptions

'Unsettling' here refers to an image of 'shaking up'. We often use the example of muesli. Muesli comprises many different types of ingredients, of different weights and sizes: rolled oats, oat bran, small grains of wheatgerm, dates, sultanas, dried papaya. Heavier pieces often fall to the bottom. Shaking the packet or jar dislodges and mixes up the layers.

What sorts of assumptions are unsettled and examined?

The assumptions that are deeper, more fundamental, or hidden or implicit are the ones particularly focused on. When the muesli is shaken, often the pieces that had fallen to the bottom are shaken to the top. These may often be the heavier pieces, which if allowed to settle become part of a lower layer that is harder to dislodge if left over a long period of time. It is precisely these pieces that are harder to access or choose if they are stuck at the bottom.

How are these assumptions unsettled and examined?

The process of critical reflection is like a process of shaking up assumptions, so the heavier ones, which have become more disguised and perhaps forgotten over time, are raised to the top. A person can then access them . . . but, importantly, they do not have to take them. What is given through access is choice. Even though I may prefer heavy raisins to wheatgerm, I do not have to take the raisins just because they are shaken to the top. What I now have through my process of unsettling is the choice of raisins or wheatgerm or rolled oats or papaya, or whatever. The process of critical reflection therefore gives choices. The decision about what to choose is then exposed as a separate decision.

In the critical reflection process the main tools used to shake up assumptions and aid choice about those assumptions are critical reflective questions, used in a group process of dialogue. Taking our muesli image further, critical reflective questions are like the spoons one might use to dig into the muesli to take particular pieces. The group is like the packet or jar that holds the muesli, and the process is more like the dynamics or movement of the jar or packet being shaken.

The aims: focused process yet uncertain outcomes

In this section we aim to help participants understand the unconventional nature of critical reflection: that although concrete outcomes are an important aim of the process, how these are achieved, and exactly what these will look like, is uncertain. This is the paradox of 'uncertain uncertainty' (Bolton 2001: 200) that so accurately characterizes critical reflection.

The ultimate aim of critical reflection is to improve professional practice, using a particular process of unsettling the fundamental assumptions that are implicit in practice experiences. The ultimate aim of the process is therefore tied integrally to the process itself. In this sense the aim of critical reflection is to improve professional practice in a particular type of way, based on a particular way of understanding the relationship between individual practices and beliefs and their social contexts. Therefore the actual outcomes of the critical reflection process may be conceptualized in particular ways that must be meaningful to the person reflecting, and therefore, in some senses, they are unpredictable at the beginning of the process. This means that the actual changes or improvements made to professional thinking and practice are not predetermined, or even necessarily determinable before the process begins, but must emerge as the process is undertaken. In this sense there are both clear, yet uncertain aims of critical reflection. The structure, theory and process of critical reflection are clear and focused – what actual outcomes and changes will emerge is uncertain. Gillie Bolton (2001: 201) characterizes the experience nicely as 'thoughtfully unthinking' and a 'process of letting go'. We would add that it is a process of letting go in order to find things that may be unimaginable, or unimagined.

Another important point to make to participants here is that 'change' does not always occur, in that everyone is not expected necessarily to radically change their practice. Some people may find their practice reaffirmed, but that different ways of seeing it will give them more options. (At this point, please refer to the student assignment written by Helen, which you can find on the accompanying website at www.openup.co.uk/fook&gardner.) We find that recognizing and naming this fact reduces potential threats people may feel, and increases their openness to all sorts of different perspectives. For instance, some people may find that, during the process, their fundamental beliefs become reaffirmed, but that what happens is they learn that there might be other ways to practise that will allow them to better enact these beliefs in different contexts.

One of the things that I [Jan] often discover about myself from modelling my own reflection process in groups is that one of my main embedded beliefs/values is social justice. However, I often realize that, in taking this position, I assume the moral high ground and therefore do not allow anyone else to take it – I implicitly and irrevocably construct 'enemies and allies' (Fook 2000) in the workplace. (Please refer at this point to the article 'The lone crusader: constructing enemies and allies in the workplace', included on the accompanying website at www.openup.co.uk/fook&gardner. This is a useful article in that it is a written version of a critical reflection on a specific critical incident, so it serves to illustrate the process of thinking and the changes involved.)

The theory

As discussed in Chapter 3, we explain the theoretical framework of critical reflection as originating from four major traditions: the reflective approach to practice; reflexivity; postmodernism/deconstruction; critical social theory. In this part of the introductory session we are primarily aiming to help participants understand three things:

1. that critical reflection can be confusing as a concept, but also very rich, because of its mixed traditions; there is no need to understand each of the traditions in detail
2. participants may build on their theoretical understanding if this is a meaningful way for them to critically reflect; for this reason we name the traditions and try to give a basic understanding
3. the main thing we want participants to take from this part of the session is a working understanding of how the different theoretical

traditions might translate usefully into ways of locating how their own hidden thinking (and choices about their own thinking) helps influence their professional practice.

Below we summarize the main points of each tradition, and how they contribute to critical reflection, for presentation to the group. We have also included the basic rationale for each tradition, and suggestions for how each might be presented. We tend to expand or compress this section depending on the group membership and available time. We have summarized the most basic points that need to be covered. (These are summarized directly from the material in Chapter 3.)

The four traditions of critical reflection

The reflective approach

In presenting the reflective approach we are mainly trying to emphasize how hidden assumptions affect practice, and also how many types of professional knowledge (some of which cannot be known consciously prior to practice experience in a particular situation) are needed in order to work effectively at any one time, in any one context. It is usually helpful to ask participants to volunteer examples of instances where they have felt they didn't know what they were doing, and what they felt guided them in those instances.

Summary: the reflective approach

- Theory is implicit in professional practice.
- Professional practice is holistic, contextual and complex, making it difficult to research and practice.
- Professional practice may be improved by closing the gap between what is implicit and what is explicitly practised.
- It helps us look for discrepancies between implicit and explicit assumptions.
- It acts as a tool for evaluation of practice.
- It acts as a tool for researching complex practice.
- It acts as a tool for developing practice theory.

Reflexivity

In presenting the material on reflexivity, we are mainly trying to communicate the point that knowledge is not just an objective thing, but that we all also participate in knowledge creation, thereby influencing what it is we know. It is often helpful to begin with a brief exercise. We sometimes ask people what they see when they look in a mirror. We ask this because people often liken reflexivity to a type of mirroring, an ability to understand the world in terms of how it is reflected. Besides eliciting a lot of laughter, the range of answers is instructive, because it serves to illustrate the range of perspectives there can be on the type of information that is elicited and the range of reasons there might be for looking in a mirror. Answers range from 'a fat 40-year-old' to 'I see how other people see me' to 'whether my teeth are clean'. It is useful to draw out the following points from the responses:

- it enables us to see things we might not normally see, such as our contexts, behind us, other people's perspectives
- what we see differs according to the reason we look in the mirror, the time of day, the context
- we often see only what we are looking for
- we only see what we want to see.

Summary: reflexivity

- It is the ability to recognize that all aspects of ourselves and our contexts influence the way we research (create knowledge) and the actual knowledge we create.
- It shows us that knowledge creation is influenced by our physicality and material contexts; our social and historical contexts; interaction; and the tools we use to create the knowledge.
- It shows us that we ourselves are therefore researchers and also research tools.
- It shows us how our own assumptions, especially about the nature of knowledge and how it is and should be created, have an influence on the actual knowledge we create and believe in.

Postmodernism and deconstruction

The main point that we want participants to understand here is the connections between the knowledge and power – how the knowledge we create or believe in also has powerful functions.

Summary: postmodernism and deconstruction

- Postmodernism involves questioning that there is only 'one truth'.
- What is believed to be 'one truth' (dominant discourse) often masks power.
- This power is able to function through the ways we communicate.
- Therefore our language plays a role in maintaining dominant discourses through:
  - disguising other (multiple) 'truths' or perspectives
  - disguising less powerful (marginal) 'truths' or perspectives
  - binary ways of categorizing phenomena.
- Therefore, by examining our language use, we can unearth the implicit assumptions that support dominant power (deconstruct), and how we therefore participate in constructing power.
- There are several specific types of thinking that might do this:
  - looking at what we believe to be 'one truth'
  - looking for what perspectives are missing or left out
  - looking at how we construct categories, and what categories we construct (e.g. our own identities and those of others, dilemmas in practice, problem types and related solutions, professional knowledge and theories).

Critical social theory

The main points that need to be understood by participants here are the connections between personal experience and the broader social context, and how these intertwine in the professional context to inform both knowing and doing. What may help to illustrate this to the group is asking participants for examples of particular beliefs, and then asking where those beliefs come from. Sometimes people respond that they hold a belief that professionals should always be objective; they will usually say it is something they firmly believe personally, but when thinking further may acknowledge that it comes from their professional training (they didn't think this before they trained, necessarily) or that it comes from broader society (e.g. 'Doesn't everyone think this?', 'I got it from watching TV shows about doctors').

Summary: critical social theory

- It shows how power is both personally experienced and socially constructed.

- Often this happens because individuals internalize beliefs that also function to preserve power at social levels (ideology).
- Sometimes these beliefs actually restrict or work against the interests of the individual person who holds them.
- This may particularly be the case if the individual and their interests are part of a marginalized or less powerful group.
- Therefore, as professionals, we may hold assumptions that actually work against what we want to achieve for service users (or ourselves) who are disempowered in some way.
- This perspective points us to look for how our assumptions might therefore function to work against our interests, and therefore how we might need to change them in order to be less restricted.

Overview of the process

In broad terms the process involves two stages, as we have already stated: the group members (and the person reflecting on their own practice experience) using questions (and engaging in dialogue) to help elicit the assumptions embedded in each other's accounts of practice (stage 1); and, through further questioning and dialogue, helping each other derive changed practices and theories about practice that result from their reflections (stage 2). The accounts of practice used are normally descriptions of critical incidents. We discuss the stages, the questions and the critical incident technique in detail below.

The stages

As we mentioned earlier, we think it important to separate the two stages of critical reflection on assumptions and critical reflection on changed assumptions and practices. The prime focus and purpose of stage 1, therefore, is to unsettle, unearth and examine fundamental and implicit assumptions. The criteria for examination, and therefore the criteria for what is fundamental, are usually identified by the person reflecting, often with the assistance of group members in clarifying and articulating what is important and meaningful to each person. At the end of the first stage the discussion therefore aims to help each person articulate some changed and meaningful awareness of their experience. This may take the form of, for example: a different or new perspective; an awareness of assumptions they were hitherto unaware of; a new feeling about the experience (e.g. may feel relieved or unburdened); clarity about fundamental meaning or importance.

To be reasonably confident the person has arrived at a point like this, we usually ask them to summarize what thinking they are taking away that they want to further reflect on. Also we always ask how they feel after the discussion of their practice has ended. This not only acts as a form of debriefing for the person, but allows us as group facilitators to gauge the nature of the learning experience for the person, and to assess how much debriefing might need to be done before the session is ready to be closed. We also follow this by a few minutes spent talking about the critical reflection process: what sorts of questions helped; what did people like (or not) about the process; did it meet expectations; what doubts do they have, and so on.

These sorts of questions are revisited at the end of each person's presentation (time permitting), or at the end of every two or three presentations, and again at the end of all stage 1 presentations. The aim of these discussions is to further participants' learning about the critical reflection process itself. In this sense the learning is on two levels: about the participant's own practice (their own and that of others), and about the critical reflection process and skills.

The winding up of the first stage also includes a briefing on stage 2, and what is expected of participants between stages 1 and 2. Participants are asked to further reflect on the changed thinking they are taking away from stage 1, and then to work out what this might mean for how they may need to change their thinking about practice further, and how they may need to change their practice. In short, they are asked what they will do differently, or what they would do differently, if they experienced the same incident again. Participants are sometimes given a set of questions to take away and use to help them structure their thinking between stages.

Stage 2 is structured slightly differently. Each participant reports on the further reflection they have engaged in, and posits further possibilities. The role of the group in this stage is to use critical reflective questions to enable clarity about each person's further reflections, and also to engage in further dialogue with each person to help them connect their theory and practices. By the end of this session the aim is to help each person be able to articulate their new theory of practice, by finding a label that represents accurately how their new thinking and new ideas about practice are connected.

Questions to aid critical reflection

Sets of sample questions are derived along the lines of each of the theoretical traditions that inform critical reflection. These are intended only as illustrations of the sorts of questions participants might ask each other or themselves. We always stress that everyone will find their own way of wording them, and that what is most important is that the ways questions are asked sets up a climate to assist a person to reflect for themselves, rather than have other people's perspectives imposed on them.

Examples of questions that might aid critical reflection are set out overleaf.

Reflective practice questions
For stage one:

- What does my account of my critical incident imply about, for example, my basic ideals or values, my beliefs about power, my view of myself and other people, what I believe about professionalism?
- Are there any gaps or contradictions between what I say I do and what is implied by what I do?

For stage two:

- What is behind these contradictions and where do they come from?
- How do I handle these contradictions?
- What needs to change about my thinking or practice to handle the contradictions?

Reflexive questions
For stage one:

- How did I influence the situation through: my presence, my actions, my preconceptions or assumptions, other people's perceptions of me, my physical well-being on the day?
- How have the tools I used to understand the situation affected what I saw?
- How might I have acted differently if there was something different about the situation (e.g. the other person was of a different gender, I was older, I was in a different role, I hadn't had the same history or experience)? What does this say about my own biases and preconceptions?
- How has who I am affected what I noticed or felt was important?
- What might be the perspective of other players in the situation? Why is mine different?

For stage two:

- How might I have acted differently so as to influence the situation the way I wanted to?
- What beliefs or preconceptions might allow me to be more open to other ways of seeing the situation?

Postmodern/deconstructive questions
For stage one:

- What words or language patterns have I used? What do these indicate about the way I am constructing the situation?
- What perspectives are missing from my account?
- What binaries, or 'either–or, forced choice' categories have I constructed?
- How have I constructed myself, or my professional role, in relation to other people?

For stage two:

- What functions, particularly functions in relation to power, do these constructions perform?
- How might I want to change these constructions to be more in line with my desired thinking and practice?

Critical questions
For stage one:

- What assumptions are implicit in my account and where do they come from?
- How do my personal experience and beliefs from my social context interact in this situation?
- What functions (particularly powerful functions) do my beliefs hold?

For stage two:

- What do I want to change about my beliefs or practices so I am less restricted?
- What might I do as an individual that will contribute to broader-level collective changes (with immediate colleagues or in my workplace)?

The critical incident technique

In this session we simply describe what we mean by a critical incident, and provide sufficient criteria to assist participants in choosing one to present for reflection. We usually provide a written sheet that participants can take away as a guide to preparing the description of their incident (refer to the 'Preparatory work' handout in the online resources at www.openup.co.uk/fook&gardner).

Below is a summary of the main features of the critical incident. We then discuss aspects of these in more detail.

The critical incident is an incident that:

- is significant or important (to professional learning)
- is an incident from which the participant wants to learn
- protects the confidentiality of other players in the incident
- is an incident the participant is prepared to expose to the group, and will minimize risk but maximize learning potential
- should be written out (maximum one page) and include in the participant's own words
    - why it is significant
    - a raw and concrete description of the context/background to the incident
    - a raw concrete description of the incident.

Copies should be made and distributed to each participant on the day of presentation.

What is a critical incident?

By critical incident we are simply referring to something (an event) that happened to a person that they regard as important or significant in some way. 'Critical' in this sense does not have to be an emergency or crisis; it may in fact have been critical because it was banal or repetitious. It should simply be important to the person for whatever their own reasons are. In some cases they may not even be able to articulate why it is important, but are clearly aware that it is significant.

What type of critical incident is appropriate? The type of critical incident you ask people to bring may vary slightly depending on the purposes of the group. We suggest that if the group is for professional learning, then participants should be asked to bring an incident that they felt was significant to their professional learning. We have often been asked whether the incidents must be negative. This is always an interesting question because we are careful never to use the terms 'positive' or 'negative' regarding incidents. However, it seems almost overwhelmingly the case that people choose what they have experienced as 'negative' incidents for reflection. For them this may mean incidents that were puzzling, traumatic, ones they couldn't stop worrying about or forget, that they regretted, thought they could have handled better, or felt strongly (negatively) about. In our experience these seem to be the ones from which people are most open to learning, ones that they want to rework in order to gain some different type of new meaning. It seems that if people bring incidents that they have felt were positive (usually because they think they did well) they have more of a vested interest in preserving their perspective on them, and are therefore less open to other perspectives. This is the key point here: participants should choose incidents they are open to learning from. It does not matter in this sense whether they regard them as positive or negative. In fact, as mentioned above, these are terms and frames of reference we deliberately do not use, as we are trying to avoid prejudgement. (We will discuss this point further later, when we discuss group culture.)

It is also important that participants choose incidents they are prepared to share in the group, which means that they need to have thought through some of the privacy and vulnerability issues for themselves. The purpose of the critical reflection group is not to encourage personal exposure for the sake of it, but simply to learn from something that may have deep personal (and therefore professional) meaning. We ask participants to take some prior responsibility in choosing incidents that they feel will maximize their learning, in which the anxiety engendered by the fear of personal exposure will not unduly diminish the potential learning. Sometimes of course a degree of vulnerability is associated with a degree of learning, but we ask participants where possible to anticipate what these levels might be for themselves. Again, this is a point we discuss further when looking at group culture, as getting the balance of anxiety and learning right is essential. It is also important, from both an ethical and a learning perspective, that the privacy of other players in the incident is protected. What is important here is that it is not the performance or the characters of the players in the incident that are being judged in the critical reflection process, so we do not want the issue of their identity to impede the learning process. Confidentiality of identities can be protected through changing major identifying details and/or through choosing incidents that happened in workplaces or at times that other group members are less likely to be familiar with. Sometimes incidents can be chosen from personal life, if the participant believes this has a bearing on their professional work life. At this point, please refer to Helen Hickson's student assignment in the online resource material at www.openup.co.uk/fook&gardner. She chose an incident from her personal life while on holiday overseas and from this made direct connections with her professional practice.

For further examples of critical incidents, please refer in the online resource materials at www.openup.co.uk/fook&gardner to: the three written critical incidents that are used in this workshop session; and the paper by Jan Fook (2000) entitled 'The lone crusader: constructing enemies and allies in the workplace' – there is a written critical incident at the beginning of this paper.

Group culture: a climate of 'critical acceptance'

In broad terms the culture we are trying to create in the groups aims to maximize the conditions under which people will be open to exposing their deep assumptions and learning new perspectives. We have termed this 'critical acceptance', building upon ideas developed earlier (Fook *et al.* 2000: 230). By 'critical acceptance' we are referring to a group culture that aims to maximize feelings of safety and respect enough to support the challenges that will induce learning. In some ways group culture, more particularly the learning culture that is set up for both individuals in the group and the group itself, is the most important aspect of critical reflection. This is particularly because the model of critical reflection itself challenges many of the traditional assumptions about learning and professional practice that participants implicitly bring to the group.

We find it can be useful to articulate and discuss these prevailing cultures so that participants are able to make a more informed choice about deliberately operating with a different culture for the purposes of (and within the bounds of) the group. Specifically, critical reflection challenges at least seven different types of cultures that influence professional learners. These are summarized from Fook and Askeland (in press) below. (This article is also available in full on the website that accompanies this book, at www.openup.co.uk/ fook&gardner, as we regard an understanding of the cultural aspects of critical reflection to be integral to its effective operation.)

1. *Cultures concerning interpersonal dialogue and relating*: many professionals have been trained to adopt empathic, listening communication styles, perhaps as part of a therapeutic tradition, and find direct questioning to be too confrontational. In addition, some national and ethic groups may also hold values about what is polite public behaviour, and may feel that delving too soon into personal matters may contravene this.

2. *Cultures regarding the construction of client identity*: many helping professionals assume that clients are less powerful than professionals, and this may carry over into the way they relate to colleagues. They therefore may have difficulty in engaging in behaviour that they feel is too confrontational.

3. *A 'task-focused' orientation*: many professionals feel pressure to provide immediate solutions, find answers or 'fix' problems. The culture of 'sitting with' and reflecting on a situation, without acting immediately, is often difficult, especially as this is not always supported by workplace cultures.

4. *Cultures of 'objectivity'*: these are perhaps related to broader learning cultures and professional therapeutic cultures, in which 'the personal' is regarded as somehow 'unprofessional'. This is often constructed as anything that involves value judgements, emotional experiences, or personal backgrounds or experiences.

5. *Self-disclosure*: related to the above, a culture of professionalism seems

to indicate that self-disclosure may be unethical, as it places focus on the needs of the professional rather than the client.

6. *Procedural workplace cultures*: current workplace imperatives to minimize risk, follow bureaucratic routines and produce identifiable outcomes against predetermined criteria work against valuing reflection, with its focus on uncertainty (Fook 2007).

7. *Cultures regarding knowledge and learning*: cultures of silence, individualism and secrecy may operate in many learning institutions (Brookfield 1995). In addition, adversarial 'argument' cultures (Tannen 1998) may prevail as the preferred way of arriving at 'truth' through debate. Overriding them all is a broader culture that tends to value technical and rationally derided knowledge (technical rationality in Schon's (1983) terms). Instead, learning from critical reflection relies on personal experience, which almost irrevocably involves an emotional component.

What are the features of the culture of critical acceptance we are attempting to establish in this introductory session?

Many of these features we have learned to articulate openly to groups, as we have found they address some of the more common 'errors' or misunderstandings that occur as people struggle to enact the critical reflection culture, while still being influenced by traditional professional and learning cultures. There are several major aspects to this, as described below.

Confidentiality

This primarily involves establishing a climate of trust and safety, based on the expectation and agreement that details will not be discussed outside the group (except for broad themes that arise, or specific material only with the express agreement of the person involved), and that identities of other players in the participants' critical incidents will be disguised.

Refraining from judgement

This emphasizes the principle that the purpose of critical reflection is to investigate 'why' (i.e. what thinking underlies practice) rather than to make judgements, approve or disapprove of the appropriateness or worth of a person's actions or thinking. This also involves the principle of creating an environment that allows people to draw their own conclusions and judgements, rather than having these imposed on them by other group members. This often proves one of the most difficult principles for people to learn and maintain. (There will be some further discussion of this in later chapters when we discuss the process further.)

Support and affirmation
This involves support of the person's morale and sense of self-worth, as opposed to support or affirmation of their actions or thinking. This is especially important if the incident that was presented was traumatic or emotionally painful. In critical reflection the principle is to support the person's sense of themselves to be able to be open to further learning (rather than paralysed by grief, fear, anxiety or self-doubt), rather than to close down learning by obviating the need to revisit the incident. In other words, the support provided should not simply be designed to make a person feel better so that they feel no need for change. It should be designed to make them feel robust enough to continue with further exploration.

Acceptance and respectful space
This principle goes hand in hand with the previous one. Specifically what we are referring to here is the idea that, for the purposes of the group, we treat whatever someone says about their incident as 'true'. The purpose of the group is not to establish the validity of the story, or what 'really' happened, or whether the person's interpretation was right. The rest of us weren't there, and even if we were, we might not have seen everything the person in question saw. The purpose of the group is to introduce the person to other possible perspectives, in order for them to become aware of the range of choices of interpretations available, and to help expose why they made the choice they did. So, for the purposes of critical reflection, the person's account is 'true' but so are many other perspectives, even contradictory ones. None negates the others, but all are worthy of examination.

Exposing choice
This follows from the principle of looking for many perspectives. We are trying to expose choice in the critical reflection process, as this then exposes the particular assumptions upon which choices were made. Sometimes asking why someone 'did A not B' can be useful, especially in situations where someone genuinely believes they had no choice.

Forever 'why' and many 'whys'
This principle supports the above. In critical reflection we keep asking 'why' (i.e. what assumptions are behind this practice), in order to arrive at greater depth. We also try to include some social connections in this. In addition, we look for many 'whys' (i.e. many different, perhaps contradictory, perspectives that have not been acknowledged before).

Responsibilities of the person reflecting
The first of these is openness; this involves a willingness to hear and understand (not necessarily accept) alternative points of view or interpretations. The

second of these is not to 'blame': sometimes focusing in depth on personal stories can be experienced as blame, as if the group is implying that the person is individually responsible for controlling what went right or wrong in a situation. This is not the principle that is intended through the process. Instead, what is emphasized is that an individual focus can illuminate some possible new options for that person, without assuming that these new options will necessarily bring about the outcomes that person intends. This cannot be predicted or controlled. However, it is hoped that this principle is about emphasizing that the person can exercise some personal agency, can act in ways that may influence the situation. Therefore responsibility in this sense is about a willingness or 'emboldenedness' to respond to a situation, rather than be frozen in inaction or a state of powerlessness because of fear of blame.

Staying outside the story

Focus on the 'story' not the situation. When people speak about their critical incident, it is often very tempting to focus on evaluating the situation or the other people in the situation. In this sense, it is easy to be 'sucked in' by the interpretation presented by the person, since obviously they will describe the incident from their perspective. Other participants often find it hard to resist taking this perspective, too, and evaluating the main players in the same way as the person whose incident it is.

> When I [Jan] present my incidents, I invariably cast everyone else in the story as in some way deficient or at fault, and I of course am faultless. (Refer to the article 'The lone crusader' in the online resource materials at www.openup.co.uk/fook&gardner as an example of this.) While this may sound like a terribly naive and arrogant position to take (which it is!) it is also worth reminding participants that this is indeed one of the features of narratives – they are in fact constructed using devices to convince ourselves of their truth (see Taylor and White (2000) for an excellent discussion of this).

It is important therefore in critical reflection not to be deceived by these devices, but to be able to recognize their operation, so that there is openness to other possible interpretations. It is also important to remind participants that the role of critical reflection is to stay outside the operation of these devices. The best way to do this is to remember that, when participants present their critical incident, they are in fact presenting a 'story', or *their version* of what happened. The purpose of critical reflection is to deconstruct the story, or the person's version, staying outside of it in order to help the person see other possible versions, rather than to get inside the story and take for granted their version of it. Another issue here can be getting sidetracked into simply wanting to know 'what happened next' or 'what happened in the end'. It is important here to remind participants that the sequence of events is important for what it says about the person's constructions, not for the happenings themselves.

An incident not a case

Many professionals are used to analysing cases and producing case studies. This often involves pinpointing all the factors involved in a case and the situation, and developing explanations of problems, as well as possible solutions. This usually also assumes that the problem to be analysed exists somewhere outside the person presenting the case, and is somehow located in the situation or service users in the situation. Critical incident analysis used for critical reflection differs in several major ways. First, an incident is very specific and happens at a particular point in time in the duration of a case. It may be as specific as a thought the person had, or it may be one sentence that was uttered by a colleague. It may be one meeting the person had, or one interaction with a service user or colleague. Second, an incident is something that happened to the person presenting it, not something that happened to a client or colleague. It may include something that happened to someone else only if that incident was actually directly significant to the person presenting it as well. For example, I might present as an incident a remark that was made to a colleague which I objected to. What is actually critical about the incident is that I felt I should have responded, or acted in a way that prevented it happening. This is the aspect that is critical (i.e. its effect on me, rather than its effect on my colleague per se), although my concerns about its effect on my colleague will be part of the critical experience for me.

Informed choice

By this we are referring to the ethical component of trying to ensure that people are aware as much as possible beforehand of what the experience of critical reflection might involve. Brookfield terms this 'full disclosure', which he sees as 'the attempt by educators to make as clear as possible to learners the qualities, risks and likely consequences of the experience they are about to undergo', arguing that it 'is a condition of authenticity in any educational encounter, but it is particularly important in education for critical reflection' (1994: 215).

While we fully agree with this, we have found it extraordinarily difficult to represent the complexity and uncertainty of the process to people before they actually undertake it. Many participants say that their idea of the process changes as they experience it, and they are often surprised by the sorts of thinking that emerge from their own material. In order to safeguard people as much as possible in this unpredictability we developed the following principle.

The right to draw limits

Recognizing that no one can predict what will be raised for some people, we emphasize that every participant has the right to draw limits to the discussion, if it is going in places they do not want to acknowledge or develop in this group forum. Of course, they have already partially done this with their choice of incident, but new issues may come up that people feel are too sensitive because they may be too personal or private, might involve what they regard as inappropriate emotion for this setting, might be too politically sensitive. We ask them simply to say to the group that they don't want to discuss that issue. Often we find what happens is that they will think about it further in private, and may discuss it further with us outside the group. Several times we have had the experience that group members have confided to us after a group that although they reflected on an incident very meaningfully, it also connected with past experiences of abuse, which they did not want to raise in the group. This is totally appropriate, as the group is not intended as a forum for exploring past traumas. (This is an issue we will return to in later chapters – that of the emotional side of critical reflection learning, and the differences between this and therapeutic learning.)

Summary: a culture of critical acceptance

- Confidentiality
- Refraining from judgement
- Support and affirmation
- Acceptance and respectful space
- Exposing choice
- Forever 'why' and many 'whys'
- Openness
- Staying outside the story
- An incident not a case
- Informed choice
- The right to draw limits

Facilitator modelling of the process

In the next section the facilitator models the process by presenting their own critical incident and then inviting the group to assist them in reflecting on it. The aim of this section is obviously to model the process in order to set up the appropriate culture, but also to illustrate the techniques of the process. This section therefore also focuses on making the process and its operation more explicit. The role of the facilitator is therefore threefold in this section. First, they are colleagues and learners, genuinely trying to learn reflectively from a piece of their own practice experience. (In fact, participants have commented that one of the aspects that makes this section helpful to them is that they can see that the reflection is 'real' for us. The less this is the case – that is, the more the reflection looks predetermined or 'staged' – the less the experience may be helpful for participants.) Second, they are teachers, illustrating the tools and techniques of critical reflection. Third, they are facilitators, working to ensure that the right group climate is set up, and that the appropriate messages about principles for relating and respecting each other are communicated and acted upon.

We usually distribute copies of our chosen written incident to all members. The purpose of this is so that participants are able to reflect on the written as well as the spoken version of the incident that emerges through further group dialogue. We usually also speak about our incident, following the written version closely.

We usually begin the group reflective dialogue by asking participants if there are any questions of clarification (that is, questions about the content of the incident that they are not clear about – for example, how many people were involved), as opposed to questions to aid reflection. This is important in helping people make the distinction between focusing on the story, as opposed to focusing on the situation.

We then begin the critical reflection process by inviting people to ask us questions that will help us unearth our assumptions. We refer them to the questions to aid critical reflection that were presented earlier in the session. We often have to assist participants in this section, as many are reluctant to speak, fearful that they may not 'be reflective' in their questioning and may 'get it wrong'. What is most important here is to encourage people just to 'have a go'. We then help them reword their question in a more critically reflective way, or may invite the whole group to help. Sometimes we might do this by reflecting back their question in a way that is more obviously reflective in its intent. For example, someone might ask, 'Why didn't you say such and such? I would have said it in a different way.' This can be reworded as, 'I wonder why you chose to say such and such as opposed to something like . . .'. This latter wording exposes the choices involved for the presenter, rather than implying they did something wrong, which the questioner would have done better! Sometimes we need to make it explicit whether we are acting in the role of person reflecting, of facilitator, or of teacher. This section is ended when the facilitator feels there have been sufficient assumptions unearthed to be able to articulate some changed thinking or awareness, which is then shared with the group.

Processing the process

Some time is then spent in both debriefing from the process and discussing the learning that emerged, including: reactions to the experience of the process; feelings that emerged; thoughts about the questions asked; feelings about undertaking the process themselves. This section is important for reinforcing group culture, as much as for actual learning about the critical reflection process. It is partly about encouraging the open airing of feelings, particularly anything that might be experienced as negative or unexpected.

Some of the comments that people make are: 'Asking questions in a reflective way is more difficult than it looks. Often I did not say anything because I couldn't think how to word it.' Our response to this is, yes, but that they should not hold back. This is something that is to be learnt here, so the whole group can help with this. Also we often acknowledge that the traditional way of questioning is not to help people reflect, but rather to communicate implicit beliefs about what people should think. Therefore it is to be expected that people will have difficulty doing this and they should not feel bad about it, but should use this forum for experimenting with new ways. A third response is to note that, at the end of the day, critical reflection is not about how we word questions, but about how we create the right climate. Participants are therefore better off trying to be aware of how everything they do might help create the right climate, so that if a question is perhaps not worded in the best way, this does not matter, since it is done within the appropriate climate. In this sense, very 'confrontational' questions can be asked in a helpful way, if the person perceives the questioner as respectful.

Winding up and linking with the next session

Time is then spent at the end of the session:

- dealing with any further questions, queries, doubts
- clarifying the expectations for the next session (stage 1), which include the choosing and writing of a critical incident
- inviting people to suggest some examples of incidents they might present (optional, if there is time).

We usually provide a written sheet for people to take away outlining the criteria for the critical incident. (See the online resource materials at www.openup.co.uk/fook&gardner, and the document entitled 'Preparatory work for critical reflection workshop'.) We also offer further consultation between sessions if anyone is not sure what incident they should present.

Participants often want to stay back after the group to consult about this, or will email us material between sessions for comment.

> **Chapter summary**
>
> In this chapter we have described in detail the content of the introductory session in a way that might easily be used or presented by other educators. We have covered: group introductions; introducing the critical reflection model (Why critically reflect? What is critical reflection? The aims, the theory, questions to aid critical reflection, the critical incident technique, group culture); facilitator modelling; processing the process; and the wind-up.

6 The second session (stage 1)

This chapter:

- begins with a brief overview of the structure of the session
- provides a description of a typical presentation of a critical incident and the process involved in exploring it
- identifies the broad principles that guide the learning process (this includes some particular techniques that might assist in achieving the basic learning principles)
- discusses some common issues that arise in conducting the second session
- links this session with the third session (stage 2).

In this chapter we describe in detail the specific guiding principles behind the structure, content and process of the second session of the critical reflection programme, as well as some specific techniques for guiding the process. Following on from the introductory session, this second session constitutes stage 1 of the critical reflection process, whose prime focus and purpose is to unearth, unsettle and examine implicit fundamental assumptions.

Overview of the session structure

With a standard-sized group of eight participants, the second session normally spans approximately a full day, or about six hours (including breaks). (A sample programme for the second session is included in the online resource materials at www.openup.co.uk/fook&gardner.)

We normally begin the second session with a brief recap of issues and questions from the previous session and a quick overview of expectations for this session. This is a useful point at which to review some of the key aspects of the group culture we want to reinforce, as well as the purpose of the session. We normally spend no more than ten minutes on this introductory material.

The main body of the session comprises successive presentations of each participant's critical incident and reflections on each. (Please see below, where we describe a typical presentation of this type.) About 30 minutes is usually allowed for each presentation, which includes:

- a description of the incident by the person presenting – either a verbal presentation by the presenter, or time to allow each participant to read a written version (usually about 5 minutes)
- group discussion of the incident, helping the participant critically reflect on their description of their incident in order to unsettle and examine fundamental assumptions (usually about 20 minutes)
- summary and recap of the discussion so that the presenter can clarify what assumptions they have unearthed, and what they will reflect on further for the next stage of the critical reflection process (usually 5 minutes)
- brief discussion of the critical reflection process, taking care to debrief the person who has just presented, and also to pinpoint learning about the critical reflection process (usually 5 minutes).

Please note that the above timings for the presentations of each person's incident are for guidance only. In fact, the time needed to arrive at a point where some fundamental assumptions have been unearthed, and the person's thinking has shifted significantly, can vary widely. In some instances this can be achieved in as little as ten minutes. In other cases, a whole hour has not been enough time to unearth significant assumptions. The facilitator needs to be flexible in managing the timing of each presentation, basically making some judgement for each person about when some fundamental new learning has been reached.

The wind-up part of the session includes:

- a discussion of further questions/observations about the critical reflection process
- preparation for the next session (stage 2 of the process), which includes questions to help with further reflection in order to develop changed practices.

This usually takes about 15 minutes in total.

A typical presentation of a critical incident

It is quite difficult to represent the dynamics and complexities of the critical reflection process. For this reason we include here a description of a typical presentation of a critical incident, in order to communicate something of how the whole experience and interactions fit together. This is a presentation of an incident of mine (Fiona's) in a group with Jan and two visiting social work professors from Israel: Riki Savaya and Julie Cwikel. We had initially planned the group as a way of demonstrating to Riki and Julie our approach to critical reflection, then decided that it would be useful to video the session for teaching. There is a DVD of the presentation, and of Jan and Riki's presentations, available; unfortunately, it was too long to be included as part of the online resources that accompany this book, but please visit the website at www.openup.co.uk/fook&gardner for details of how to access it.

Below we describe the process, noting the main features of it as they are exemplified by my (Fiona's) presentation and the reflection with group members surrounding it.

Description of the incident

Participants may read this, speak about it, or allow participants to read it for themselves. I choose to speak about it, saying that the incident involves a student (Leonie) making a complaint to me in a previous role as head of a university programme about an assignment grade given by a sessional staff member, Megan. Leonie believed that her mark of 83 per cent was not high enough given that no negative comments were made. At this point I say that the incident is critical for me because it made me question assumptions regarding absolute or relative marking scales, and what educators are trying to achieve.

Often during this initial description of the incident, the group might also ask clarifying questions to ensure they understand what the person is stating about the 'facts' of the incident. Here, as often happens, when group members ask me for a little more clarification I volunteer information that is not included in the written version of the incident. I offer further background information about what say the student body had in deciding on the current system of assessment: that students had been asked whether they wanted marks or pass/fail grades. This additional information also forms part of the 'story' of the incident for reflection.

Clarification questions at this point are, however, normally confined to the more concrete aspects of the story that people feel they need to be clearer about in order to help the person presenting reflect on the incident accurately. This might include aspects such as clarifying the names and roles of the people involved, or the actual time span of the incident. (In the recording this section spans roughly minutes 25–29.)

Moving into reflection: clarifying why the incident is 'critical'

This is important both to clarify why the person has chosen this particular incident (that is, what it means for them), but also what they hope to learn from critical reflection on it. Different participants will have thought this through to different degrees and may or may not be able to articulate this clearly. With my incident, Jan enquires about this aspect, by asking about what causes the 'angst' for me. Here she is trying to pinpoint what is most significant (using emotion as a pointer or flag) – is it having to approach Megan, or is it questioning my own assumptions that feels most problematic for me? (In the recording this section can be found roughly at minute 29.)

Looking for what is missing, and using emotions as a flag

Sometimes an easy starting point for unearthing deeper assumptions is to look for what is missing. Often, what is left out of accounts are people's emotions. Therefore trying to pinpoint whether the emotional aspects are missing, what they are, and what they might signify can be an aspect that it is relatively easy to identify, but that might yield a depth of further information. At this point, Jan takes the 'angst' question further, notes that my account seems rather 'rational', and asks where the feeling is for me. I reply that Megan felt some irritation at the student Leonie, as Leonie was seen as one of those students who had 'read more than the staff' and 'knows everything'. I somewhat identified with these feelings and also thought it might have been me in Megan's situation – giving Leonie this mark. Jan quickly moves to normalize this by acknowledging that these might be common feelings, and introducing some humour. Perhaps this is because she senses that I may feel some implicit blame about these feelings, or it may be from her own reaction. Participants often identify the need to distinguish between their own and the presenter's reactions: similar to this example, participants often resonate with other people's incidents. (In the recording this section spans roughly minutes 20–31.)

Attending to social contexts

Often normalizing people's reactions or feelings is a step towards connecting personal experience with social or cultural influences. Julie asks about the influence of the marking culture in the department, which leads me to talk about the history in the department of 'agonizing' over assessment and marking criteria. Riki then asks about the power dimensions in the incident, focusing on the idea of the 'revenge element' and that there might partly be an issue of 'letting students know their place'. Jan translates this as a 'social-izing' element of marking, that the process may be functioning partly to socialize students into their relative power position. (In the recording this section can be found at minute 32.)

Framing the issue in meaningful (language) terms for the person presenting

This is possibly one of the most important aspects of the process, since the language used to express the fundamental assumptions must be language that represents a meaningful discourse for the person themselves. I follow on from this idea of 'socialization', and speak instead about a 'subjective' process. In talking about this further I focus on the idea that, while there is perhaps some-thing about Leonie that clouds this issue, I am certain that it is the idea of the '85 per cent glass ceiling' that is the more problematic issue for me. This elicits further discussion about grading norms in the group, with different group members (Julie and Riki) talking about their own norms. Sharing different perspectives can be useful, provided that the focus remains on enabling the presenter to become clearer about their own views. (In the recording this section spans minutes 33–34.)

Looking for contradictions in assumptions that cause discomfort or unease or that may point to conflict

Once the more fundamental assumptions are articulated in the language terms of the person presenting, it is often helpful to examine these for elements of discomfort or unease. That is, it is useful to examine further why the funda-mental assumptions that have been unearthed are problematic in some way for the person. Sometimes it may not necessarily be the assumption itself that is problematic, but the environment in which that assumption is enacted. However, the main point at this stage is to assist the person in further examin-ing what is critical about this fundamental assumption. At this point, Jan attempts to help do this by reframing the fundamental issue as being to do with our ideas of perfection, and how this may involve some contradictory assumptions: that marking is a subjective process, but that it is also assumed to be objective, in that there is an ideal '100 per cent' that is attainable. It is like 'having our cake and eating it', 'marks do and don't mean something', 'a mark is really 85 per cent but it is also really 100 per cent'. In making these state-ments Jan is attempting to highlight a problematic contradiction inherent in assumptions about perfection, which are being played out in this con-crete incident around marking. These statements connect both the original issue raised by the incident, as well as the implicit fundamental issue made apparent through the critical reflection process. By doing this they also function to make the potential problems with the fundamental assumptions clearer, by posing them as stark contrasts. (In the recording this section spans minute 35.)

Looking for where the fundamental assumptions come from that may cause the conflict

In trying to understand the power of fundamental assumptions, it is often useful to look at where they might come from. For me, this comes from my family background – my parents were teachers who brought me up to believe there was 'always a higher bar'. Jan immediately draws a further connection with the broader social environment. She normalizes this by saying, 'Isn't this something we all share? Does this mean it comes from somewhere else as well?' (In the recording this section spans minute 36.)

Unearth the fundamental assumption that underlies all situations

Continued discussion and group reflection on the fundamental assumption, sometimes using the experience of other group members to illustrate points, fills out how this fundamental assumption might underlie, and function in, other situations. Riki talks about her own experience in grading papers, of needing to differentiate between 'being perfect' and 'writing a perfect paper'. She notes how perhaps, if we can't make this differentiation, it says something about our own expectations of being perfect, and therefore what we are really doing when marking is comparing ourselves to our students. (In the recording this section spans minute 37.)

Further discussion of whether this assumption is the fundamental one

This further tests out how fundamental is the assumption that has been unearthed. I acknowledge that Riki's foregoing statement 'gets to the heart' of the issue in the incident. Riki comments further that if this is the case, then it is unfair to students if this implicit assumption about perfection, and the implicit comparison with ourselves, is operating. In an ideal critical reflection group process, I would make these judgements myself. However, Riki does not pose these remarks in an accusatory way, but includes herself (and by implication all educators who do this), so this is an appropriate way of furthering my (and the whole group's) reflection on what might be problematic with these assumptions about perfection and how they are enacted. (In the film, This discussion occurs roughly in the first half of minute 38.)

Discussion of how making this assumption explicit affects the original issue

This is important so the person can link the learning about their fundamental assumption (and the associated issues) with their original incident and their original concerns. Sometimes such discussion can carry implicit values about what is more or less desirable, as well, although these sorts of judgements are best when they emerge from discussion. In this case Jan attempts to make explicit the links with the original concerns by reframing the crucial question as: 'Is assessment relative to stated criteria or to some other unknown thing that is not articulated?' Riki introduces an evaluative element by adding that, if we are stating that assessment is based on stated criteria but not acting on it, then it is problematic. The group appears to concur that if there are stated criteria for the assessment of assignments, then people should be able to fulfil them. Again, in an ideal scenario, these conclusions would be arrived at by the person presenting, in relation to their own work. Alternatively, the group can identify points of view for the presenter to consider. Here, the group articulated my perspective clearly and I simply agreed with it. (In the recording, this discussion occurs in the second half of minute 38.)

Wind-up

This includes a summary of the assumptions that have been unearthed, how they are connected, and what can be further reflected on for stage 2. Jan asks me, 'Where has it [the discussion] gone for you?' I note my awareness of my original assumption that marking is a rational process; I am now more consciously aware of the contradiction – that while I believe there is a rational process, I acknowledge that there is also a subjective (and hidden) nature of assumptions about marking; how the hidden nature of these assumptions means that making them explicit in regard to assessment might help; and that examining assumptions about what is perfection, as opposed to what might reasonably be expected, might be helpful. The aim here is to make sure the person has reached a point of clarity about their underlying assumptions. It isn't that the issue must be 'resolved' for the person concerned, but it is important that they feel they have enough clarity so that they can continue reflecting on their incident and fundamental assumptions for the next session. (In the recording, this discussion occurs in minute 39.)

Looking forward to stage 2

This involves packaging the reflections from this session's learning in a form that can be further reflected on, and for development into practice. Jan asks me, 'What are you taking away to work on for the second stage?' I reply that I will formulate some new assumptions about marking, and also relate this to some of my current work. (In the recording, this discussion occurs in the first half of minute 40.)

Debrief

This involves checking the feelings of the person presenting, particularly to see if they feel they can move on from where the present discussion has left them. Jan notes that sometimes the process dredges up other feelings that people haven't necessarily talked about. (In the recording, this discussion occurs in minute 41.)

Discussion of the critical reflection process and learning about this

This addresses important observations or queries about the process. Julie notes the relative 'safety' of the incident, and that it is possible to learn from experiences that are not necessarily 'earth shattering'. Riki notes that we can learn from 'banality'. I point out that although the incident was a relatively simple one, I chose it (and participants sometimes do) because it linked clearly with current incidents (which I could not discuss for confidentiality reasons). So in some ways this was a 'representative' incident for me. The discussion finishes with the issue of taking notes, recording and using observers in critical reflection sessions. (In the recording, discussion spans from the end of minute 41 to minute 45.)

Broad principles and techniques

Above we have described a typical presentation of an incident and the sort of process the critical reflection discussion might follow. We want to stress that, while the beginning and ending of most processes will be similar, the sort of format each follows is for the most part fairly unpredictable. What seems to work best for us is keeping in mind broad principles, and having in mind what the session is aiming for, that the facilitator aids the group members to best bring that about for each presenter in a way that works best for them. With this in mind, we have attempted to articulate below what these guiding principles are, with some suggested techniques for enacting them.

Beginning by clarifying the significance of the chosen incident for the person

This involves clarifying why they chose this incident, why it is 'critical' to them. This acts to begin the process of working out what is fundamental about it for them and can be a crucial pointer regarding some major assumptions. The most common reasons for the choice of critical incident are:

- wanting to improve or change their practice in some way
- simply being shocked or puzzled by something that has happened
- the incident evoked some strong emotions that the person finds it hard to forget (e.g. anger, hurt, sadness); one incident that stands out for me (Jan) was presented by someone to which it happened 20 years earlier in which the worker had had to remove a child from a family; the pain and trauma of that incident were still felt keenly
- incidents involving what the person regards as unfair treatment
- incidents that involved a turning point
- incidents that are significant in forming learning and therefore later experience
- incidents that crystallize a realization
- incidents that participants want to explore the emotional effect of.

Sometimes at this early stage, it is not easy for participants even to articulate what is significant for them. For example, we are sometimes told that people have chosen their incident because they have to write an assignment on it shortly! While this is obviously a legitimate reason for their choice, the challenge is to move them to a position where they can see what other significance learning about the incident might have in terms of their self-directed learning. So, to some extent, the principle of focusing on implicit assumptions, even at this early stage of understanding why an incident is critical, is crucial right from the initial starting point. For instance, to help people move on in such a situation, it might be useful to clarify what assumptions they have about learning (e.g. 'What is important to you here then?', 'Are you saying that it's most important to do your assignment properly?', 'What assumptions are you making here?').

Enacting appropriate culture

One of the major issues that arises in critical reflection workshops is making the appropriate cultural shifts in order to maximize the learning from critical reflection. In Chapter 5 we discuss the culture of critical reflection, and the difficulties in building and maintaining such a culture, given its non-traditional nature, within many existing mainstream professional and learning cultures. We find it is all too easy to slip back into traditional ways of learning. Three of the major ways in which this is manifested are:

1. focusing too much on techniques (asking the 'right' critical reflective questions)

2. difficulties in maintaining a spirit of non-judgementalism and not imposing one's own views
3. focusing on the situation, not the person's 'story' about the situation.

Focusing on technique

With regard to a focus on technique, we often find participants get sidetracked from the dynamics of the process and listening to what the person has to say, into trying to ask what they believe are the right sorts of questions, in the right sorts of ways. This usually masks an assumption that questions are either inherently reflective or not, and that therefore being reflective equates to mastering some techniques. While we do agree that being reflective does involve mastering some techniques, this is by no means the totality of being critically reflective. In fact we often find that focusing solely on techniques inhibits people from interacting, as they are reluctant to speak unless they 'have it right'. What we therefore try to emphasize is that being critically reflective is more about a culture of thinking – it is about a mindset or attitude, rather than simply mastering a set of techniques. Questions are therefore not necessarily inherently critically reflective – rather it is the climate for learning they create, and the sorts of responses they facilitate, that are important. For this reason, it is crucial to model different ways of asking questions that might elicit further thinking and reflection for a person, as opposed to asking questions that might be more inclined to close a person's thinking down, or implicitly impose a way of thinking, rather than invite a person to think it through for themselves. Most importantly, it involves being open to seeing the effect of different types of questions on a person; but again there are no hard-and-fast rules here. For instance, in my (Fiona's) incident, questions were asked in a variety of ways, but always with the intention of helping to get to my assumptions. Sometimes, for instance, group members might even make statements about their own thinking or practice, but always with the intention of illuminating my thinking.

There are many ways of ensuring a focus on the person's thinking, including: giving the person enough space and time to answer; checking with the person that particular ideas or wordings fit with their way of seeing things; as the facilitator, 'translating' participants' questions or statements into the person's own terms, or translating questions in ways that allow the person to reflect more easily. Obviously, open-ended questions may assist reflection better than closed questions, but sometimes closed questions are necessary to help a person clarify options (e.g 'Why do you think you chose A and not B?'). For example, in trying to help someone identify the source of their assumptions, a form of 'critical questioning' (Fook 1993: 98) might help people separate whether their expectations are more personal or come from social contexts. For example, 'Is that because you think this, or because you think you are supposed to think it?'

Maintaining a spirit of non-judgementalism and non-directiveness
Our participants often say that this is one of the aspects they have the most difficulty with. There is a tendency to look for blame, either in a system or people. This tendency to individualize and pathologize problems is matched by a corresponding tendency to focus on solutions – once blame can be apportioned, or a problematic cause identified, there is reflex action to fix it by finding a solution. A related culture is that of assuming that learning is simply about the teacher getting the learner to think in the same way as the teacher. (We have had many experienced teachers shamefacedly admit this to us!) These sorts of cultures often manifest as participants either looking to blame themselves for what they believe went wrong in their incident, or to blame other people in the situation. Other participants are often quick to judge a person in terms of their own (rather than that person's) perspective and experience, or simply seek to tell the person how they should think, or what they should have done. This often means they will simply ask the equivalent of 'Why didn't you do what I would have done?' or 'Can't you see why what you did/thought was problematic?' Or they may simply start lecturing the person as to the 'right' way to see things. As facilitators we move quickly to stop this kind of questioning or activity, as these work directly against fostering a spirit and climate of reflection. Such questions may be reframed in terms of 'I wonder why you didn't choose to do such and such?' or 'I wonder why you saw it in those terms?' The latter types of question throw the focus back onto the thinking of the person reflecting, rather than the thinking or the actions of the questioner. When other participants start 'lecturing' the person, we usually interrupt them and ask them to reframe what they are saying as a reflective question. We invite all group members to help with this.

Focusing on the situation, not the person's 'story' about the situation
This is another common problem that arises in our experience. Participants are often 'sucked into' the story. After all, a narrative is told in a way that is intended to convince the listeners of its veracity (Taylor and White 2000). In workshops participants have a tendency to want to find out 'what happened next', or to get sidetracked into analysing the different players in the situation, or the situation itself. Rather than making judgements about the person who is presenting their incident, they feel it is OK to analyse and assess in detail the actions or character of other players in their story. When this happens we try several different things. Sometimes we might ask why a participant wants to know 'what happened next' – how does it help to get to hidden assumptions? If it seems there is too much focus on other players in the story, we might reframe questions: instead of 'Why did X do that?' we might reframe the question as 'Why do you think that X did that?' or

'Why did you see X in that way?' In this sense questions are aimed at returning the focus to the person who is reflecting and what their thinking or constructions are.

Learning how to critically reflect while also learning from critical reflection

Participants are learning on three levels while participating in workshops: they are learning from their own practice experience using a process of critical reflection on it; they are learning about their own practice experience through participating in reflection on other people's experiences; and they are learning how to critically reflect. It is important therefore to ensure that both the learning about experience (one's own and other people's as it applies to one's own) and the learning about the critical reflection are made explicit. Part of this is achieved by having debriefing sections at the end of each reflection session, which specifically focus on learning about the critical reflection process. However, it is also achieved by the facilitator explicitly modelling different critical reflection techniques (as we have mentioned elsewhere this may sometimes involve 'translating' participants' questions into terms that are more conducive to reflection), and sometimes making direct links between the questions asked or statements made, and the theory of critical reflection that is behind them. For example, we may sometimes preface what we are going to say with a statement like 'I'm just trying to make some links with the professional context here: do you think that thinking comes from your own assumptions about what it is to be a professional, and where did you get those ideas from?' or 'I wonder if there might be a binary here?' or 'Just linking this with critical theory a bit more, do you think your thinking has a role in preserving your power?'

Connecting the personal and social

This of course is one of the main principles of critical reflection in our model. Specific focuses might entail the following.

- *Identifying both personal and social influences on assumptions and looking at overlap and interaction*: for example, in my (Fiona's) presentation, we acknowledged both my family background but also linked this with broader organizational contexts and cultural norms relating to 'perfection'. One does not misplace the other – my family background in this sense may have contributed to me simply taking on board cultural norms of perfection with greater emotional conviction.
- *Identifying how particular ways of thinking may mirror, and contribute to existing structures or power relations*: in my example, Riki highlighted

how hidden assumptions about perfection could function to disadvantage students.

- *Identifying perspectives that are missing can also be a way of identifying dominant discourses (and therefore hidden functions of power)*: for example, in my presentation we discussed how emotional discourse was missing (i.e. the story was constructed as rational). This of course played into a dominant way of thinking, which denied that educators may also be subjective. This helped to preserve the more dominant way of thinking that educators are objective.

- *Identifying the sources of fundamental thinking and assumptions*: this is helpful as a way of differentiating personal and social expectations, and provides a basis for understanding their interaction and making further choices about desired (and more empowered) thinking. The techniques of critical questioning have been discussed in the section entitled 'Focusing on technique', above, and are also relevant here. In my case being able to identify both family background and cultural sources of the idea of perfection helped to give me some choice about what I wanted to preserve in this idea and how I wanted to enact it.

- *Normalizing*: by the idea of normalizing we are referring to the principle of putting the person's experience in social context so that they can see some links between their own thinking and that of their social and historical environment. This functions of course to help them understand the connections between themselves as individuals and their social worlds, but also of course may function to help them feel supported and less isolated. The latter may or may not be useful in a critical reflection process, and judgements about this need to be made in the context of the process at the time. For example, if a person seems unable to continue to learn about their own assumptions because of some self-blame, then normalizing can help them accept their past thinking/actions enough to enable them to move on. On the other hand, normalizing an experience may function to make a person so self-accepting that they see no need to further examine their thinking or practice. If this latter situation occurs, one of the things we do as facilitators is to continue to normalize the practice/thinking but own it as a broader social problem that can be further deconstructed on that level. For example, one of the common assumptions unearthed is about professional objectivity – people either believe it exists, or it is a prime value to be striven for. Without being critical of such a value in principle, however, participants often present incidents where this type of thinking has proven problematic in some way – for example, it doesn't allow them to acknowledge and value their own personal abilities or reactions and consequently they have cast themselves as inadequate professionals. We often normalize this situation by deconstructing where the broader thinking about objective professionalism comes from, what functions it performs for different people in the group, and so on. This reduces the personal threat to the individual person who is presenting their incident, but at the same time it addresses the issue directly and reinforces the social nature of much of our thinking.

The complexities of getting to meaning and changed thinking

It is important to remember the main purpose of the first stage. Although in technical terms this does involve unearthing, shaking up and examining fundamental assumptions, what we find is that this inevitably kicks off a broader process that actually involves articulating the fundamental meaning of the incident as a forerunner to changing thinking about this. So while we are hunting for deeper assumptions, we are also looking to frame this learning in a way that articulates the meaning for that person. To make matters more complex (and more exciting), what is meaningful will differ. For some people the process may function as 'therapeutic' in a professional sense – that is, they may find it healing (freeing them from some burden or dilemma); they may simply feel emotionally supported; they may feel it reduces self-blame or enables them to accept some part of themselves they had found problematic before; it may release them from some thinking or behaviour about which they had been 'stuck'; they may feel better able to integrate some aspect of their personal life with professional identities or activities; a potential resolution of previously irresolvable issues; it may help to articulate dissonance so it can be accessed and reworked; it might restore integrity – that is, an ability to achieve a congruence between personal values and professional activities.

We need to be as open as possible to guiding the discussion so that each person will understand what is meaningful to them about the incident they have presented. We find it easiest to stay mindful of aiming, by the end of the first stage, to help each person articulate some changed and meaningful awareness about their experience, which may take different forms. For example, a different or new perspective; an awareness of assumptions they were hitherto unaware of; a new feeling about the experience (e.g. they may feel relieved or unburdened); clarity about fundamental meaning or importance. To be reasonably confident the person has arrived at a point like this, we usually ask them to summarize what thinking they are taking away that they want to further reflect on. The following point picks up further on this issue.

Articulating the main concern/what is worrying the person

Sometimes the process of unearthing assumptions functions simply to articulate what is the person's main concern, what is important or what is worrying the person about the incident. These are all interrelated issues of course. This may be particularly the case if the person chose an incident that they simply could not forget, or about which they felt some strong emotion. Part of their reason for wanting to critically reflect on a particular incident may be because they cannot articulate what it is that bothers them about it. This means that they may not have the relevant language to express their concerns, or the discourse within which to understand it.

In these cases we sometimes find it helpful to coin new terminology or invent imagery or metaphors as a way of articulating the person's own perspective. This can be similar to the skill of reframing, or simply finding a new discourse that frames or expresses the person's fundamental and desired assumptions in a way that fits with their experience. Often common colloquialisms can be useful: 'You feel like you've been asked to move a pile of sand'; or perhaps common cultural images: 'You are a bit of Sisyphus – all that effort to roll the rock up the hill only to have it roll down the other side.' Sometimes common (shared) stories are helpful: 'You were a bit like Red Riding Hood in this story – unaware of the Big Bad Wolf'; 'You were like the boy with his finger in the dyke.' Sometimes using language that is associated with service users can be very moving, but can also hit the nail on the head, perhaps because often as professionals we resist using discourses we might normally reserve for clients. One situation where this was striking was for a family worker who related an incident of seeing a young child chased around the room by her mother brandishing a newspaper. It was difficult to pinpoint what was critical about this incident, to get at the fundamental assumptions and concerns, until someone said, 'You felt traumatized because you felt you had to witness this abuse and were powerless to change the situation.' The word 'trauma' captured the worker's experience, and she was able to move on and articulate her basic values and expectations of herself as a worker.

Exposing choices and supporting a sense of agency

Part of the function of critical reflection in exposing assumptions is to expose the choices one had in making those assumptions. Exposing choice also reinforces a sense of agency, or personal power or decision making (see Fook 2004e for further discussion of the transformative aspects of critical reflection), and a sense therefore of influence in situations even where people did not necessarily possess official authority or power over others. One of the common techniques we use to expose choice is to ask 'Why did you choose to do/ think this, not that?' Sometimes this can be couched in more contrasting terms – for example, 'I wonder why you didn't choose to . . .' (fill in whatever more extreme type of behaviour might have been possible but was obviously factored out by the person).

An example of this occurs in my (Jan's) discussion of my critical incident (featured in the DVD of the group, details of which are given in the online resources at www.openup.co.uk/fook&gardner), in which I feel forced into an escalating confrontation with a boss. The incident is partly critical because I feel like I am being forced into acting in a way that is against my principles. To expose my choice (and to expose the extent to which I participate in constructing the situation in this way) it would be useful to ask: 'I wonder why you chose not to leave the room?', 'I wonder why you chose to stay and listen to her if you thought she was being abusive?'

Using emotions

The role of emotions in critical reflection is a complex area. Emotions can be understood in many different ways (Bilson 2006) including as an aspect of personal experience, but also as socially constructed phenomena that may also influence social dynamics. In the critical reflection learning process there are at least three main ways in which emotions are useful: as a flag or pointer towards what is important (e.g. strong emotions often point to strongly held values or beliefs); as an impetus to initiate change; as a resource in sustaining difficult changes. We find that often when it is difficult for people to articulate what is critical about an incident, or what their fundamental assumptions might be, focusing on the emotional aspect of their experience, trying to label it accurately and what brought it about, can be a helpful starting point. For example, we might simply ask 'What were you feeling?' or 'What were you feeling most strongly about?', 'What feelings do you remember?', 'What are you feeling when you look back on it now?', 'I wonder how your feelings at the time affected what you were assuming?'

Acknowledging emotions also functions to validate a part of their experience that may hitherto have been ignored or devalued. Participants often also feel that this goes some way to legitimizing their experience, and therefore themselves, as whole people. There is a need though to be wary of focusing on emotions for their own sake, as this runs the risk of misdirecting the purpose of the learning away from professional learning, towards more purely therapeutic ends. It is important to remember that critical reflection may serve therapeutic functions but only in the service of professional learning (Fook and Askeland, in press).

Inclusivity

Clearly learning may take place in different ways for different people. While there is some acknowledgement that critical reflection may not be an effective learning process for all people (for example, it may be that a certain resilience or emotional maturity is needed (Fook and Askeland, in press), the goal is to try to maximize the learning for as many different people as possible. This means, at the very least, that facilitators need to be able to use a range of different techniques, and able to frame questions in a range of different ways, as well as, of course, being open to a range of different perspectives. These abilities might have to be used in 'translating' some participants' questions or points to others. The facilitator's own self-reflexive ability is mandatory. Brookfield (1995) notes the importance of educators themselves being prepared to be critically reflective about their own practices. Specific questions can be helpful in prompting more inclusive thinking in the group. For instance, asking 'Why do you think you chose to do this and not that?' exposes the fact that there may have been other choices. Asking 'What do you think other people's perspectives might have been?' or 'How do you think X might have seen it?' are other ways of asking a similar kind of thing. Sometimes we try a brainstorming exercise: 'Let's all try to think of as many different ways of interpreting this situation/action as possible.' The latter technique reduces the threat of focusing on one person's perspective and puts the onus on the whole group to try to be inclusive.

Pinpointing impossible situations or forced-choice scenarios

Sometimes incidents are critical because they involve situations in which the participant might have 'boxed themselves in', or constructed a scenario in which they could not win. A common technique therefore involves simply articulating this in imagery that highlights the impossibility: 'So you felt you were in a "no-win" situation?', 'You felt you were up against a brick wall, you had nowhere to turn?', 'You were "damned if you didn't" and "damned if you did"?' Notice that colloquialisms are often really useful here, as they seem more accessible as common ways of talking about experience.

Framing questions

As mentioned earlier, the ways questions are framed may be vital in allowing the person to gain awareness of deeper assumptions. The framing needs to be in a form meaningful to the person. Often this involves just having lots of different phrases and terms available, and to keep trying different ones until there is one that works. To this end, although we supply examples of questions to aid critical reflection (see Chapter 5) it is important to recognize that these questions are not necessarily worded in ways that might best elicit reflective responses. For instance, it has been raised by participants in many workshops that asking 'why' can be experienced as quite confrontational, and those who are trained counsellors or therapists often state that they were trained never to begin questions with 'why'. On the other hand, asking 'why' can be just the sort of challenge someone needs to probe their thinking further. The facilitator can often assist the reflective process by helping participants reword questions in ways that encourage reflection, rather than close down thinking. Often asking hypothetical questions, especially about ideal situations, can help a person more easily access their fundamental values. For example, 'What would you ideally have liked to have happened?', 'If that happened what do you think you would have done or thought?', 'What thinking was behind that?'

Identifying constructions and assumptions and how they fit together

What often happens in the critical reflection process of stage 1 is that a whole variety of assumptions are unearthed, some more fundamental than others. One of the difficulties of this stage is to identify how the different sets of assumptions may be linked. This is particularly problematic given time constraints. However, we often find that identifying the more fundamental assumptions also serves to link other assumptions. In this sense, the assumption that links or underlies other assumptions may also be the more fundamental one. So, looking for an assumption that links other assumptions that have been identified may lead more quickly to the fundamental assumptions. (At this point, please refer to Jan's paper, 'Beyond reflective practice: reworking the "critical" in critical reflection' on the book's accompanying website at www.openup.co.uk/fook&gardner. This analyses the three assignments by Belinda, Helen and Lynne, also on the website, showing the process of how many different assumptions were at first unearthed, and how often more fundamental assumptions and meanings were identified only in connection with experience.)

Below we have listed some of the more common types of fundamental assumption that are unearthed in the critical reflection process. These might provide a useful guide in facilitating the process, as sometimes we find that some structuring is needed to identify the more fundamental assumptions in short periods of time, especially when participants are confused or present incidents that are complex and include a whole range of assumptions which, superficially, may appear unrelated. In the process of unearthing the kinds of assumptions we have listed below, we are also usually aiming to introduce an analysis of these assumptions that demonstrates to each participant who is reflecting how these assumptions may in fact be restrictive of their practice. Ideally, however, the person reflecting should discover this for themselves through the process, rather than have it imposed by other participants.

Binaries/dilemmas

(See also the above discussion of 'forced choices'.) This can be helpful to focus on if participants appear to be constructing 'either/or', 'all or nothing', 'black or white', 'victim/perpetrator' (see Lynne Allan's assignment in the online resource materials at www.openup.co.uk/fook&gardner for examples of the latter). We often find that highlighting the binaries provides an easily accessible analysis for participants, and one that seems readily credible for many of them. Because binary thinking tends to rule out more complex ways of thinking it also tends to rule out more options for action. So identifying binaries is often seen by participants as offering a relatively simple route for reworking or reconstructing their thinking in ways that are more complex and at the same time more freeing.

Identity and othering
It is often useful to unearth what people's fundamental assumptions are about who they are, and who others are in relation to them. Not only does this indicate how they value themselves, and what are the sources of this self-value, it also says a great deal about how they value and construct other people in their situations. This framework is very useful in helping people see the connections with the way they want/need to see themselves, and the way they want/need to see other people, and can pinpoint how they may construct other people (and indeed their social worlds) as partly a function of their own needs and desires. It is therefore an important part of being reflexive, in that people can be helped to see the connections between the way they construct their own identities and those of other people, and therefore the way they participate in constructing their own social worlds. For example, simple questions like 'What power do you think you have?' can lead to assumptions about a powerful/powerless identity, and therefore how other people's powerful or powerless identities are created accordingly. For example, we often find that participants construct themselves, in the stories of their incidents, as powerless (seemingly regardless of what positions they have; even people at management level do this). They often invest other people in the story with power. So part and parcel of feeling powerless in a situation is having a powerless identity, and constructing others as powerful.

This type of analysis can point out how constructing more complex identities can allow for more complex activities, and therefore more choice of actions.

Professionalism
Not surprisingly, assumptions about professionalism are often fundamental to professional practice. These include assumptions about what constitutes a professional person (professional identity) but also what constitutes professional conduct (ethics) and what constitutes professional ability (competency). Interestingly, much angst arises because many of these assumptions are couched in abstract terms that are perceived to be in conflict with what is possible in a work environment. A common example that arises is the difficulty of

maintaining professional objectivity, which many participants interpret as not being emotional or making subjective decisions. Unfortunately many of the incidents that are critical to them involve being emotional, and often in fact using and expressing emotion in their work. (One participant told of an incident when she had phoned a client's home, only to learn the client had died recently. She remembers bursting into tears, only to be told by a colleague that she was 'too emotionally involved' and therefore 'unprofessional'.) As a result they have often constructed themselves as 'unprofessional'. There is clearly a binary dilemma they have constructed here as well: 'professionals are by definition not emotional' – that is, being professional is equated with being rational; being unprofessional is equated with being emotional.

This type of analysis points out how there may need to be a reworking of what professionalism means, to allow for the more personal and perhaps human side of practice to be incorporated.

Knowledge and theory

Many assumptions about the nature of knowledge (and theory) and their relationship to practice seem to be crucial determinants in professional practice. Knowledge (including relevant information and theory) may be seen on a continuum from 'rules' that determine practice, to more flexible ideas that are formulated in interaction in new situations. (For example, in the online resource materials at www.openup.co.uk/fook&gardner, Belinda Hearne notes in her student assignment how theory became almost a guidebook that was intended to keep her from the possibility of abusing her power – ensuring that she followed feminist principles became almost her talisman to prevent her being abusive to others.) Sometimes knowledge is equated with control – that is, having the relevant knowledge (information) about a situation before-hand allows for preparation and therefore control in new situations. Usually in critical reflection sessions the aim is to assist people towards a more flexible view of knowledge, to put them in the driver's seat in relation to constructing relevant knowledge.

Power

There are many different assumptions about power, often that it is finite, invested in people through position (formal power), and often determined from outside. These roughly equate with modernist views of power (see Fook 2002: 48). We often find that these views of power can be very restrictive, as people often see the sources of power as being external to themselves, and therefore outside their control. This reduces their sense of agency. They often also have constructed identities for themselves as passive victims. Yet, oddly enough, participants may at the same time harbour implicit assumptions about themselves as responsible and all-powerful in many situations, taking sole responsibility for events, and blaming themselves when things did not go as they had planned or wished. (If you refer to Jan's article, 'The lone crusader', in the online resource materials at www.openup.co.uk/fook&gardner, you will see these themes come across strongly. Jan in some senses sees herself as a 'victim' of Annette's perceived racism. Yet she also sees herself as having responsibility to right it, and to get Annette to think in the same way she does. In this sense, she feels she has failed if she cannot get Annette to not be racist, when in fact what she overlooks is that Annette has agreed to actions that are fair for the Asian student.)

What we are working towards in these instances is a sense of power as a complex entity, able to be created in many different ways by different players, and able to be exercised in different ways. We aim to expand people's ideas about power, seeing more possibilities for their own power, and the creation and use of that power. In Jan's case (in the article mentioned above) we might ask what power Jan thinks she has, and how she has changed the situation. What has she been assuming about her own power in relation to Annette? What power does she think she needs to wield, and what would be a sign that she has it?

Values

Often, fundamental assumptions are demonstrated as fundamental values – that is, beliefs that the person holds as most important in their working lives. Incidents are often critical because people perceive them to involve a conflict between their fundamental values and what happens in the incident. In the critical reflection process it can be helpful simply to clarify and articulate what these values are, and then to examine the assumptions behind the conflict they perceive. In this sense, what often happens as a result of the critical reflection process is a clarifying and reaffirming of fundamental values, as a basis for restoring a sense of integrity for a person.

Change

Assumptions about change – what it is, the extent to which it is desirable and possible – form one of the fundamental areas of thinking that are unearthed in the critical reflection process. As written about elsewhere (Napier and Fook 2000), many social work professionals seem to assume that only major change is enough, and to devalue any other sorts of changes they may bring about. Incidents may often be critical for people because they feel they did not do enough towards making structural changes, or because they feel only large-scale changes are good enough. One example cited in Napier and Fook (2000) is of the worker who felt that her inability to have a corrupt worker sacked was not good enough. Despite the fact that she had complained about the worker to the board of management, she felt she had not done enough, and took responsibility for the fact that the board did not sack the colleague immediately.

In these sorts of instances, we are trying to get participants to examine whether their assumptions about change are relevant, appropriate or realistic to the situation at hand: 'How do your assumptions about change fit this situation?'

Winding up and linking with stage 2

In the wind-up phase of this session it is important to:

- ensure that all participants feel they have something to take away for further reflection on their own incident
- address any further queries about the critical reflection process
- prepare participants for the next stage of the critical reflection process.

Some examples of questions that are useful in the wind-up are:

- What sorts of reflective questions helped?
- What did people like (or not) about the process?
- Did it meet expectations?
- What doubts do they have?

We often find that a very positive culture prevails at the end of the session (i.e. people are often very enthusiastic and also respectful towards each other and to different viewpoints). We of course value this, but it is important to make space for more negative views to be heard as well. It may be helpful therefore for facilitators to air some more negative reactions, such as 'The process can feel very unstructured', 'You might have felt it was too personal', 'Do you think it would be possible to undertake critical reflection like this in all environments?', 'What about if there is a lack of trust – how might you deal with this?'

We usually provide participants with a set of questions that will guide their thinking for the next stage. These consist of one main question broken down into smaller questions, as in the following example.

Broad question: 'How does my practice, and my theory of practice, change as a result of my reflections?'

- What fundamental assumptions were unearthed for me in stage 1, and what main themes do I need to reflect on further?
- How has my thinking changed as a result of these reflections (how do I want to change my fundamental assumptions)?
- What might I do differently as a result of this changed thinking? (Sometimes in answering this question it is helpful to ask, 'What

would I do differently if I were to experience this incident again, and how does that relate to my changed thinking?')

- How might I label my new theory of practice (putting these new ideas and new practices together)?

We usually ask participants to bring brief notes to the next session, to hand out to other group members, or to make rough notes that they can speak from.

In the online resources at www.openup.co.uk/fook&gardner we have included a 'troubleshooting guide' that discusses common practical issues that arise in facilitating critical reflection groups.

Chapter summary

In this chapter we have described in detail the structure and processes involved in conducting stage 1 of the critical reflection model. We have presented an analysis of a reflection on a critical incident presented by Fiona and have drawn out the broad principles and techniques of critical reflection, including: clarifying the significance of the incident; enacting the appropriate culture; learning how to reflect while learning from reflection; connecting the personal and the social; the complexities of getting to changed meaning and changed thinking; articulating the main concern; exposing choices and supporting a sense of agency; using emotions; inclusivity; pinpointing forced-choice scenarios; framing questions; identifying how assumptions fit together. Finally, we discussed the winding up of the session and suggestions for linking to the third session (stage 2).

7 The third session (stage 2)

This chapter:

- considers what happens for participants between sessions and what this means for their approach to stage 2
- outlines briefly the overall structure of the third session
- describes stage 2 in detail, continuing to use Fiona's incident introduced in Chapter 6
- explores ending the critical reflection process
- identifies the broad principles behind the process and specific techniques that are useful for stage 2.

Overall, the aim of this second stage is primarily to move from exploration and analysis. This means identifying how the participant will operate differently, changes in and/or affirming of assumptions and values, a framing of the person's new 'theory of practice', and developing the capacity to act in new ways. Before exploring this second stage, we want to acknowledge that the space between sessions is an important part of the process.

Between sessions

Participants finish stage 1 with an introduction to stage 2, which outlines the key aims and questions for this stage. The time between each stage is important, allowing the participants to 'sit' with the material from stage 1. At a conscious or unconscious level, this allows integration of new ideas or assumptions, or the validating of existing values. We are explicit about people doing what they can in terms of reflection between workshops: for some participants the workshop is time out of a hectic life and they will say they cannot think about anything outside of it; others talk about wanting to read more, think about what has happened or possibly try to operate in a different way.

Clearly it is preferable and to their advantage for participants to take time to consciously reflect on their experience, but we encourage them to come back no matter what they have or have not been able to do; stage 2 still works whatever has been done at a conscious level.

How participants approach stage 2 divides them into three main groups, although of course there are always variations.

Stage 2 already?

This first group has thought very little consciously about stage 1. They are often apologetic, saying that they have been too busy, caught up with work or home and haven't had a chance to think further about their critical incident. This doesn't necessarily mean that nothing has happened. Once they start to talk about their incident, they often realize that they have shifted their perception or begun to feel differently about it. The change seems to have happened at an unconscious level and is then made conscious in the workshop. Occasionally, participants will really not have thought about the workshop or their incident at all on any level, but will do the work in the session.

Thinkers

This group has reflected on what happened for them in stage 1. Some say they have thought a lot about the workshop or some aspect of what emerged for them and have found it helpful to write notes about how their reflections have developed; others have thought a 'little bit' and have jotted this down. For some, what emerged from stage 1 has been surprising or intriguing; for others, a shock. This has stimulated them – or meant they could not stop thinking about the implications. Some people have a 'niggle' that they haven't got as far as they could have in thinking about their incident and so puzzle away at it. For some, a question or comment that they dismissed during stage 1 keeps coming back until they pay attention to it – and find that there is some new understanding there.

Carlene worked at Youthworks with a colleague, Jane, with whom she had been friendly since they trained together several years before. Jane was the union representative and when Carlene was promoted to supervisor expressed disappointment in her taking on a management role. This led to some conflict between them and Carlene's manager mediated between them. Carlene's incident focused on her manager's lack of skill in mediating. One of the group asked her what this meant for her friendship with Jane, but she said that wasn't relevant. When she returned to stage 2, Carlene said that that question had stuck in her mind and really was the crux of the incident; she realized that she had made an assumption from this experience that she should separate work and friendship and, as a result, had often felt isolated at work. She now wanted to focus on changing this and related assumptions about managing difference in relationships.

Doers

The participants in this group have decided to try something out as a result of stage 1, perhaps a new assumption, a different action or way of being, and want to talk about that in the group. Nearly always, this change has been successful in some way and of course this is encouraging for everyone in the group – change really is possible!

Frieda's incident was about conflict with her supervisor, who she had described as being cold and unsupportive. The group had worked with Frieda to explore what else might be happening for her supervisor, what other perspectives there could be about her supervisor as a person and worker. Nobody else in the group knew Frieda, so suggestions were often unrealistic, but this did trigger Frieda saying she could see that her supervisor might herself be under pressure and appear more negative than she meant to. In the week between sessions, Frieda suggested to her supervisor they meet for coffee and talk about their different perspectives on supervision. She discovered that her supervisor was regretting taking the job, feeling pressured from above and below, and that being 'brisk' and task focused was her way of dealing with this. This changed the dynamic of their relationship and Frieda came to stage 2 feeling much more positive about her supervisor, and also about her own ability to act and seek change.

Stage 2: overview of structure

Stage 2 is also generally run across a full day (i.e. six hours including breaks) for a group of about eight participants. (A sample programme for the third session is included in the online resource materials on the website that accompanies this book, at www.openup.co.uk/fook&gardner.)

The second session normally begins with a brief discussion of any general issues and questions emerging from stage 1, as well as a reminder of the programme for stage 2. How long this takes does vary: some groups are focused on moving on to stage 2 without delay; others want more exploration of some aspect of the critical reflection process. For groups that have struggled with the process, it can help to reiterate the culture and to reconnect with what emerged as useful in the previous session (stage 1).

Occasionally, there will be a particular reaction from one or several group members that needs to be explored before the group is ready to move on. For example, a participant may have come to feel she had been pushing a particular view and want to acknowledge that in the group. This can lead to a useful discussion about process – how to focus on the other person's perspective rather than reacting from your own. Alternatively, several participants may be feeling the need to talk about how other people in the organization are reacting to their involvement in the group, a perception that they are operating differently. The importance of addressing these issues has to be balanced with ensuring that there is enough time for each person to participate in stage 2. Normally, this part of the process takes between ten minutes and half an hour.

Most of the session follows a similar pattern to stage 1 in that each participant takes it in turns to look at their incident in terms of this stage of the process. This usually takes each person about 30 minutes. The process includes the following stages.

1. The participant:
    - briefly reminds the group about their incident; this need only be one or two sentences; group members usually remember each other's incidents very clearly and simply need a memory prompt
    - summarizes what emerged for them from the first stage – key themes, awareness of assumptions, values, changes in feelings, thinking, understanding or perception
    - articulates where they are now – what changes in thinking or awareness are there; what, if anything, has shifted from stage 1; what, if anything, have they done differently; what is their reaction to that
    - addresses what they want to change, how they might want to be different or act differently; this might be about acknowledging a shift in assumptions or affirmation of values; the aim is also to ground these by exploring what that would mean might be different in practice – what actions or strategies might be used
    - may also articulate and label their new theory of practice (i.e. how they would describe their new ideas and how they will be put into practice).

    Again participants vary in how much of this they are able to articulate at the beginning of their session. Nearly everyone covers the first three, most at least begin to address what they want to change, some people have thought about all of these areas. This usually takes between five and ten minutes.

2. The group works with the participant at the point that seems most useful for them. This may mean some further refining of their understanding of the key issues, with the aim of clarifying what is new and how this new understanding will be translated into practice. For some participants new assumptions and values will be identified. For others the focus is more immediately on addressing change, including developing specific strategies to ground the new theory. Each participant finishes with a clear label for their new theory of practice. This usually takes between 15 and 20 minutes.
3. The group stands back from this presentation, while checking that the presenter is ready to move on. There is then a brief discussion of the critical reflection process and any emerging issues related to practice. This usually takes five minutes.

    Again, as in stage 1, the timings suggested here are approximate and it is important to be flexible. Sometimes a participant will be clear about all they have learned from their incident in ten minutes and ready to move on. As the group becomes more practised, the resolution of stage 2 often speeds up.
4. The winding-up part of the session includes:
    *   general reflections on the critical reflection process
    *   input and discussion about how critical reflection can be used within or outside the workplace
    *   exploring how participants will ensure that they keep using the process, including brainstorming about possible strategies
    *   evaluation.

A typical stage 2

Here we will continue to use my (Fiona's) incident; the first stage of this was discussed in Chapter 6 and we have outlined the main features of the process of stage 2 below.

Participants have a list of the areas to be covered in stage 2, which they were given at the end of stage 1. Each generally talks about as many of these as they are ready to before group discussion starts, although group members may ask questions of clarification or make suggestions along the way.

Brief reminder of the incident

Participants are asked to begin by summarizing their incident briefly. This really need only be one or two sentences to prompt group members. My (Fiona's) incident is a good example of this. I summarize here very briefly, saying the incident is about the student who wanted to have a higher mark and a session staff member who wanted to give her a lower mark. This seems to be enough detail for the group and I very quickly go on to the next area.

Some participants want to tell their story in detail again and need to be reassured that this isn't necessary – group members often reinforce this by saying something like 'Oh yes, of course' once the participant begins. Interestingly, some participants 'remember' their incident differently, perhaps emphasizing another angle related to their new perspective. This only matters if they are missing something important from the original telling of the story. It is usually better to wait and see whether it is relevant to go back to the original perspective.

In the DVD mentioned in the online resource materials at www.openup. co.uk/fook&gardner, this discussion begins at 5 minutes, 40 seconds.

Summary of what emerged from the first stage

Here I, as participants often do, say 'but really what it was about for me was . . .'. I go on to talk about the assumptions that I had become aware of in stage 1, such as that the aim of assessment is to get the perfect answer. I also identify questions that emerged for me – for example, what is it we are trying to do with assessment? Again I move quite quickly to the next area.

What participants talk about here will obviously vary, as will how they talk about it. Some are clear – they may have written down what emerged and will read it back or will have simply remembered what was key for them. Others are clearly trying to remember what happened given that they are now seeing what happened differently. Some find it helpful if the group prompts them to remember by saying, for example, 'What stood out for me was . . .'. Often participants say it is useful to remember where they were at – for some because they have forgotten some of their new understandings, for others because they have moved a long way from there.

In the DVD, this discussion begins at 5 minutes, 55 seconds.

Articulating where they are now

Again, on the film, I quite typically say 'So where I've got to now is . . .'. I go on to say that there is a need to work out with assessment what it is you are trying to do for each subject and topic. I have realized that my assumptions about marking have changed – rather than assuming nobody can be perfect, so the top mark can only be 85 per cent – I now give marks up to 100 per cent, but I realize that I haven't articulated my old or new assumptions to other staff and this causes conflict. I have had discussions about these issues at a rational level but not at this 'underneath' level.

At this stage the group begins to explore what this means, clarifying where

I have got to and enabling me to articulate my 'new theory' more clearly. This happens in several ways:

- *paraphrasing and summarizing* to articulate new assumptions – for example, Jan says 'So you do it [articulate new theory about assessment] with students but not with colleagues?'; when I answer 'With some colleagues' she uses a
- *probing question* – 'Why haven't you done it, do you think?', which leads to me realizing I have made another assumption – 'I assumed we had all changed'
- *checking connections and challenging thinking* – Julie asks about power and whether holding on to power over students is part of the issue; I explore this and conclude that this is not a major part of what is happening for me in the sense Julie has suggested
- *other participants articulating what their experience has been* to see whether this is relevant – this can be helpful in moderation; it provides another perspective, such as Riki pointing out that her colleagues would have very different values about this.

Exactly what is covered depends on what has happened for participants between sessions, as articulated above. Ways in which participants identify where they are now include:

- changing focus significantly, unearthing new assumptions that feel more fundamental to them about the incident and their understanding of it
- feeling stuck with trying to take their new understanding further
- wanting to consolidate what they have learnt from trying out new actions
- having a sense of inner change, a new awareness of how they might be able to be different
- uncertainty about how new understanding can lead to changed action
- a new perspective about other people they work with and changed assumptions related to that
- awareness of how something they thought was a professional issue also influences their personal life.

In the DVD, this occurs between 6 and 8 minutes.

How might they want to be different or act differently?

Depending on how the training has been organized – and how much time there is between stages, some participants return to stage 2 saying that they have already noticed change in how they are reacting or acting. Some say their new perception of 'how things are' means they are responding differently, perhaps asking questions rather than giving answers, or not accepting that there is only one way that a crisis can be 'fixed'. Some may have tried out new assumptions in the form of new actions – for example, deciding to raise difficult issues with a manager or colleague, or proactively suggesting change in work processes. In our experience so far, this has nearly always had positive results: the new action reinforces the new assumptions and often reveals more to explore in stage 2. Where the new actions haven't been effective, participants usually return saying they can now see how they need to develop greater clarity about how to put their new assumptions into practice, rather than rejecting the new assumptions. Participants also wrestle with the issue of how their change will connect with seeking to change the generally large and unwieldy organizations they work in, and we often return to this issue at the end of the workshop.

In practice, this and the previous area are often explored together. This is illustrated by my (Fiona's) incident: as I articulate where I am now, I also start to work out what this means about what I could do differently. The group moves backwards and forwards from further exploration of assumptions to thinking about possible actions. This particular group was held over one day, so there was little time between stages for participants.

In moving towards clarity about how I might act differently, I say that I realize now that I and my colleagues have not explored assessment, 'looking at this underneath level'. I suggest that I would now raise this issue in a different way with colleagues, looking at the hidden assumptions rather than assuming the discussion is a purely rational one. This becomes more explicit through the discussion: 'That's what I think I have to do differently – I think I assumed that we had all changed.' As the group continues, what needs to be named differently becomes more explicit: Julie says it's about 'making an explicit framework for assessment'. I agree with this and relate my values of how to work with colleagues with this.

Finally, Julie asks whether I would use this learning in other contexts – an important and useful question for thinking about how transferable the learning is. I respond by connecting this to other possible areas of practice.

It is important that there is time for this aspect of the process: grounding the learning from stage 1 in specific ways. The aim is that the participants leave the workshop with some clear ideas about how the shifts of stage 1 can be expressed, ideally ideas about strategies or possible actions. At the same time, it is important that the new learning is seen as applicable to practice in a general way, not only this incident. The discussion needs to vary to include both.

In the DVD, this section runs from just after 8 minutes to 19 minutes.

Articulating and labelling their new theory of practice

Although some participants arrive for stage 2 with their 'label', most develop it through the process of stage 2. The idea of the label is for participants to find a way to summarize what they have learnt in a way that integrates theory and practice (i.e. brings together the new ideas with how they can be put into operation). One participant called this a 'mantra', others a 'motto', or a 'metaphor'. Ideally, the label is also a reminder of the new learning, something participants can use to prompt the new way of acting in a similar situation. For some people it is important the label is also a metaphor, for others that it is humorous. What is really key is that it epitomizes what the participant has learnt, in language that is satisfying and meaningful to them.

Some examples of labels include:

- conflict is interesting
- I can be powerful in positive and constructive ways
- there's more than one way to skin a cat
- anything can be seen in many ways.

In my incident Jan as the facilitator prompts focus on the 'label', asking 'So if you had to put a label on your theory of assessment practice . . .'. It seems that I am not ready for this and the group spends more time exploring assessment and what my new theory of it might be. Jan eventually suggests a possible label of 'reflective assessment', which I accept as useful, combining the values and assumptions I have been developing about assessment.

One of the issues here is about timing: at what point is the participant clear enough about their new theory to be able to give it a label. Sometimes the participant is so caught up in the reflection that it is helpful, as in this incident, for somebody else – the facilitator or other group members – to make suggestions.

This process also enables people to make connections between their own theory and the more formal theories that may be written up in professional literature; this is generally an empowering process and crucial if participants are undertaking critical reflection as part of a formal degree programme.

In the DVD, this discussion occurs between 12 and 19 minutes.

Ending the workshop

The final session for the workshop – at the end of stage 2 – has three elements, as described below.

Reflection on the critical reflection process for this group

This session begins with some general discussion on the group's experience of the process – usually how they have felt about the process, what they found useful, any remaining questions or comments. Some groups focus on a particular aspect of the process that they have particularly valued or struggled with. A group might, for example, have wanted to move too quickly to change rather than exploring each incident sufficiently, or struggled to ask open questions.

In some groups a common theme emerges across the incidents – usually, though not always, with participants from the same organization. The group may then want to look at how they can work together on this issue, reinforcing their learning. For example, in an agency for victims of sexual abuse most of the group had incidents about conflict with a worker they supervised. It became clear that there were common unhelpful assumptions, such as that supervisors were either caring or controlling staff and couldn't do both. As it became clear that this was a common binary, they linked this with the agency's work with clients: how to convey clearly that clients are cared for and that abusive behaviour is not acceptable. The group wanted to spend some time on how they could collectively reinforce a new assumption: that supervisors can support staff and maintain a high-quality service.

A group of on-the-ground workers had expressed common themes about feeling powerless to make changes in the work culture. In stage 2 participants began to identify how they could feel more powerful and, as a group, reframed this to 'managing up'. What this meant for them was:

- team meeting – setting own agendas
- using time in team meetings for own issues – take hold of agenda
- educating managers
- checking management views/actions
- asking for clarification
- telling managers when their behaviour is disappointing
- recognizing the tension between independence and accountability
- looking for sources of power and support
- seeing managers' roles as different, not better.

Exploring how this new learning can be sustained and developed

This is a major issue for many participants who fear that the learning from the workshop may be swamped by the busy-ness of returning to work. On the other hand, some participants feel that the process and learning has been so significant for them that they cannot imagine it not being an integral part of practice. The group explores how they might sustain and continue to develop their learning both individually and collectively. The options can include:

- building in time for reflection individually – using travelling time, setting aside time in the office or somewhere quiet, thinking about how critical reflection can become part of ongoing practice rather than a separate activity
- using critical reflection in individual supervision – either formally or informally (see Chapter 9)
- making an agreement within the group that participants can call on each other for a 'critical reflection session' as needed
- pairing up with another participant and agreeing to meet on a regular basis, dividing the time so that each has an opportunity to reflect critically on an incident
- using critical reflection in ongoing team meetings or some kind of group or peer supervision (see Chapter 9).

Evaluation

This stage of the process is useful in providing closure as well as an opportunity to consider the process overall. Ideally, there is time for discussion about this as well as people filling in their own evaluation forms. We are looking here for feedback about the process, but also about what people feel they have learnt and how they might use the critical reflection theory and processes. Hearing their own and other people's feedback articulated helps them to consolidate what they have learnt and want to change.

We do also ask participants to fill in an individual evaluation form (you will find a copy of this in the online resource materials on the accompanying website at www.openup.co.uk/fook&gardner). Ideally, participants complete this and hand it in. Some people prefer to take the form away and send it back, so they can think more fully about what they want to say. The problem with this is that it often gets lost once people return to practice so we prefer participants to hand it in at the end of the workshop. The individual evaluation form aims to have people identify what they learnt from the workshop and what difference they think this will make to their practice. Results from the evaluation forms are discussed in Chapter 8.

Broad principles and techniques

Reinforcing the culture

By stage 2, groups have generally achieved a greater sense of trust in each other and the process. Because everyone is expected to participate – and by this stage has participated, there is more feeling of knowing each other, understanding where others are coming from and being able to work together.

It is still helpful to reinforce the culture of critical acceptance, particularly as the group moves to stage 2. The group might choose to look again at their stage 1 notes about the process and what worked. This can alert them to particular issues they had with the process – for example, to do with asking open questions or retaining the focus on the presenting participant's experience.

Starting with each participant's experience

As identified above, participants arrive at stage 2 at quite different points. It is important to recognize this and work with it. This doesn't necessarily mean that someone who hasn't thought about their incident will take longer at this stage than someone who has. It may be that a participant needs to spend more time initially on deeper clarification of where an assumption has come from and what it is, then can move quickly to the implications for change. What doesn't work is trying to move participants on too quickly when they have not sufficiently understood where they were coming from. This validates in a very direct way the underlying critical reflection theory: the assumption that there are many ways that this process can work, and that participants will vary in what is effective for them. This connects with the following point.

Identifying what matters

Just as in stage 1, participants need to focus on the essence of central themes of their incident rather than getting distracted by minor issues or surrounding detail. Once the major themes have been identified it is important for the group to concentrate on where the participant wants to go with these.

Remembering that the process is not necessarily linear

Although we talk about the elements of this stage as if they follow each other in a linear sequence, in practice participants may experience and so express them in a more complex and intertwined way. Some participants will also see connections to other parts of their work and want to make links with these.

Such a participant may need to go back to their incident to bring to mind what the essence of their learning is – the fundamental assumptions and values underlying the incident. It helps at this stage to keep an overall view that the focus should be on moving from analysis to change.

Focus on moving from analysis to change

The movement from understanding to action is a critical part of stage 2. The expectation is that participants will identify – with help from the group – what it would mean for them to operate differently. By 'operate' we mean both how might participants 'be' different and how might they 'act' differently.

Participants often talk about how they feel they are different as a result of the critical reflection training: they have new assumptions or perceptions, and/or have affirmed existing assumptions and values. They perceive themselves differently and may perceive other people differently, see new possibilities and choices that they haven't been aware of before. Some feel different about their incident and the others involved in it. Participants might say 'I am different so I will be different.'

To integrate their learning, participants need to ground this new sense of being more specifically in identifying what it might mean for them to act differently. Some people, of course, will already have tried some kind of changed action. Most participants imagine how they might act. Some start by going back to the original incident and thinking about how they might act now. Others might think about a similar incident arising where they are now, others still of how they would apply their learning in a more general way. Participants generally find it useful to be specific at this point, though some find this easier than others. The group can help with this, if needed, in the following ways.

- Asking questions to encourage exploration of change, such as:
  - How might you use your new assumptions? What difference would it make having these assumptions?
  - What difference might having the new assumption make to practice?
  - If you were faced with a similar situation again, how would you react now? What strategies might you use?
  - How else might these new assumptions (or affirming assumptions and values) change your practice?
- Asking questions to encourage specific strategies and plans. For example, some participants will explore how to change in a general way, but not be confident they have the skills to enable them to manage change. Given time, it can help to get them to be more

specific – even, for some, to develop a plan of action. Checking how realistic their plan is can help: what will they feel able to do, rather than what would they do in an ideal world? For example, a participant exploring how to operationalize a new assumption such as 'I can raise difficult issues in productive ways' might want to think about 'How might I raise issues?', 'What language would I want to use?', 'What strategies would make this more successful, such as timing, place?', 'What do I mean by productive?' Some questions that can help here are:

–   So can you give an example of how you would use your new assumption?
–   In your example, what steps would you take?
–   What would you do if it didn't work? What would your fallback position be?
–   How else could you work with the new assumption in this example? What else could you do?
–   What skills or knowledge do you need to refine or develop?
–   What outcomes would you be satisfied with?

•   Brainstorming possibilities: the facilitator or the participant can ask the group to help by brainstorming possible changes or strategies. It is important that this be done in a non-judgemental way, offering a smorgasbord of ideas to choose from rather than implying 'right' ways. This need not be based on reality (i.e. the group doesn't need to know the details of the presenting participant's workplace or practice). Brainstorming like this enables the participant to stand back from responding directly to the group and allows them to listen in to ideas that might work or that might spark other possibilities that are more realistic for their workplace.

Connecting the individual and social

Again groups vary in how clearly they make these connections. Some groups are already familiar with thinking in this way; or individuals within a group may readily link their own experience with dominant thinking in terms of gender, age, culture and ability. Differences in power are often more obvious for participants given that many work in large organizations where almost everyone, even those in senior positions, is conscious of their relative lack of power compared with someone else. This often leads to discussions about power and how it could be used, and the assumptions made about power individually, organizationally and socially.

The case study overleaf shows the connections made in one group when they wrote up what had emerged for them in the group.

Members of this group all came from a large public service organization. At the end of the workshop they identified what they felt were common themes in the group. These were:

- gender issues
- link to feeling less powerful in the organization
- able to stand back from gender and also see links to experience and maturity (i.e. others don't have the capacity to see this at this stage)
- personalities different, not everybody operates in same way, same style
- affirming commitment to public service as consistent with their values and how and where they want to make a difference
- implications of culture/refugee family background in seeing difference.

Making connections with learning about critical reflection

The training continues to operate at both levels: participants are applying stage 2 to their own incident and at the same time are learning about critical reflection theory and processes. Participants may name theory that they have found particularly useful – such as recognizing the binaries they use, the reflexivity involved in their incident or the multiple perspectives they now see. Looking at the process after each incident allows space to stand back and gain a different perspective. Writing comments on the whiteboard builds a more complex picture of the process. Participants often comment that being able to look back at the comments helps them see more clearly how the process works and to link aspects of the process to theory.

Again, some groups and individuals find this easier than others; some participants are familiar with some of the theory from their past training and so use it more readily. One of the advantages of working in a group is that participants hear others naming the connections in relation to their incident and can then adapt that learning to their own. This can mean that certain aspects of theory become more common in terms of group language than others. Part of the facilitator's role is to help make the links back to theory and the underlying process.

Chapter summary

In this chapter, we have explored the second stage of the critical reflection process: moving from analysis to change, including what happens between sessions. The structure and processes of this stage have been outlined, as have the processes of ending and evaluating the workshop. Broad principles and techniques have been identified, including: reinforcing the culture, starting with participants' experience, identifying what matters, remembering that the process is not necessarily linear, focusing on moving from analysis to change, connecting the personal and social, and making connections with learning about critical reflection.

8   The benefits and outcomes of critical reflection

In this chapter we present:

- the main themes that emerge about the benefits and outcomes of critical reflection, both from our own findings from our own course evaluations and from a brief review of relevant literature, and
- the main issues involved in evaluating critical reflection.

Identifying the concrete benefits and outcomes of critical reflection is arguably one of the most difficult aspects of the whole exercise. Given the diversity of thinking about it, and the unpredictability of how the process will be experienced by different learners, it is difficult to even speak about it in terms that will satisfy those who are more sceptical about its claims. In addition, little systematic research has been conducted on critical reflection generally (Ixer 2000; Hargreaves 2004; Fook *et al.* 2006), let alone research that attempts to delineate or measure the more concrete outcomes of the process. Of that which does, there is even less that attempts to specify these in terms of changes in the workplace. Nevertheless it is important in the current professional climate to be able to pinpoint specific benefits and outcomes, both for individuals and their workplace contexts.

Given the extent of the material involved, we include only summaries of main themes at relevant points in this chapter. Full analysis of our evaluation forms is included in the online resource materials on the website that accompanies this book, at www.openup.co.uk/fook&gardner.

In referring to benefits, we mean the perceived usages and positive contributions of critical reflection to learning and professional practice. In using the term 'outcomes' we are more explicitly addressing the sorts of changes in learning and practice that occur through and as a result of the critical reflection process. There may of course be some overlap between the two.

We begin with a brief summary of some of the issues involved in evaluating critical reflection, before summarizing the main research findings, from the literature and from our own evaluations.

The issues involved in evaluating critical reflection

Ironically the lack of research on critical reflection is probably the major drawback in conducting further research. Yet there may be good reasons for this lack. As we have noted several times, critical reflection is notoriously difficult to research in more 'objective' ways. Its meanings are diverse and sometimes amorphous, and there is little consensus (Moon 2004: 9). It can be approached from so many different perspectives that it is perhaps difficult, or sometimes meaningless, to translate its significance into different frameworks. The experience of the process itself is uncertain, and its outcomes unpredictable, often making it too limiting to simply use a predetermined framework. It is difficult to isolate the factors about the process that may contribute to learning, as so many factors are involved and intertwined and their relative influence may be indeterminate (e.g. the role of the facilitator, the influence of previous education, other learners, the work/learning context). Critical reflection has also essentially been developed for learning and professional development, which means as a concept it has not been operationalized for research, so few validated measurement instruments exist, particularly with regard to workplace context (Van Woerkem *et al.* 2002). And when findings are made, it is difficult to assess their significance, given the lack of existing material to which to relate them.

A second major issue surrounds the questions of what are we evaluating, and for whom? Clearly, what is focused on in the evaluation, and the relative worth of the findings, will depend on framework and perspective. Critical reflection may be evaluated in several main ways:

- an evaluation of the effectiveness of or satisfaction with the actual teaching/learning programme
- an evaluation of the actual learning/changes involved for learners
- an evaluation of the application or use of this learning.

These three different focuses may also be evaluated using differing theoretical frameworks (as we have addressed in earlier chapters), ranging from frameworks that see reflection as more about task and problem solving, to those that specifically address the questioning of power. And, within these approaches, there may be differing value placed on differing outcomes, depending on whether an individual or an organizational focus is taken. Of course, it is even debatable how meaningful it is to separate discussion of outcomes from an understanding of the whole process of learning involved. In addition, as

Greenman and Dieckmann (2004: 241), quoting Schor and Freire (1987: 34), so nicely remind us, 'transformations come in all sizes'. But of course, different sizes will be valued differently by different people, and especially by participants themselves (Fook and Napier 2000). Definitions may also vary, depending on how rational or cognitive the focus, or whether values (Ixer 2000) or emotions are taken into account.

Methodologies obviously also differ. Most studies are conducted from the point of view of the learner (that is, they involve methods that seek to identify the learner's perspective), and use either interviews or analyses of written material (such as journals, narratives or critical incidents) that students have submitted during the course of their formal programme of study.

In our own evaluations we have tried to address all three focuses, and have incorporated both reflective and critically reflective frameworks, all from the point of view of the learner, but with some attention paid to potential organizational gains (from the perspective of the individual worker or manager). We have used interviews, focus groups, analysis of written assignments, and analysis of written evaluations.

The issue of timescales is also problematic: does the learning from critical reflection change over time (Redmond 2004)? Few studies exist that specifically test this dimension. We have tried to address this in a preliminary way with our own programmes by including evaluative studies that are one-off (conducted immediately at the end of a programme), follow-up (conducted between six months and two years after a critical reflection programme), and longer term (conducted over a spread of time with one group of learners).

The four studies we have conducted on our own programmes comprise several different designs and methods. The full reports on each of these are included in the evaluation articles section in the online resource materials on the accompanying website at www.openup.co.uk/fook&gardner. In summary these involved the following aspects.

1. A study of the critical learning achieved, using a framework of 'reflexive modernity': this study analysed the responses on the evaluation forms of 154 participants from 20 workshop programmes conducted between 2002 and 2004. Some results are reported below where relevant and the full version of these results is included in the online resource materials (in the article 'Social work and civil society: reclaiming the links between the social and the personal'); another version has been published elsewhere (Fook and Askeland, in press).

2. A more general study of the responses on the evaluation forms of 396 participants from 54 separate workshop programmes conducted from 2002–2006: some of these results are reported at relevant points in this chapter, and the full results are also included in the online resource materials.

3. An analysis of postgraduate student assignments, submitted in two courses designed to teach critical reflection: the main paper is included in the online resource materials: 'Beyond reflective practice: reworking the "critical" in critical reflection'.

4. A follow-up study of participants who had undertaken the workshop training more than one year previously: some results are included below, and the full paper ('Creating a climate for change: critical reflection and organisations') is included in the online resource materials.

The benefits of critical reflection

What are the claims made about the potential benefits of critical reflection in the literature? These are broadly congruent, and often little attempt is made to justify them, given the huge popularity of the idea (Moon 2004: 9). Mezirow's early claims that critical reflection brings with it more 'inclusive, discriminating, permeable and integrative' perspectives (Mezirow and associates 1990: 14) are generally borne out by later writers. Brookfield (1995) points to the possibilities of more informed choice, developing rationales for practice, less 'self-laceration', emotional grounding, more enlivened teaching, and an increase in democratic trust. In broad terms, these benefits have been translated as contributing towards improved professional practice (and better theoretical development of it), coupled with an ability to research practice more directly (Fook 1996). The ability to learn directly from individual practice experience is seen as a plus in terms of organizational learning, and generally in terms of what it may teach us about more generalized workplace cultures (Johns 2002).

Some more specific uses of critical reflection have been underlined more recently. For instance, there may be a contribution towards improvement of professional relationships (with service users and colleagues) through the development of more collaboration and dialogue (McKee 2003). There may be a direct contribution to the development of professionalism, through regaining a sense of professionalism (Yip 2006) and through the ability to actualize social work values (Yip 2006) and, more particularly, social justice values (Rossiter 2005). More pragmatically, incorporating reflective methods into other training may strengthen its impact (Moon 2004). While the potential individual emancipatory benefits of critical reflection are well documented (Fook 2004e), there is some question about what this might mean for the workplace.

The human resource development framework has some relevance regarding the implications for the workplace. Van Woerkem (2004) summarizes the different perspectives on critical reflection from this framework. On one level it may primarily be about trying to solve workplace problems. Taking it further, it may be about trying to change workplace values or culture (this view is similar to Argyris and Schon's (1996) 'double loop learning'. A final level (incorporating a critical dimension) is about individual emancipation in relation to the organization. What of course is less clear is how individual emancipation contributes to organizational interests. Van Woerkem argues that there is clear benefit to the workplace if individuals question whether they really want to be in the job (2004: 185) and that there is a need for deeper thinkers in today's workplace. Looking at the potential of critical reflection more broadly, she argues that if individuals are able to learn how social and organizational norms have an impact on their own identity, then critical reflection can aid an understanding of how individuals are made in a workplace context. An understanding of this process can help better accommodate individual needs and capacities, and can contribute towards workers' capacities to deal with an unknown future, by linking work and personal lives.

In our experience, it is quite easy to identify major themes that indicate the nature of the critical reflection experience for participants. We include them here as a backdrop to the themes identified more systematically from our analysis of evaluation forms.

First, there is a broad sense of participants moving from feeling disempowered to empowered. Participants use words and phrases like feeling empowered, liberated, freed in talking about their response to critical reflection training. For some it is integrating new theory about their practice that is liberating. For example, participants are often unfamiliar with postmodern approaches (Rolfe 2000; Fook 2002) and find that the idea of multiple perspectives literally opens up new ways of seeing. This is reinforced as they begin to relate this to a particular incident, for example, in asking what are all the ways this particular experience might be seen. Such theory provides a counter to organizational contexts that expect a 'right' answer. For some practitioners new theory and the ability to use it means they can assert something they have sensed intuitively but haven't felt able to express. This generates a new feeling of confidence about being able to work effectively, of being empowered.

How power is perceived is also part of the background theory to critical reflection. Engaging with the notion of power as exercised not possessed (Healy 2000; Gardner 2006) often emerges in the process of reflecting on incidents. Participants say this is a powerful idea: it transforms their assumption that the more senior you are, the more powerful you will be. Instead they take on board that power is complex and that they too can and do exercise power in various ways – the power of commitment, passion or experience, for example. This opens up possibilities for new ways of acting, with participants saying they feel enabled or empowered to think about change.

For others the experience of sharing as part of a group process is empowering. This may be because their organizational context does not allow or encourage this kind of analysis or exploration of what is happening. Identifying underlying assumptions and values puts specific issues into perspective; they become part of a broader outlook (Brookfield 2005). Hearing from a number of participants also generates a sense of shared understanding of issues and the links between what is individual and what is structural. A frequent comment is something like 'This isn't just my issue.' Awareness of issues as common rather than individual depersonalizes them and sometimes visibly lightens the sense of feeling oppressed, or overwhelmed, by them.

Second, participants often see new possibilities for change. Exploring what new understanding means in terms of change is a critical part of the training process. Planning and allocating time for considering change as well as analysis is a visible reinforcement of the expectation of change. Participants say that this means that change starts to feel more real during the process – they are aware of change in themselves as well as at least the possibility of generating change outside themselves. Rather than being left to come up with new approaches on their own, they feel supported and encouraged to develop specific ideas about what will be different. This can be particularly powerful in a group where there is a cumulative effect of seeing how other participants approach being different and doing things differently. It is especially reinforced if one of the participants has already tried a different strategy – and even more so if it has worked (see Chapter 7).

Participants also see from both the theory and the process that they are always making choices – about whether to act, how to act, what attitude to take. Having made this conscious they can then choose whether to be a more conscious agent of change (Kondrat 1999).

Cate's incident was about a conflict with her supervisor. She thought it was pointless to talk about change: her supervisor had the power to make the decision. As she began to articulate her assumptions about power and change, the group challenged her by asking whether she had examples where she had been able to influence what happened. She gave several examples, then realized that she been able to exert considerable influence because of her past experience and respected position in the organization. Her assumptions about being powerless shifted; she laughed and said she felt a weight had lifted from her shoulders; she could see that there were many ways she could tackle this conflict.

Third, there is an acceptance of the integration of the personal and professional. 'This feels very personal' is a frequent comment from participants about critical reflection training. It is always said with a tone of surprise; sometimes almost one of indignation. So where are participants coming from? We have been surprised ourselves by the number of participants who say that both their organizations and their professions expect them to separate the personal and professional. There are different meanings of this: some mean that professionals should not be emotional or express their feelings; others that professionals should operate according to the organization's procedures and not have input from their own values; others that the professional's own reaction to what is happening is not relevant. This certainly fits with the issues that we looked at in Chapter 1: the expectation that human service professionals operate according to rules and procedures determined by their organization (Gould and Baldwin 2004) or the prevailing professional culture. However, as Bolton (2001: 45) says, 'we do not practise with one part of ourselves, and live a personal life with another, all the elements of ourselves are each a part of the other'. Participants generally found that in reflecting critically it made sense to integrate the personal with the professional: reflecting on their reactions to a work incident had parallels of some kind to their personal life, and vice versa.

This is a major issue in using critical reflection. The theory and the process affirm the need to work with the whole person. Participants frequently comment at the end of a critical reflection process on how they now feel more connected as a worker, able to use their own feelings and reactions as valid information in deciding how to act. They also feel more in touch with underlying values and assumptions that inform what they see as important and how they want to act in their organization. Schon (1983: 300) would suggest that reflective practice encourages a shift from wanting to be seen as the expert to looking 'for the sense of freedom and of real connection to the client, as a consequence of no longer needing to maintain a professional facade'.

Another part of this for participants was recognizing that they wanted to have fuller, more honest relationships with clients. They wanted to be able to respond in a human, holistic way, rather than merely as the representative of a bureaucracy. They did not want to offer the kind of service one participant experienced as a client of an organization, of three social workers asking the same questions in the same order. Binnie and Titchen's (1999) experience of developing patient-centred practice in a hospital ward fits more with what participants saw as desirable. They found that once nurses focused on patient needs rather than the demands of the system, they developed new kinds of relationships

> with new demands and responsibilities [with] extraordinarily privileged access to the patient's private world ... and the nurses recognised that this difference called for a personal, as well as a technical, response ... the trust itself demanded a human response. It meant that nurses were involved as people and were called upon to give something of themselves. (Binnie and Titchen 1999: 159)

A distinction that participants find helpful here is between who they are as a person/professional and the separation of their private life from their work life. They affirm that critical reflection enables them to see they cannot separate who they are as a person from how they operate as a professional – the expression of their personality, values, assumptions, the influence of past experience. If they try to separate off who they are as a person, they feel as if they are working more like a robot rather than a person in relationship with other people. On the other hand, they can, and do, make conscious choices about how much of their private life they want to share at work. Again this is experienced as part of the critical reflection process: participants see that they inevitably express who they are as a person, but can choose whether to talk about their private life.

During supervision, Millie used critical reflection to explore her angry reaction to people not washing their own mugs or lunch dishes at work. She talked about her values of respect for others, for order and cleanliness, but these didn't seem to tap into the depth of her reaction. Her supervisor asked 'Where does this come from?' Millie thought for a few minutes, then said, 'Oh I think I've got it, but I'm not sure if I want to talk about it.' She thought further then said she would: that she realized that her reaction came from being in a family where no one ever bothered about any routine or order; she felt like the only one who ever washed dishes before they ran out of them. Once she recognized this she was able to see that the strength of her anger was out of proportion and tackle the issue more positively.

Fourth, finding the place of emotions appears to be significant for many participants. Getting to the feelings in critical reflection training is often what generates the recognition of what is really important – the underlying assumptions and the values behind them. The importance of emotion in generating change is well recognized in critical reflection training (Taylor 2000; Bolton 2001; Fook 2002) and this is explored as part of the introduction to the theory (see Chapter 2). Mezirow (1991: 38), for example, affirms that 'if the emotional stress of a conflict of beliefs causes us to transform a meaning perspective dramatically, that transformation will be remembered'. The depth of feelings may be about the particular incident being discussed or connect to other past experiences either at work or with a connection from the participant's private life.

The validity of expressing emotions is a related issue for participants in linking the personal and professional. It may seem surprising that in the health and human service field, participants felt there was an embargo on talking about emotions. Not all participants felt this by any means, but it was an issue for a significant number. Gibbs (2002: 307), who explores the experience of child protection workers, sees this as a major concern: 'anxiety cascades through each level of the organization leaving workers drowning in a whirlpool of angst, uncertainty and distress. These feelings, rarely acknowledged and poorly contained, do not go away.' She suggests that the lack of recognition and exploration of emotions contributes to ineffective work and high staff turnover.

This was an issue for participants both in their work with clients and in their relationships within the organization. Some felt they were supposed to remain distant from clients; others that the pressure of work demands and expectations of working in routine ways meant there was no opportunity to develop more meaningful relationships. This then often translated into relationships with peers and supervisors who had also internalized an organizational culture that discouraged emotion.

Kara, an occupational therapist, had been working with a family with a severely disabled child for six months. The family had been doubtful about her suggestions initially, but she had finally established positive relationships and the child was beginning to respond. Her incident was about a supervision session where her supervisor indicated that, given the agreed timelines for working with families, she needed to withdraw. While Kara could see that this was fair given the vast waiting list, she felt deeply frustrated and disappointed, and was close to tears. Her supervisor then said, 'Well it's clearly time you moved on from this family, too much involvement there.' Kara left supervision feeling misunderstood and angry. The other participants validated her feelings and she was able to articulate her values about treating families respectfully and allowing them time. She decided to talk with her supervisor and her team about other ways to organize work, including dealing with the waiting list.

Given this experience, participants talked about feeling 'liberated' by the view that expressing emotions is a legitimate part of work. They agreed that recognizing their own feelings often provided useful cues in work with clients. Those who had had positive experiences reinforced the value of expressing emotions so that they could move on. Participants also affirm that the recognition and expression of emotions is a vital part of being yourself and an important aspect of critical reflection.

Lastly, the therapeutic nature of critical reflection recurs constantly. 'Is this supposed to feel therapeutic?' is another reasonably frequent comment from participants. The tone of the question here is still surprised, but positively so. More often, participants ask this at the end of critical reflection training. We were initially surprised, too, that people used the word therapeutic; we hadn't thought about the process in that way. Once the questions were asked, we started to explore more about what people meant. We also started to ask how being therapeutic might fit with our expectations of critical reflection.

Being therapeutic is clearly not limited to formal therapy. Writers use 'therapeutic' in all sorts of ways: some in terms of community environments that are life enhancing for residents (Delgado 2000), or community centres that are therapeutic both in the direct service and the community connections they provide (McMahon and Ward 2001). Ellis, Kiesinger and Tilmann-Healy suggest that research can be therapeutic when it makes a difference in people's lives (cited in Hertz 1997). Although narrative therapists reject much of traditional approaches to therapy, they still talk about narrative therapy (Morgan 2000; Payne 2000).

What is consistent about this – and about participants' comments – is creating an environment that enables some kind of positive shift or change. Family therapists seek change within families, psychotherapists change within individuals. Often, for participants, being 'therapeutic' is connected to what they call, for example, an 'aha' or 'ouch' experience: a shift of perception at a deep level that generates a feeling of growth and new understanding. From this inner shift it becomes easier to contemplate external change, acting differently.

Reasonably often, this 'aha' experience came from making a connection to an issue in participants' personal as well as their professional lives. Connecting back to past individual or family experiences is also part of what people mean by therapeutic.

Penny worked as a speech therapist for a community health centre. Her incident was about her frustration with her colleagues who often arrived late to work. Even though she knew that they worked later to make up the time, she still felt angry with them about being late. When she explored her incident she realized that what really frustrated her was her own inability to go home on time, when her colleagues were still working. Digging deeper, she realized that what was important to her was being seen as a perfect worker. One of the participants asked 'Where did this come from?' Penny suddenly connected this with her experience as a child and young person of being noticed for doing well. This was an 'ouch' moment for Penny: she could see that this worked badly for her at home as well as at work. She started to work on affirming new values about who she is rather than what she is seen to be doing.

The five themes discussed above are echoed in the more formal evaluation responses of our participants, although they do not always use the same language. Below we have summarized and categorized these responses. Four main themes emerged from our systematic analysis of these:

1. learning and professional development, which incorporates the ability to be able to learn directly from one's own practice experience
2. therapeutic uses, which refers more to the ability to address emotional aspects of work, and to be able to better support and care for the 'self'
3. the ability to integrate personal and professional spheres, which refers in the main to the idea that critical reflection has uses in both professional and personal lives
4. workplace uses, which encompasses several themes around supervision, team management, improved practice and better organizational practice.

These themes fit broadly with the benefits noted in the literature, but also provide far more specific detail from the perspective of participants. In particular it is worth noting that therapeutic uses contained well-considered details regarding how critical reflection could assist workers to 'move on' from emotional or personal issues that threatened to restrict their practice. These sorts of details require further research and exploration if critical reflection is to be used in meaningful ways in workplace settings for both individuals and organizations.

The outcomes of critical reflection

To what extent does the research conducted on critical reflection bear out these claims about its benefits? In this section we focus on literature based on empirical research studies of critical reflection. It is probably correct to state at the outset that research in general does bear out the claims made, but adds a note of caution to the broad optimism that abounds, and much more detail to our understanding of the process, too. Let us start with the more generalized, and cautionary, findings first. Please note that we have focused here on studies that were primarily focused on learning about the critical reflection process, the learning or changes made by the learners, and any workplace application; we have not included studies that were primarily evaluations of a particular teaching programme.

What is the nature of the critical reflection process?

The right conditions are needed for critical reflection to happen optimally (e.g. Issit 2000). It involves self-evaluation and is experienced as challenging (Issit

2000); it is not necessarily an enjoyable experience for all. It may initially involve a great deal of anxiety about the newness of the learning method itself (Wong *et al.* 2001). Obviously, learners become more comfortable with this over time. However, several studies indicate that, more often than not, it is only lower levels of reflection that are attained and not the deeper or more sophisticated critical levels (Hatton and Smith 1995; Duke and Appleton 2000; Griffin 2003; Whipp 2003; Thorpe 2004). However, there is clear indication that it is possible to move to more critical levels (Hamlin 2004).

Learning in the process is helped by listening (Knights 1985), self-questioning, opportunities for reflection, as well as interactions with significant others (Pedro 2005). There is a note of caution sounded, though, about the barriers to reflective learning. Platzer *et al.* (2000) note that previous educational experience, the context and culture of the reflection, and others in the learning group will influence how and whether learning occurs. Some research also indicates that there may be no difference between the learning attained through a reflective approach and through a more traditional approach (Lowe and Kerr 1998), although a reflective approach does aid learning (Lee and Loughran 2000).

In our own studies participants identified a wider variety of helpful factors, which included in particular: the learning environment (safe, supportive, comfortable, inclusive, empowering); the experiential and practice nature of the learning; the linking of both theory and practice; the group nature of the experience, particularly the group participation; adequate time; the quality of the facilitation; the clear and practical nature of the model; the illustration of specific techniques. It is important to note that many different aspects may be experienced as helpful by different participants, and that it is perhaps the way these are combined in the environment that may be crucial to successful learning. This came across quite clearly from many participants, who framed what was helpful more in terms of the broad experience of the process, rather than specific aspects.

What is involved in the change process itself?

We analysed student assignments to identify patterns in the learning process. (A full report on this is included in the online resource materials, as well as copies of the student assignments – see www.openup.co.uk/fook&gardner). Overall the process seemed to involve a complex interplay of reflecting on specific personal experiences, filtering out different sets of assumptions, and again using the prism of personal experiences, particularly the emotional element, to distil some fundamental meaning (theory of practice) that connects the disparate assumptions. Sometimes part of this fundamental meaning involves the awareness of the importance of the past experiences in identity formation, or in emotional politics. This fundamental meaning is then scrutinized against current contexts (literature, current experiences, other perspectives) and remade in ways that seem more appropriate in these con-texts. This remaking involves turning the fundamental meaning (theory of practice) into an issue that is researchable and actionable in the current work-place context. What is particularly noteworthy about these findings is the important role personal emotional experience plays in assisting learners to pinpoint what is meaningful and of fundamental importance. We believe that more work needs to be done in understanding the role of emotions in critically reflective learning.

What specific outcomes have been identified?

- Increased self-awareness (Tsang 2003) and self-discovery (Maich *et al.* 2000) couple with the idea that critical reflection functions as a self-evaluative process (Griffin 2003). This may also enable an overcoming of personal fears (Griffin 2003). Learners also develop a better under-standing of the relationship between emotion and learning (Grant 2001). From our own general evaluations we found a strong theme of being better able to resolve or work through dilemmas and tensions in the workplace, and a strong recognition of the power of emotions and its recognition in professional practice.
- Better awareness of connectedness with colleagues occurs (Maich *et al.* 2000), which often goes along with more collaborative notions of power (Fook and Napier 2000). They may also display a different attitude towards cases, taking a less 'forensic' and more 'relational' approach, prepared to analyse a case in more dynamic terms and in terms of their own involvement (Fook 2004a). Our own studies particularly bear out the idea that critical reflection engenders an increased sense of shared experiences and values.
- There are changes in thinking that can have direct spin-offs for prac-tice. For instance, some learners report being 'less robotic and reactive', taking more time to think about their practice (Fook 2004a), and reducing 'knee-jerk' reactions. Learners may also simply think more deeply and broadly about their work (Griffin 2003), taking into account different and multiple perspectives (Griffin 2003), particu-larly the perspective of the client (Redmond 2004). Or they may be more rigorous about evidence for their practice, thinking more cri-tically (Maich *et al.* 2000) or using coursework and research to support what they do (Griffin 2003). In some cases learners report having more practice strategies at their disposal and being better able to make decisions (Fook 2004a). This latter point is borne out particularly in our own general evaluations: participants reported a better ability to think through issues and therefore better decision making. Many of our participants saw themselves as becoming more 'soul searching',

stopping to ask themselves 'Whose needs am I meeting?' or 'looking more closely at how hidden ideas can cause conflict'. Many conceptualized their changes in thinking as 'not a solution-driven approach', and saw themselves as becoming more skilled in the process.

- Some learners may experience a 'professional awakening' (Maich *et al.* 2000), and others may remake their notions of professionalism and themselves in relation to it (Napier and Fook 2000: 219). For many of our own participants this took the form of recognizing the inevitable connections between themselves as people and as professionals, and accepting and valuing those connections.

- The ability to abstractify may increase (Tsang 2003), and learners may develop broader understandings of theory (Napier and Fook 2000: 219). For many of our participants this latter took the form of being able to develop a more personalized theory, which many found affirming.

- There appears to be a greater tolerance of ambiguity (Grant 2001) and uncertainty (Tsang 2003), which may also link with developing a more complex and multi-dimensional perception of the job (Tsang 2003). For our own participants there was much mention of a greater recognition of the unpredictability of practice, and the inability to be able to control it all. With this came greater acceptance: 'It's OK to be human' was one phrase that captured this aspect well.

- How emancipatory is critical reflection? Some studies report an increase in personal agency and feelings of power (Schon 1995: 224; Fook and Napier 2000) and certainly that learners feel more responsibility in situations (Griffin 2003). Learners also report a more empowered sense of self in many different ways (Fook and Askeland, in press). Maich *et al.*'s (2000) learners were able to 'identify and break free of oppressive forces' and 'give voice'. Johns (2002), in analysing the narratives of reflective learners, notes a reclaiming of control of the self. In our own studies we looked at the issue of empowerment in two ways. In the first instance we used the framework of reflexive modernity (Beck 1992), and in the second we used a framework derived more directly from our own framework of critical reflection.

First, the framework of reflexive modernity and the related concept of 'life politics' (Giddens 1992) was used to analyse how critical reflection might assist people in encountering current challenges conceptualized in these contemporary terms. (The full version of this paper, 'Social work and civil society', is included in the online resource materials at www.openup.co.uk/fook&gardner.) This analysis demonstrates that individual workers can use critical reflection to reconstitute themselves as potentially powerful, able to exercise agency in influencing situations. This involves a revaluing of self through: shifting the source of self-value from social environment to themselves; valuing characteristics that were formerly thought to be non-professional, and reintegrating these characteristics into their professional identities. Choices are also reconstructed, moving usually from framing choices in 'forced choice' terms to provide multiple choices, and sometimes from a more fatalistic frame ('dilemma') to a more empowered frame ('opportunity'). These ways of reframing understandings of practice provide more opportunities for new practices. In this process participants also experience a 'liberation' or empowerment, as if freed from ways of constructing a situation that restrict options and ways of doing and being.

Second, using our own critical framework, we found that one of the dominant responses was an increased awareness of links between personal and social spheres, a greater appreciation of shared views and experiences, some further awareness of the operation of dominant discourses, as well as the ability to envision changed actions as a result of changed awareness. Self-validation and belief formed a large component of participants' views of their own empowerment through the process.

One way of looking at empowerment was, interestingly, one that we had not predicted. Many participants specifically focused on what they believed to be the possibility of positive, healthy outcomes, through the use of critical reflection. Not only did they feel the process encouraged positive change, but because it did not involve just focusing on negative perspectives, they believed it to be a 'healthy' way to view personal and professional boundaries and experience. Someone spoke of the process as 'enabling me to gain strength and learn from incidents rather than drain me and reinforce negative thinking'.

- For many of our own participants, a particular outcome of learning critical reflection was the ability to use the process in a way that integrates different aspects of learning directly for professional practice. The following quotes illustrate clearly how some participants put the whole process together.

> 'I developed an awareness of how being open to personal reflection and listening to others' perspectives can have a profound impact on how we frame what has happened and what can be done to move forward.'

> 'Critical reflection is a process that allows for the deep reflection and questioning of one's previously unexamined assumptions and values, but that provides strategies to evaluate one's core integrity and remain not only intact but also respected.'

'I learnt about trust, shared meaning and experiences . . . about hope, power, the use of self . . . the power of self as opposed to theories. Hard to dig to the deep level required for this process but the rewards were huge. Really throwing away my assumptions/ truths and being really open to the situation regardless of the vulnerability we feel.'

What is the longer-term impact of these changes?

Maich *et al.* (2000) note that learners had a plan of how they would implement continuing changes. This accords with Tsang's (2003) finding that learners had an action plan based on their increased self-awareness. Griffin's (2003) learners had also already attempted to make changes. Studies of the longer-term effects of Mezirow's transformational learning, while not quite the same as critical reflection, are useful to note here. For instance Taylor's (1997) review of 39 studies of transformative learning confirms most of these outcomes.

Our own follow-up study of 20 participants (the full paper is included in the full analysis of evaluation forms in the online resource materials at www.openup.co.uk/fook&gardner) indicated that there was clear chance for a wide variety of individual changes, including awareness of multiple perspectives and the impact of self, leading to more openness in relationships. Changes with regard to organizations were less clear, however, and limitations to organizational change were noted.

Where to from here?

On the whole the findings from most studies of the outcomes of critical reflection support the broad claims made about its potential benefits, although of course the studies provide far more detail and complexity regarding the actual experience of learning, and the sorts of conditions that are necessary to foster that learning. Studies to date also indicate that there is a need for more understanding of how critical reflection might be applied in the longer term, and how it might be practised and supported within the workplace.

Chapter summary

Although critical reflection is under-researched and under-evaluated, it is important to attempt to pinpoint specific benefits and outcomes for both individuals and workplaces.

Some major issues in evaluating critical reflection are: the diversity of perspectives; the indeterminate nature of the process; the differing frameworks and methods that are used.

The main benefits (perceived uses and contributions) of critical reflection fall into several main categories:

- rational – more informed choices and better rationales for actions
- emotional – self-awareness, support
- values – increased democracy, trust, inclusiveness and emancipation
- practice – improved relationships, collaboration, professionalism, organizational learning.

The main outcomes (changes and learning that take place) of critical reflection incorporate the fact that the nature of the change/learning process is complex and involves a range of factors. The learning environment is crucial.

Specific outcomes include:

- those related to rationality – better abilities to abstractify and understand theory, more considered and evidence-based actions, contributing to better decision making and more choice; better ability to tolerate and work with uncertainty and multiple perspectives
- the self and emotions – increased self-awareness, an ability to overcome personal blocks, resolve dilemmas, and recognize and harness the power of emotion
- value-based practice – more inclusive (and less judgemental) emancipatory practice, more agency and awareness of personal agency
- direct links with practice – enhanced sense of professionalism; better connectedness with colleagues; practice not focused entirely on solutions that, ironically, may lead to a sense of having more skills; ability to better integrate the personal and professional realms; ability to use the whole process for better learning.

PART III
Application of the Critical Reflection Process

9 Using critical reflection in organizational settings

This chapter aims to:

- explore the use of critical reflection in organizational settings, particularly in relation to the following three areas of organizational life
  - management
  - supervision
  - programme development
- consider briefly current thinking that provides a context to critical reflection in organizations, particularly ideas about organizational learning and the learning organization
- outline specifically how critical reflection might be used in each area of organizational life (i.e. management, supervision and programme development).

The theory of critical reflection provides useful background for managers and supervisors, as well as a specific process for working with individuals, teams and organizations. Participants suggest that critical reflection prompts managers to think broadly and analytically, to consider context and question their own as well as organizational assumptions. The process of critical reflection can be used to inform management, supervision and programme development processes generally as well as being a particular way of working within supervision or in teams. How critical reflection is used will depend partly on the culture of the organization. How supervision is perceived, for example, will make a difference to how critical reflection can be used. Critical reflection as a process can also be used in developing specific programmes or projects.

Managers and supervisors say they currently face conflicting expectations about how they will operate. On the one hand, there are the pressures that we considered in Chapter 1: the pressure to operate according to a more market-orientated approach to service delivery with narrow funding guidelines; the use of procedures and routines to manage the fear of risk and fragmentation of service delivery. On the other hand, there is an increased expectation of operating as a 'learning organization' or engaging in 'organizational learning'. This is often expressed as a desire to create a flexible and open culture in organizations both in terms of the organization as an entity and the individuals within it. Both are expected to operate creatively, to engage actively with change and, particularly, to question current processes (Coulshed and Mullender 2001).

Ideas about the learning organization originated in a business culture (Senge 1990), but have permeated widely in human service organizations (Boud and Garrick 1999). Writers debate the difference between organizational learning and the learning organization. Argyris and Schon (1996: 180) see the literature divided into 'the practice-oriented, prescriptive literature of "the learning organization," promulgated mainly by consultants and practitioners, and the predominantly skeptical scholarly literature of "organizational learning" produced by academics'. Gould (2004: 3) suggests that the distinctions are less important than what is common. He suggests two basic assumptions that are shared:

> First, individual learning is a necessary but not sufficient condition for organizational learning . . . Second, the learning experience is more pervasive and distributed than that delivered through a specific, designated training or education event; learning incorporates the broad dynamics of adaptation, change and environmental alignment of organizations, takes place across multiple levels within the organization and involves the construction and reconstruction of meanings and world views within the organization.

This connects to new approaches to learning and work across professional practice. These suggest that in the past we thought about education or training for practice as separate from practice: you completed training in a course then became a practitioner with perhaps extra short courses for specific new skills or knowledge. Now the expectation is that practitioners are 'life-long learners' (Tosey 2003: 145) with learning seen as a continuous process and part of work. The need to be life-long learners is associated with being able to adapt to a constantly changing environment – the 'supercomplexity' discussed in Chapter 1. Schon's thinking about reflective learning has been influential: that people learn by reflecting on what they are doing (reflection on action), but also ideally develop the capacity to reflect while acting (reflection in action) (Schon 1983). Others talk about 'action learning' (i.e. that practitioners learn from experience) and suggest that education and training need to encourage this. Cherry (1999: 8), for example, says the key to experience-based learning is that the individual is asked to access direct personal experience and practice in 'real life' situations: this contrasts with reading about other people's experience and ideas or simply thinking about ideas in a training situation. The role of the educator is to facilitate ways in which people can create, access and reflect upon their experience.

Critical reflection and management

Given this context, critical reflection offers managers and supervisors a useful framework for exploring issues in a way that leads to constructive planning and/or change. This can be helpful in reviewing existing service delivery, for example, or for planning how to manage a new policy initiative. Managers say that the theory underlying critical reflection reminds them to:

- think about the context – How does this particular issue or change fit with what currently exists as well as the proposed change? How do current structural issues impact on the situation?
- consider the different perspectives of team members and other stakeholders
- take into account that many ways forward are possible – there is no 'right' answer
- work in inclusive and collaborative ways
- identify underlying values and their potential impact
- value the knowledge base generated by workers 'on the ground'.

One of the current issues in critical reflection writing is whether organizations should focus more on critical reflection as an organizational process rather than an individual one. Reynolds and Vince (2004: 1) suggest that current writing has concentrated too much on the individual and 'that less emphasis needs to be placed on reflection as the task of individuals, and more emphasis needs to be put on creating collective and organizationally focused processes for reflection'. This is supported by Boud, Cressey and Docherty (2006: 16), who advocate what they call 'productive reflection' where the focus is on embedding productive learning through the 'creation of contextualized workplace learning that allows and releases the capacity of the workforce, via de-centralized and flexible project groups, the use of multi-functional networks and multiple stakeholder perspectives'. This approach would require an organization to formally adopt productive reflection as a way of operating. Our own research suggests that both are important and that there is a complex interaction between the individual and their organization (see Chapter 8): some individuals see themselves as generating organizational change as a result of being involved in critical reflection workshops; others believe that the organization needs to more formally adopt critical reflection processes for real change to occur.

Certainly, from a worker perspective, managers need to take seriously the implications of critical reflection training: if workers feel more empowered to seek change as a result of workshops endorsed by management they will feel very frustrated if their suggestions are not treated with respect. Critical reflection does offer managers a process for considering organizational issues in a way that respects the knowledge and experience of those at all levels of the organization, as the following case study illustrates.

An organization primarily providing employment services for people who have been long-term unemployed is planning how to deal with new government policies that expect people with disabilities to work for at least 15 hours a week unless assessed as medically unable to. Some of the team members have expressed concern about how realistic the policy is, fearing that it will make people with disabilities feel even less able. The team manager suggests that the team use critical reflection to explore this issue. Copies of the new policy are available to staff before the discussion. The discussion covers the following points.

- The context: the changing labour market, the ideology of the current government and reactions to it, changing expectations culturally about difference.
- Underlying assumptions and values: the team generates a vast list of the assumptions they see as embedded in the new policy, such as that people must work to be valued; people who are not in paid employment are not seen as contributing to society and so are seen as worth less; current standards of living must be maintained instead of being questioned; some people will not work unless they are forced to.
- Varying perspectives among team members: about their own assumptions and values and how these are similar to and different from those embedded in the policy.
- Differing attitudes: to change in general and particularly to this change; views about power and who has it; how possible it is to work with and/or around the policy.

Once the team manager felt the team had analysed thoroughly, she summarized where she thought they were up to. Overall, there were mixed feelings about the new policy. Team members were not in agreement with many of what they perceived as the policy's underlying assumptions and values. However, they also knew from their experience that many of those not employed wanted to be, and the new policy came with some extra funding that would support their efforts to gain employment. They agreed that social values meant that people felt more valued if they had work; they felt caught between wanting to change these and wanting to support people who wanted to be able to work.

This led to discussion about strategies. The team decided they would implement the policy, but would also document systematically where they considered the policy to be ineffective or detrimental to individuals and that, depending on the results, they would use the results to argue for change. They also agreed that they would emphasize work with clients in a way that conveys respect for them as individuals to try to minimize people feeling undermined as the policy is implemented. Where appropriate, part of this would be exploring clients' and the policy's underlying assumptions and values in the hope that clients would not internalize negative messages from the policy.

Critical reflection and programme development

The critical reflection process can also be used for programme or project development, review and ongoing management. The management of organizations is generally divided into programme or project areas, each with its own context – both organizational and the broader structural context including the political context. Depending on the programme there may be more specific guidelines about how it is to operate, which also have their own assumptions and values.

Using critical reflection can be useful for programmes at many stages: planning, implementation and review or evaluation. The following questions can be used to enable a team or worker to consider the programme.

- What is the context for the programme?
  - How did the programme develop?
  - Who was involved and what were their assumptions and expectations?
  - What was the political and social context?
  - How has the programme been funded and what are the implications of this?
  - How does the programme fit with the organization?
- What are the aims of the programme?
  - How were the aims developed?
  - What assumptions and values are implicit in the aims of the programme?
- Who is involved?
  - What are the different perspectives on the programme?
  - Whose voices are being heard?
  - Are there voices not being heard?

- What is expected of the project?
    - Are specific outcomes expected?
    - What is the balance between process and outcomes?
    - How will the project be evaluated?

Critical reflection and supervision

Historically, supervision was associated with social work and psychotherapy, but has now become more embedded in other disciplines such as nursing (Rolfe *et al.* 2001; Winstanley and White 2002) and allied health disciplines such as occupational therapy and physiotherapy (Rose and Best 2005). Most workers in human service organizations would expect to have supervision, but how this is defined and operationalized varies considerably. The traditional definition of supervision as a combination of support, education and adminis-tration (Kadushin 1985) has remained a fundamental part of supervision edu-cation (Brown and Bourne 1995). Interestingly in nursing there is a similar widely used combination of restorative, formative and normative supervision (Bond and Holland 1998). This type of supervision also tends to take the form of a more senior practitioner meeting individually with a more junior practitioner, usually on a regular basis through some kind of structured meet-ings. How exactly this is organized will vary depending on the organizational context as well as individual expectations about how much the relationship is hierarchical rather than collegiate, how the three functions are expressed, and what assumptions there are about learning and development.

Currently, participants in critical reflection training often see supervision as having become overly administrative or management orientated. Rather than an avenue for support and the exploration of issues, the emphasis is on control of workload and compliance with operational standards. This reflects the more market-orientated approach of human service organizations dis-cussed above, where organizations seek to control workers through procedures and routines. The fear of risk is a significant part of this: trying to ensure that nothing will go wrong. Gibbs (2002) suggests this is a major issue in child protection, for example, where the organization seeks to reduce anxiety by proceduralizing and codifying the work, with supervision often focusing on what is being done rather than how workers feel about it or what they need to learn. Jones (2001) found that this was a common experience in human service organizations, with practitioners becoming increasingly stressed and without opportunities to have such stress recognized and addressed. On the other hand, Gibbs (2002: 222), from her research in child protection, found that what made a difference in terms of staff retention was a positive early super-visory relationship: 'they consistently talk about feeling cared for and valued as well as having some control over their learning'.

Summary: definitions of supervision

Clinical supervision is regular, protected time for facilitated, in-depth reflection on clinical practice. It aims to enable the supervisee to achieve, sustain and creatively develop a high quality of practice through the means of focused support and development. The supervisee reflects on the part she plays as an individual in the complexities of the events and quality of her practice. This reflection is facilitated by one or more experienced colleagues who have expertise in facilitation and the frequent, ongoing sessions are led by the supervisee's agenda. The process of clinical supervision should continue throughout the person's career, whether they remain in clinical practice or move into management, research or education. (Bond and Holland 1998: 12)

... supervision in social work continues to serve several purposes at once ...: managerial, education and supportive (or enabling) ... it is the norm in social work to hold these functions in a fruitful tension. (Coulshed and Mullender 2001: 163)

Changing approaches to learning and ideas about the learning organization have started to encourage thinking about the diversity of ways that supervision can be understood and operationalized. There is more interest in exploring how supervision can be part of creating a new culture of managing change and expectation of ongoing learning, with reflection of some kind an integral part of this. Bond and Holland (1998: 4), for example, advocate a framework for supervision where 'people weave their own pattern rather than a model that sounds prescriptive'. Deprofessionalization and job fragmentation can mean that practitioners are looking for new ways of being supported and educated rather than expecting one person to provide all of these functions. There are more models of supervision – from the developmental, which assumes supervision changes as the worker becomes more experienced, to the cyclical, which is based on forming a contract about learning (Ooijen 2000; Page and Wosket 2001). Bishop (1998: 6), for example, sees supervision for nurses as therapeutic, 'something for nurses' rather than a 'disciplinary or critical event', and relevant to the context of the particular practitioner. Lahad (2000) suggests being more creative in supervision, using images and characters from fiction or films, metaphors and letter writing; Wood (2003) talks about creative supervision, suggesting the value of play using, for example, objects such as puppets and toys as symbols and metaphors or for visualization.

There is now more diversity of forms of supervision, such as group supervision, either with a supervisor as facilitator, or as peer supervision. Group and peer supervision are more often used for mutual support and education than for accountability (Hawkins and Shohet 1989). Peer supervision is essentially where workers meet on a regular basis to discuss aspects of their work and provide some elements of supervision for each other – providing information, education and mutual support (Hawkins and Shohet 2000). The group usually begins by establishing what it will do and how it will operate. Facilitation of such groups is generally shared, with workers taking it in turns to assist the group process. These forms of supervision affirm the value of practitioners sharing ideas and perspectives, and can offer a more empowering environment – particularly peer supervision with workers at the same level in the organization.

One of the advantages of using critical reflection in group and peer supervision is that the group may find common experiences, so begin to see them differently – as collective or organizational issues rather than or as well as personal ones (see Chapter 7). Finally, team or peer supervision can encourage the development of a team learning culture, which can be an essential source of support for workers. Gould's (2000: 590) research in a national child care agency, for example, showed that the team was 'a critical context for learning', with teams being able to maintain their own culture in a time of stressful organizational change in spite of changing workers.

Critical reflection can be used in a variety of supervision contexts: in individual as well as group or peer supervision, or in mutual peer partnerships. Using critical reflection in supervision fits with expectations of developing a learning organization (Gould and Baldwin 2004). As discussed in Chapter 2, how critical reflection is named varies here: some writers talk more about reflective practice, which is seen as an important part of supervision in nursing (Driscoll 2000; Ghaye and Lilyman 2000; Hawken and Worrall 2002: 48). Hawken and Worrall (2002) talk about reciprocal mentoring supervision:

> structured, reciprocal learning relationships between peers (two or three) who wish to work together, where trust, support, and challenge encourage honesty, in-depth reflection and constructive analysis on practice and related personal and contextual issues, enhancing self confidence, personal and professional learning and promoting best practice.

Practitioners in critical reflection training often bring examples of incidents connected to supervision, which suggest the importance of supervision to practice and organizational culture. In the final session, participants often comment that they can see the potential of using critical reflection as part of supervision both as a supervisor and as a supervisee. Critical reflection is seen as offering a means of balancing the management focus of supervision, opening up different kinds of supervision conversations.

Participants often make a distinction between formal and informal supervision, and what could be called 'formal' and 'informal' use of critical reflection. By informal supervision they mean the, usually short, incidental 'on the run' interactions they might have as opposed to planned formal sessions usually in the supervisor's office. Formal critical reflection would happen when both parties agreed to use this as part of a supervision session. Participants said they would often have integrated a critical reflection approach into their thinking, so that they might ask questions in a critically reflective way even if they didn't use critical reflection formally. When critical reflection is used formally in supervision there are a number of issues to think about, as discussed below.

Why is critical reflection being used as part of supervision?

What is the aim here? Whose idea is it to use critical reflection? Participants have different views about this: some feel that they can negotiate agreement within their own team about using critical reflection individually or as part of a group process. Others consider that their organization should formally endorse this approach so that time is allowed for it to happen and be done well. As we have already established, critical reflection can be a challenging process at a personal and professional level. There needs to be clarity about how and why it is being used. This fits with the following point.

How to establish the right 'climate of critical reflection'

How much this is an issue will vary depending on the organization and/or the team perception of supervision. If supervision has previously been primarily an administrative or management tool, this change will need to be negotiated. Part of this is establishing trust that the process will be used for exploration rather than judgement. It also means engaging with the following point.

Power issues in the supervision relationship

In most human service organizations supervision is between two people with different levels of power, in the organizational sense at least. This can be inhibiting to critical reflection: if the process is about using a critical incident, for example, the supervisee may feel that they are opening themselves to judgement that may be detrimental at least to how they are perceived. Ideally, there will be enough trust in the relationship to make this work, but the issue needs to be acknowledged and dealt with in some way. This might be by agreeing that such incidents will be written up only if they need to be, in a way agreed to by both parties. Alternatively, it may be more appropriate to have a group supervision for critical reflection rather than individual sessions.

Mutuality of process

Generally, critical reflection is seen as a mutual process and this is likely to be the case in a group or peer supervision but is not likely to be the case in a traditional supervision relationship. This may or may not matter depending on the supervisory relationship, but again needs to be acknowledged and resolved.

Pat's experience of critical reflection training reinforced the value of having supervision where workers could explore issues rather than focusing only on administrative tasks. She questioned her own assumptions and values about supervision, seeing that in practice supervision had low priority though her espoused theory was that it was fundamental to good practice. She talked to each worker she supervised about their assumptions, expectations and hopes for supervision, developing a plan with each for a balance between her and their preferences and the organization's requirements. Her commitment to supervision changed: she rarely changed times, made sure there were no interruptions to sessions and became more flexible in her approach.

Using critical reflection to develop or articulate a model of supervision

Although many organizations provide staff with supervision, the model or theory behind the supervision is not always clear. As well as being used as part of individual or group supervision, we have used critical reflection to develop or articulate the organization's 'theory of supervision'. The process provides a way for the implicit knowledge that staff have from their experience of supervision to be made explicit and then translate into specific policies and processes the organization can use.

This process can be used in an organization that is starting to think about supervision and how it might operate in the organization as well as those where supervision is already established. In either situation, staff members are asked to come to a critical reflection workshop with an example of their experience of supervision. Depending on the organization and the aim of the workshop, it may help to focus the examples more: in an organization thinking about developing supervision, participants will need to bring past examples of supervision – or examples where they think supervision would have been useful. For these participants it may be equally useful to bring an example of when supervision worked well, with the focus in the critical reflection process being to articulate why it was positive. In an organization where supervision is well established, it is likely to be more helpful to ask participants to bring examples that they feel are significant and uncomfortable – those that are likely to evoke deeper thinking, as we suggested in Chapter 5.

Session 1: stage 1

As each staff member talks about their incident, it is important to work at three levels, particularly with incidents that have left participants feeling uncomfortable. First, the incident is explored in the usual way in a critical reflection process. Second, again as is usual in groups learning critical reflection, the group considers the process: what seems to make the process work well, what needs to change to improve the process. Third, the group stands back from the incident to think about what it means for supervision in the organization. This would include a consideration of questions such as:

- What does this incident suggest about supervision in the organization?
- What is the experience of supervision like here?
- How do we and other staff feel about supervision?
- What are the assumptions and values from this incident that are significant in the organization?
- What is the influence of the context as described here?
- What processes and procedures have been identified and what is their impact?

The responses from each incident are documented (e.g. on a whiteboard). These are accumulated over the process until the responses about all the incidents from the group are written up. Between the two sessions – stage 1 and stage 2 in critical reflection – the responses are written up in a more coherent way according to what seem to be emerging themes. This means that the participants can be presented either between sessions or at the beginning of the next session with a beginning 'theory of supervision'. What this looks like will depend on the particular staff group. While there are likely to be some common themes, there is also a great deal of variation between organizations or even staff groups within an organization (see the case study below). Having a visual sense of their 'theory' is very reinforcing for participants about the value of the process – it makes the idea of generating theory come alive.

Session 2: stage 2

At this session, participants revisit their incident as they would in the critical reflection process. Similarly, some will have come to a different understanding of their incident; others will have shifted assumptions or affirmed values.

Some may have tried to do something differently; others may not have thought about the process at all. The aim is that as each person explores their incident there is movement towards change – of assumptions or values, articulating of possible new strategies or processes, shifts in feelings or attitudes and, finally, identifying a new theory of practice. Again, the group then stands back from the incident and examining the process, to look at what this means at an organizational level for supervision. This time the group takes into account their beginning theory of supervision developed in session 1 to consider questions such as:

- What new assumptions and values have been articulated and/or existing ones affirmed?
- What changes in approach – processes, policies, strategies – have been identified and how might they be established?
- What other changes need to be considered?
- What other theory needs to be included?

Example of workshop

Staff from Agecare were concerned about supervision practices in their agency. Although in theory supervision was valued by the agency and staff, in practice it seemed to be a low priority. New staff often commented that they missed having supervision, there was a general feeling that supervision was both idiosyncratic and taken for granted instead of being applied consistently across the organization.

The senior staff agreed that critical reflection workshops would be held for all staff providing supervision. Each staff member would bring an incident that illustrated something about their supervision practice in the agency that they were not satisfied with. In the workshops, the group first explored what the incident meant for the individual supervisor, and then considered what it meant for the agency. Comments and questions were written up on the whiteboard, then themes were identified and checked with each group. By the end of the workshops, the staff had clearly identified issues needing more work and some beginning ideas about how to work on these.

The themes identified were as follows.

Stage 1: thinking about context

1. Broader/structural context:
   - Who is powerful about supervision and how does this reflect dominant discourses? For example, having a group of staff trained over 30 years ago at base-grade level.
   - What is the impact of gender? What is the impact of having younger women supervising older men, for example?

- How does supervision take into account the diversity of ethnicity in both staff and clients?
2. Organizational context:
   - What is the history of supervision in each area? What do the differences mean?
   - Contradictory messages about supervision – such as espoused theory vs theory in practice (e.g. space and time for supervision).
3. Professional context:
   - Organization's perception of different professional backgrounds – expectation that social workers will provide supervision.
   - What are the perceptions and assumptions about social work supervision?
4. Personal context:
   - For each supervisor – how do I perceive myself as a supervisor, very different expectations of self.

Thinking about supervision processes
Key questions:

- How is good supervision/practice defined?
- How is supervision constructed?

Processes of supervision
Beginning supervision:

- Need to clarify expectations – making expectations explicit on both sides.

Managing/valuing differences – what are the implications?

- Different expectations
- Style
- Learning

How will supervision be organized?

- Preparation
- Setting and its implications
- Who will do what?

Types of supervision:

- What will this supervision include? What will be the focus? Formal and/or informal.

Ongoing supervision
Reviewing and checking expectations.
Supervisory role – how to balance:

- supportive relationship and task focus
- logic and intuition

- support and challenge
- agency issues and worker issues
- accepting and exploring emotion, and getting work done.

Question of how to build in reflection.

Stage 2
Here the group moved to start developing principles of good supervision from the assumptions they had made about supervision and also the new assumptions they wanted to work from.

Developing principles about supervision
1. Supervision is a shared responsibility between supervisor and supervisee. This means that both actively take part in supervision, make times that suit both, bring issues to be discussed, agree to goals and make supervision a priority.
2. Feedback is part of supervision and should be expected and scheduled in both directions.
3. Boundaries about what is not accepted as part of supervision need to be explicit.
4. Supervisors need to recognize, allow and affirm difference within acceptable limits.
5. Supervisors are not perfect and do not have all the answers. Good supervisors know their own limitations, make this explicit and refer on if necessary, and are prepared to explore issues together with supervisees.
6. Supervision should be seen as a place where it is safe to express emotion as a way of moving forward.
7. Supervisors do need to maintain standards, clarify what attitudes or actions are not acceptable.
8. Silence is useful as part of supervision, allowing time for processing.
9. Supervisors can and ideally will be role models for self-care, while acknowledging that other workers may use different strategies.
10. Supervisors need to recognize when staff are reacting to their role and not take reactions personally. Supervision is an important investment in an organization and should be allocated adequate time and other resources.

Areas needing development
The team then decided to continue to work on:

- articulating a clear policy about the place of supervision in the agency
- developing agreement about flexibility of supervision arrangements (i.e. under what conditions supervisees should be able to choose a supervisor or change supervisors rather than having purely a line management arrangement)
- exploring further what working with difference means in supervision – how flexible supervisors should be about matching preferred styles of supervision.

Chapter summary

This chapter has focused on exploring how critical reflection can be used in organizations as part of management, programme development and supervision. The chapter began by considering the influence of current thinking about the learning organization and learning in organizations. Critical reflection can be used by managers to inform their practice; managers also need to be aware of the impact of using critical reflection in the organization in terms of worker expectations. Possible questions for use in programme development were outlined. A significant proportion of the chapter explored using critical reflection in supervision: whether individually or in peer or group supervision. The background thinking about supervision and the place of critical reflection was outlined. The chapter finished by using supervision as an example of how critical reflection can be used to identify how workers experience an aspect of their organization, and how they might affirm their experience as well as name needed change.

10 Using critical reflection in research and evaluation

This chapter aims to outline briefly:

- the current background to research and evaluation, particularly the developing interest in evidence-based practice
- how this relates to critical reflection approaches to research and evaluation
- the similarities and differences between research and evaluation.

It will also explore how practitioners can use critical reflection as:

- a framework for research or evaluation
- a way of researching their own practice
- a way of providing processes for research and evaluation.

Defining research and evaluation

Research and evaluation are, of course, defined differently depending on the values and theoretical perspectives of the writers. Generally speaking, research is seen as more focused on general explorations of issues and the creation of new knowledge or understanding. Stringer and Dwyer (2005: 3) suggest, for example, that 'Research may be defined as a process of systematic investigation leading to increased understanding of a phenomenon or issue of interest.' Evaluation generally has a component of making a judgement about effectiveness: 'in practical evaluations, the evaluator must make a series of interrelated decisions in order to make a judgement of worth' (Owen and Rogers 1999: 14).

However, views are mixed about how distinctly to define research and evaluation. In a sense, both are about wanting to find out more about what is happening – in a programme, service, with an organization, an approach or a policy. However, some research is evaluative: Winter and Munn-Giddings

(2001) talk about action research as a form of responsive evaluation. Evaluation can focus on identifying significant processes rather than outcomes. Royse *et al.* (2006: 1) sees programme evaluation as 'that aspect of professional training which is aimed at helping you to integrate research and practice skills'. Some writers focus on what both can offer: Braye (2000), for example, on the need for both to be used to promote user participation. Action research provides a way to encompass research and/or evaluation: the researcher/ evaluator and participants are jointly involved in a cycle of reflecting, planning, implementing, analysing, reviewing and reflecting. It can be more helpful to see both as fostering 'critical curiosity' (Gardner and Nunan, forthcoming). This also recognizes that 'the variety of research and professional issues demand answers of such a diverse nature that the adoption of a single epistemological and methodological position is not commensurate with the demands of ethical and competent practice' (Tsang 2000: 73).

Current interest in evidence-based practice

There are increasing expectations for practitioners with regard to ensuring that their practice is well researched or 'evidence based' (Cheetham *et al.* 1992). Funding bodies and consumers alike require organizations and their practitioners to demonstrate that what they do is effective, although this research or evaluation tends not to become part of agency practice (Frances 1997; Shaw 2004). Clearly it is reasonable to expect practitioners to justify their effectiveness; practice has changed significantly over the years, with practitioners relinquishing approaches that they once believed were effective (Brechin and Sidell 2000). Evidence-based practice, for example, would include an expectation that practitioners review relevant research to check that their approach is appropriate, ethical and effective.

However, there are also tensions related to evidence-based practice. A key issue is what evidence is considered to be valid (Rolfe 2005). Some researchers or evaluators see the only valid research as scientifically based empirical research providing 'the answer' to a particular, usually clearly and narrowly defined, research hypothesis; for example, that introducing compulsory testing of literacy rates in primary schools will increase literacy. Some advocate the 'gold standard' of scientific research (Webster and Osborne 2005): using randomized control trials where one group receives services or resources and another doesn't so that outcomes can be compared. This is clearly difficult in much of the human service field; there are ethical issues around resourcing some groups and not others. It is also at least difficult, if not impossible, to demonstrate that the groups are similar enough for comparison and that there are no other confusing influences. This kind of research often also leaves many questions unanswered: you may know that one community now has more people participating but not be clear about what was significant in making this happen. The preference for this kind of research often reflects the pressure to practise in outcome-orientated ways.

Other writers advocate a broader approach to evidence-based practice, suggesting that a wider range of research approaches are valid and more appropriate. Winter and Munn-Giddings (2001: 45) for example, say, 'It is thus highly misleading when the advocates of so-called "evidence-based practice" attempt to hi-jack the term "evidence" to mean, exclusively, statistical evidence of the sort generated by randomised control trials'. Instead, they suggest the need to ask 'what sort of judgements are to be made and what sort of evidence is therefore appropriate?' Randomized control trials might be useful for some situations and disciplines such as comparing the impact of medical treatment, but less useful in exploring the impact of a community development initiative aimed at increasing participation in community life. Brechin and Sidell (2000) point out that practitioners draw on different 'ways of knowing', formal empirical research, theoretical knowledge and also experiential knowledge, which is harder to make explicit but an equally valid form of knowing. Such approaches are also more likely to acknowledge that all research and evaluation has an implicit worldview that needs to be acknowledged (Rolfe 2005).

Another concern about evidence-based practice is whose voice will be heard and, particularly, will the voices of those most affected by the research processes or outcomes be heard. Smale *et al.* (2000: 8), for example, say, 'there is much emphasis now on evidence-based practice but social problems are not like physics and engineering and the knowledge on which we base our practice must include the experience and expertise of users and carers as well as research'. Alongside, or perhaps in response to, the development of evidence-based practice, there has been a major increase in interest in participatory forms of research and evaluation where those being researched are more active participants. These include collaborative evaluation (Cousins and Earl 1992), empowerment evaluation (Fetterman 2000) and evaluative inquiry (Preskill and Torres 1999), as well as various forms of action research (Wadsworth 1998; Cherry 1999). Some of these approaches more than others see the process of the research or evaluation as achieving change in itself. All would recognize that research is not value free, and have processes for reflection and collaborative work. Cooperative inquiry, for example, emphasizes that the researcher/ evaluator and those involved as participants are seen as co-researchers. Heron (1996: 19) stresses that this form of research is '*with* people not *on* them or *about* them. In its most complete form, the inquirers engage fully in both roles, moving in cyclic fashion between phases of reflection as co-researchers and of action as co-subjects. In this way they use reflection and action to refine and deepen each other.' The aim is for the research process to be mutually beneficial.

A related concern about evidence-based practice is that the underlying structural causes of issues may be ignored – it is easier to look at results or outcomes than what the issues represent in terms of meaning for users of services, or the broader connections. If the introduction of testing for literacy does not lead to increased literacy rates, for example, is the reaction to look for other 'solutions' or to consider links between poverty and literacy or to explore in a more participatory way with parents, teachers and children why children are finding it hard to learn to read? White and Stancombe (2003) suggest that the focus has been so much on 'What works?' that the question of 'What's wrong?' is being lost. Everitt and Hardiker (1996) point out the dangers of 'managerial evaluation', where evaluation is 'applied as a tool of social control' rather than contributing 'to the development of good practice'. Finally, too much focus on scientifically focused evidence-based practice can inhibit the development of innovative programmes that have not yet been able to demonstrate their effectiveness. Practitioners may feel that it is too risky to try a new process that has not been tested. They may also feel unnerved by inconsistencies in research results and feel unable to act according to their own 'ways of knowing'. Research and evaluation then become distanced from practice: something that 'experts' rather than practitioners do.

A critical reflection approach to research and evaluation

What then might it mean to use a critical reflection approach to research and evaluation? Again writers in research and evaluation write about this in different ways. Some see critical reflection as a form of research on their practice, carried out by the practitioners involved (Bolton 2001); others see critical reflection as part of their approach to research (Winter and Munn-Giddings 2001). Bolton talks about creating a 'spirit of enquiry' through encouraging students to reflect on experience; Winter (1987: 67) about research as 'a form of inquiry located in biographical experience'; Winter and Munn-Giddings (2001: 23) about 'creating a "culture of inquiry" in practice settings ie building in continuous evaluation' supported by a climate including respect, harmony and supportive criticism.

Some forms of research are particularly congruent to and articulate their links to critical reflection. Kemmis (2001: 92), for example, distinguishes between three forms of action research: the first with a focus on effectiveness; the second focusing on process, how change happened; and the third a critically reflective process that:

> aims not only at improving outcomes and improving the self-understanding of practitioners, but also at assisting practitioners to arrive at a critique of their social or educational work and work settings. This kind of action research aims at intervening in the cultural,

social and historical processes of everyday life to reconstruct not only the practice and the practitioner but also the practice setting. It aims to connect the personal and the political in collaborative research and action aimed at transforming situations to overcome felt dissatisfactions, alienation, ideological distortion, and the injustices of oppression and domination.

Critical reflection also offers a way of considering and evaluating research. Gardner (2003) suggests a number of criteria for evaluating whether community-based research or evaluation projects have been critically reflective. These can in turn be used to think about how to create research or evaluation that is congruent with practice. Her criteria include:

- involving a variety of individuals and groups so that the range of perspectives is more likely to be representative
- the views of those least likely to be heard need to be included
- recognizing values and assumptions about self and others for all those involved in the evaluation process including the evaluator
- paying attention to processes as well as outcomes
- making connections between individual and social issues
- the evaluation or research process itself should be part of generating change in a way that is meaningful for participants.

Critical reflection in research also provides a way for professionals from different disciplines to connect – the concepts are familiar even if the language may be different (Redmond 2004).

Using critical reflection in research and evaluation

Critical reflection as a framework

Critical reflection provides a framework for approaching research and evaluation and can be used to complement many approaches. For example, critical reflection theory suggests that researchers and evaluators need to acknowledge the values from which they are operating and to operate in socially just and inclusive ways. More specifically, the theory:

- prompts taking a 'researching' or 'inquiring' attitude – standing back from what is familiar and seeing it in new ways
- helps us to be open to new understanding or knowledge – to ask about what is happening and why, rather than taking things for granted
- encourages us to see researching/evaluating as something we can do that is an integral part of, rather than distinct from, practice

- reminds us to look at the variety of points of view in a given situation – as researchers this might mean having interviews/focus groups with people from many different perspectives
- remembers to ask whose voices have not been heard, particularly those of users/consumers of services
- notices the language that is being used
- encourages user participation in research – using tools and processes that enable users of services to be involved in research and evaluation processes, including those that recognize social difference (Gibbs 2001)
- generates the capacity to explore and tolerate uncertainty – to affirm research and evaluation that explores interpretations and constructions rather than seeking uniform answers (White and Stancombe 2003)
- expects that research will lead to change – and ideally that participants in research or the services being researched will be involved in the processes
- validates research that acknowledges
  - the importance of process as well as outcomes
  - reflexivity in the sense of 'critical self-reflection of the ways in which researchers' social background, assumptions, positioning and behaviour impact on the research process (Finlay and Gough 2003)
  - the importance of naming values
  - the influence of broader social structures and the importance of context.

Critical reflection processes for research and evaluation

The processes of critical reflection can be used as part of research or evaluation. In this book we have particularly focused on using critical incidents and these are used in many related forms for research or evaluation: Crawford talks about using 'learning moments' (2006) for students undertaking research studies; McDrury and Alterio (2002) about using stories, and others about using discourses or narratives (e.g. Finlay and Gough 2003). What these have in common is taking a particular experience and exploring it in a critically reflective way.

Other processes include critically reflective journals or critically reflective questions. Stuart and Whitmore (2006) use reflexive journals and focus groups as part of researching the impact of teaching a research subject to social work students. Such processes can be used like any other research processes, such as questionnaires or interviews. They provide a method for carrying out the research, gathering the data in a way that is congruent with the values often expressed in human service agencies. Here we are talking about them being used within the context of a critical reflection approach.

Such processes can be used with individuals or families or in groups, depending on the context and aim of the research. They can complement other research or evaluation processes – for example, a researcher might choose 'biographical methods' (Chamberlyne *et al.* 2004) as their process (exploring a person's history with them) but decide that they want to focus the biography by asking those interviewed to talk about incidents related to specific themes or times in their lives using a critical reflection approach to underpin the process.

A researcher on the experience of users of maternal and child health services, for example, might begin the research process by meeting with a group of service users to explore with them their interest in the project and introduce the critical reflection framework she is using. She might then ask each parent to keep a journal reflecting critically on their experience of the service, and then use the data collected to analyse the service's effectiveness from the parents' perspectives. Alternatively, she might meet individually with each parent, or parents, using the service, asking them to bring an incident that they see as typical of their experience or one that is of concern to them in relation to the service. These then could also be used as data for her research.

The questions in the box on p. 170 were used by Gardner and Nunan (forthcoming) as part of a research project that aimed to explore the development of a research culture in an agency called St Luke's. The project's Reference Group decided to ask for expressions of interest from teams or small groups of staff in carrying out some kind of research or evaluation project. The aim was that staff would primarily do the research but be supported by a combination of:

- a research worker and/or
- other members of the Reference Group and/or
- the outside evaluator of the process.

Two teams were selected: the youth team, which wanted to work on a research project about funding services for young sexual offenders; and one of the mental health teams, which wanted to evaluate some tools being used with people with a mental illness.

Each group used the set of questions in the box on p. 170 as a beginning exploration of their own projects and revisited them as the projects developed. Over the life of the projects, the following themes emerged in relation to the critical reflection process.

- *The importance of articulating and questioning assumptions:* it quickly became clear that participants had quite different assumptions about the project and its goals as well as about the content and context for their project. Articulating these led to greater clarity about the complexity of issues involved and the need for discussion to come to agreement about how to work together.

- *Acknowledgement of feelings and thoughts, particularly that this can be an unsettling and uncomfortable process:* the clearest example of this was the frustration experienced by some participants about the questioning of assumptions. This led to a period of uncertainty about how to proceed when the team had been clear about what they were aiming to do initially. Different attitudes and views about the project were also hard for some people to accept from others.

- *Awareness of subjectivity:* that assumptions may be personally and/or socially determined and are likely to be both; as thoughts and assumptions were shared, workers were surprised at times by their own reactions and those of others, realizing that they had taken on board embedded attitudes without realizing it – for example, about the difficulty of achieving community change.

- *Affirmation of the value of the experiential and tacit knowledge via the reflective process:* this did affirm the value of workers' practice knowledge. Reflecting critically demonstrated that the workers had considerable knowledge and experience.

- *Awareness that in any situation there will be a variety of views and perspectives and commitment to ensuring that the voices of those potentially or actually marginalized are heard:* workers were very conscious of this with both sets of clients, feeling that they were certainly marginalized.

- *Understanding of the importance of context and the influence of culture:* both groups were very aware of the mixed and often stereotyped views in the community about the groups they worked with. For the youth team particularly, the thought of trying to change community attitudes was challenging.

- *A desire to use awareness to lead to positive, socially just change:* workers wanted to change the service and social context for their client groups.

Overall, critical reflection was a useful approach for these practitioners: it encouraged a more critical approach to projects, particularly in identifying the differing and common assumptions and values in the teams. Critical reflection also helped generate a 'culture of inquiry' more generally about practice. However, the workers also identified the need for resources – time, quiet space for reflection and input – in order to be able to use critical reflection effectively in their practice.

Useful questions to think about for critically reflective research

What is the issue to be explored?

How is it constructed as a problem?

- Who sees it as a problem?
- What variety of views are there?
- What specifically do people want to consider?
- What are the underlying assumptions and values?
- Why now – why has it come up as an issue now?
- What is the history of this issue?
- Is there a range of views about the background? What impact does that have on how the issue is now being seen?

Has the issue been thought about by other people? Who, where, what? What did they think? What conclusions did they come to? What questions did they raise?

Why are workers interested in this issue?

- What range of views are there?
- What do workers hope will happen?
- What do workers know from their experience?
- What do workers assume from their experience?

What needs to be asked/explored? What kind of information is needed? What is it that you want to know? For example, specific questions or general questions and prompts, factual information, views, ideas, beliefs.

What voices need to be heard about this issue?

- Are there particular voices that are likely to be harder to access?

How will people be involved? What ways of asking people for information are likely to work with these groups, particularly people experiencing the issue?

What resources are needed? What are the timelines?

Critical reflection for researching your own practice

Given the increased expectations and pressures on agencies, practitioners tend to see research and practice as distinct entities instead of integrally connected (Darlington and Scott 2002). Ideally, though, research and evaluation are built in to practice. Reason and Bradbury (2001: 12) say 'research can be thought of not as an *interruption* of work, but as a means for *furthering* and *developing* the work we are already engaged in'. There is growing interest in what is called 'practice research' (Dadds and Hart 2001) – that is, research undertaken by practitioners generally using designs and methods more accessible to practitioners and able to be applied to immediate practice concerns. Practice research usually builds on data either already available or readily accessible in the workplace, including the reactions and experiences of practitioners themselves. In writing about qualitative research, Fook (2001) points out that practice research recognizes the importance of tacit knowledge of the practitioner: 'if the qualitative researcher is self-reflexive, then she or he recognizes that the self is the lens through which they see the world. The lens itself therefore becomes an important part of the research, as instrument but also data'.

Critical reflection can provide a framework for practitioners to use in researching their practice (i.e. taking a research attitude to practice). Some writers would talk about this as a 'spirit of inquiry' or training people to 'notice' what is happening in a systematic way. The idea of 'noticing as research' is a research method which Mason (2002) suggests is particularly suited to practitioners interested in researching their own practice'. Like critical reflection, noticing is about paying attention to what happens in practice in a systematic way so that the information collected can be used to generate change. Riemann (2006: 198), for example, encourages social work students to be 'ethnographers' of their own practice (i.e. to make their 'own practice strange' to 'foster a self-critical and egalitarian discourse'). Students present written field notes about a particular aspect of their practice and these are then 'researched' by the student and the class using a critical reflection approach.

Using the questions in the box below, participants in workshops bring an incident from their practice that they want to 'research' as an example of their practice: to understand why it worked – or didn't. They want to stand back from their experience so that they can see it in a different way and develop new theory about their practice. They may then choose to further 'research' their practice through their own observations and reflections, or to develop this more formally as research on their own or with colleagues.

Questions to aid using critical reflection to research practice

- What did I do?
  - What happened?
  - What worked – and what does 'worked' mean?
  - What didn't work – and what does that mean?

- What were the different perspectives? What range of views were there about what worked and didn't; are there any missing perspectives?
- How did I/others influence the situation?
  - My and others' perceptions
  - My/others' assumptions and values
  - My/others' presence and actions
- What was the influence of power?
- What does my experience imply about:
  - my theories of practice – espoused theory and theory in action
  - other theory that I would find useful
  - theories of practice that I would want to use
  - theories of practice that other people use
  - new theory that I want to develop?
- How can I try out my new theory?

Sarah wanted to research an incident from her practice where her work with a family had gone well but she wasn't sure why. She wanted to identify what had worked so that she could build this more coherently into her practice. She was working in a family and children's services agency and the agency philosophy was to work with all family members wherever possible in order to strengthen family links and mutual support. She was conscious that it seemed to be harder to involve fathers and was wondering whether her practice contributed to that.

The incident involved a family she had been seeing for about three months on a weekly basis. She generally visited the family at home and the father, Paul, was on shift work and often not present. When he was present he often looked uninterested in being part of family discussions and would sometimes leave the room. When asked about this, he would say that Miriam, the mother, was really more involved with the children. The incident was one where Sarah had been able to borrow a car seat for one of the children on a long-term basis, but she and Miriam couldn't get it to fit. Sarah asked Paul if he could help them and he came and fixed the car seat. He then participated in a conversation with both Sarah and Miriam, which shifted on to family issues. They all moved inside and continued to talk over coffee about the issues that Paul had previously seemed unwilling to talk about.

As Sarah 'researched' the incident, she articulated some of her assumptions about what worked with male clients: she realized that she often assumed that men would be less interested in talking about family issues so tended to 'give up' on their participation. With Paul, she had assumed that he would see his role in the family as the breadwinner, which reflected the social culture she grew up in and thought she had left behind. She had also assumed that family members who wanted to explore family issues would be engaged by talking about them and that being in the family home would 'break the ice' compared to them coming to the office. As she thought about the different perspectives involved, she remembered noticing that other clients, particularly men, seemed to talk more easily when not facing her directly – if they were engaged in a task, for example. She realized that she saw her role as talking rather than doing, and that this might be an unhelpful binary. She developed new theory to be researched further in her practice in the form of new ideas to be tested:

- to engage men, I need to work more flexibly and actively, looking for opportunities to do something together and allowing conversations to emerge
- I need to change my assumptions about how men see themselves in relation to their families, and make opportunities to hear from men – and women – about their perspectives
- I need to value explicitly the different things that parents bring to relationships and the care of their children.

Sarah decided to also 'research practice' with her colleagues, to share her research process and the conclusions she had reached and see how these fitted with their experience. She also decided to treat this as an action research cycle: she would consciously try out her new theory and note the results in a reflective journal. After two months she would look at the data she had gathered and evaluate the effectiveness of her new theory.

Refer at this point to the article 'Critical reflection in community-based evaluation', by Fiona Gardner, which is in the online resource materials at www.openup.co.uk/fook&gardner.

Chapter summary

In this chapter we have considered the relationship between critical reflection and research and evaluation. Research and evaluation can be seen as having a different focus but also have much in common, and critical reflection can be useful for both. The current interest in evidence-based practice has been explored as a background to using critical reflection in research and evaluation. More specifically we have looked at critical reflection as a framework for research and evaluation, critical reflection processes (including useful questions to ask from a critical reflection perspective) and how critical reflection can be used by practitioners to research their own practice.

11 Critical reflection and direct practice

How can critical reflection be incorporated into practice? This is a question often asked and explored towards the end of critical reflection workshops with workers in direct practice. We have already explored how critical reflection can be used as part of supervision and/or management (Chapter 9) and in research and evaluation (Chapter 10). While these are ideally closely connected with direct practice, this chapter will focus on using critical reflection in direct practice itself.

Direct practice is defined in various ways depending on the field or professional background of practitioners (Gardner 2006). In work with individuals and families, for example, social workers generally talk about casework, psychologists talk about counselling, and nurses or occupational therapists about clinical work. Nurses, social workers, community workers and allied health workers may also work in practice that is community orientated: again using a range of language depending on background and the kind of community practice. Some would talk about community organization, development or social action, others community health nursing or having a public health orientation. Policy development is also seen by some practitioners as direct practice because policy work connects individual concerns and organizational and/or government responses.

In this chapter we explore critical reflection and direct practice in three areas:

1. working with communities
2. working with individuals and/or families
3. policy development and implementation.

In some ways we would hope that this division into areas of work is an artificial one. A critical reflection approach would suggest that all of these are integrally linked. A worker with individuals and families would always be aware of the community and policy context; a policy worker would be aware of the need to check with individuals and communities about the potential impact of a new policy. Because of this we will begin to explore critical reflection and direct practice by identifying what is common. Given that practitioners do tend to work in distinct areas, we will then explore how what is common can be applied in each area, giving specific examples of direct practice.

Common themes for direct practice using critical reflection

The theories underlying critical reflection generate a common approach that informs direct practice across these areas. A critical reflection perspective has the following benefits.

- It enables us to stand back from what is familiar and see it in new ways. Practitioners often gain a new view of their practice using critical reflection. Hearing other people's responses to their incident often surprises participants and enables them to understand it in a different way. A common response is 'I wouldn't have thought of that' or 'I wouldn't have seen that person like that.'
- It prompts us to articulate underlying assumptions and values. Participants say that, as direct workers, they are often caught in an overly busy work environment where the need for action means they don't take time to question where they are coming from. Using the critical reflection process enables them to see that this means they have operated from assumptions that may cause harm, or at least are not how they would consciously prefer to act. Alternatively, participants find that they are reminded of the assumptions and values they do work from and want to assert more clearly. Articulating values is seen by participants as useful in reminding them that values are central to their practice and provide a foundation from which to work. This then reinforces the importance of taking time to articulate their assumptions and values, and explore them before acting.
- It reinforces a socially just approach to practice. Critical reflection is not value neutral and reminds practitioners that they are advocating such values as fairness and equity whoever they are working with. For participants who are direct service workers this again orientates them to where they want to operate from – their value base rather than simply accepting agency rules or funding guidelines.
- It enables participants to be open to and act on new understanding or knowledge. Participants in direct practice say that critical reflection

encourages them to be open to other ways of seeing. This includes taking on board or actively seeking new knowledge that will improve work quality. This might come from exploring an incident with others who make suggestions about relevant knowledge or from a sense of dissatisfaction with how practice is going.

- It encourages us to make connections between individuals, communities and broader social structures. The 'critical' in critical reflection particularly prompts participants to look beyond their incident or practice to see the broader context. Direct service workers say this helps put what they do into context, reminding them of the other perspectives that need to be considered as part of their work.
- It reminds us to look at the variety of views in a given situation and particularly to seek out those who are marginalized. Participants, as direct service workers, see this as helping them not to become entrenched in a particular perspective. It also fits with their social justice values of asking which voices are not being heard.
- It encourages the capacity to explore and tolerate uncertainty. Direct service workers say they live with constant uncertainty; critical reflection enables them to see this as part of practice rather than something to be 'dealt with', and to develop strategies accordingly.
- It suggests an accessible and enabling process that can be used with individuals and groups. This is more variable for direct service workers. While many can see how to use critical reflection in supervision and with colleagues, they find it harder to imagine how to use this in their direct practice. However, some do and examples for each area are given on p. 177.
- It validates:
  - the importance of process as well as outcomes – direct service workers are very conscious of the centrality of processes in their work and appreciate these being validated in a critical reflection approach; this also, they say, enables them to be more assertive about valuing and seeking recognition for these in their organization; this might, for example, be about asserting the time needed for change for individuals or communities, or the importance of using a variety of models for work rather than a 'one size fits all' approach
  - paying attention to subjectivity, intuition and creativity – direct service workers are also aware of the impact of their 'selves' in their practice, what they come with in terms of their own history, experience, values, and their capacity to respond intuitively and creatively. Again critical reflection affirms this approach.

How to use critical reflection in direct practice

How to carry out critical reflection also has common themes. We have separated these into four main areas, but of course they are not mutually exclusive or the only ways to use critical reflection.

Using critical incidents for critical reflection

Direct practice workers can use a critical incident, as outlined earlier (Chapters 6 and 7), for themselves in considering their own reactions to practice. They can also use critical incidents in their practice: this might mean exploring a critical incident with individual clients or with a family group, with volunteers, with community groups or groups involved in consultations. In the same way as this process is illuminating for workers about their practice, it can also be illuminating for clients and communities. Examples for each area are given below.

Using critical reflection informally/implicitly

Participants in workshops suggest that how they will use critical reflection will often be in more informal or implicit ways; once they have incorporated the theory and processes into their thinking, these will become part of how they operate all the time. The way questions are asked in their practice might change to include more reflexive questions, to allow for multiple understandings or to include marginal perspectives. In this sense, critical reflection might inform or reinforce other approaches. Some participants, for example, have talked about how they see critical reflection complementing and supporting a narrative approach.

Using journals or other tools for critical reflection

Much has been written about using journals or other forms of writing as part of critical reflection (Bolton 2001). While this generally focuses on practitioners, these processes can also be used in direct practice. A worker might ask an individual client, for example, if they are interested in writing a journal to map their experience of depression; a community or policy worker might ask community members to write about stories that illustrate their experience of community life around a specific theme related to a project. These could then be used either individually or collectively to generate critical reflection processes.

Some critical reflection practitioners are also using other tools, such as art, or using images or symbolic figures to generate reflection. Schuck and Wood

(2006), for example, once they have established a safe environment, divide workshops (usually over a day) into a series of short, powerful and fun exercises. Depending on the group, this might include asking participants to express themselves with crayons, meditate, visualize, use puppets, toys or shells, or take part in role play. They also use this approach with individuals and in supervision. They suggest that some of the creative exercises work better for some people than others, and this varies depending on how they are at a particular time.

Using critically reflective questions

Writers about critical reflection have often developed a list of questions as possible or suggested prompts (e.g. Johns and Freshwater 2005; Lehmann 2006). A list of possible critical reflection questions was presented in Chapter 5 as a starting point for participants. The danger of using a list of questions can be that they are seen as definitive rather than possibilities. In direct practice, it makes sense for practitioners to develop critical reflection questions that fit with their language and context (see boxes on pp. 181 and 184 for examples). These questions can then be used to begin a critical reflection dialogue.

Using critical reflection in community work

Community work currently has a variety of labels, each with its own underlying assumptions and values. Here we are using 'community work' simply to mean direct practice that involves workers in primarily working with a community focus, whether the community is geographic or a community of interest. Currently such practice is often labelled as 'community capacity building' or community strengthening or community capacity enhancement (Delgado 2000). Ife (2002: 1) points out that people use words such as community work, community development, community practice and community change often interchangeably 'and although many would claim that there are important differences between some or all of these terms, there is no agreement as to what these differences are'. Writers might also talk about more discipline-specific forms of community work, such as community social work (Smale *et al.* 2000) or a public health approach (Kellehear 2005).

Historically, community work or community development has been based on values and assumptions that are very congruent with critical reflection. Ife (2002), for example, considers the foundations of community development as ecological and social justice perspectives. Lane and Henry (2001) see community work as focusing on marginalized groups.

However, community development processes can also be used in less empowering ways and it is important to check underlying assumptions and values. Lane (1999) says 'community development is under siege as a process-oriented, contextually sensitive means of promoting participation in civil society and politics'. Funding for community work is more often tied to predetermined outcomes rather than allowing the outcomes to emerge from the community work process. Ledwith (2001: 180) reinforces the need for community work to 'rearticulate its mission in a more rigorous way', enabling questioning of existing structures and transformative change.

A critically reflective approach is useful for community workers. Participants in workshops say the theories underlying critical reflection challenge them to act from what they identify as compatible community work values. The process enables them to identify not only their own underlying assumptions and values about community work but also those of the particular organization and/or funding body they are working for. A Conservative government department, for example, may choose to fund a community-strengthening programme based on the assumption that this will encourage volunteerism, increase community self-reliance and reduce the need for other resources. This might contradict a community worker's values of advocating for more equitable distribution of resources for marginalized groups. Participants say that using critical reflection to identify the conflict between their assumptions, their agency's assumptions and those of the funding body makes them better prepared for dealing with the inevitable differences in expectations.

The following critical reflection processes can be used in community work.

Critical incidents

Community workers can use critical incidents:

- in small groups for a specific purpose
- at community meetings to explore or raise general issues
- with individuals
- for themselves.

The purpose of using critical incidents can vary to suit the needs of particular individuals or communities. The aim might be to identify what community members are finding challenging about community life, and possible directions for change. Alternatively, workers could ask for examples of positive experiences of community building to identify and explore what is working well and build theory about how to operate in this community. Some examples of using a critical incident are presented below.

- *Exploring community practice:* for example, asking people on the management committee to each bring an experience of how the community handles difference, then using these to identify the underlying assumptions and values of each and what that means for how difference is perceived in the community. This could then lead to discussion about what values the committee does want to generate and how this might be done.

- *Identifying the embodied nature of the community:* asking people to come to a community meeting with examples of what are important places to them in the community and lead a critical reflection discussion on why. This starts to give a sense of the significant geography of the community (O'Looney 1998), and the importance of place and environment.

- *Exploring what people see as issues of concern in the community:* ask community members in small groups to each bring an incident that concerns them about their community, then explore what these mean for the individuals concerned and what they say about the community itself. This can also start to build more sense of community as people make connections with each other.

- *Establishing a dialogue with a disgruntled community member:* for example, by asking them to explore with you a particular incident that is bothering them.

- *Asking volunteers for an incident that is symbolic of what they value about their work.*

- *Looking positively at what the community has to offer:* by again, for example, having small community meetings where community members are asked to bring a positive experience of living in the community.

- *Deconstructing a critical incident yourself:* perhaps combining this with one of the other approaches – for example, writing the incident up as a story, writing it again from the perspective of someone else involved in the incident.

Informal/implicit use of critical reflection

In community work settings, practitioners might use a critical reflection approach as a general framework for how they go about their work. For example, one participant suggested she would be more likely in meetings with individuals or committees to slow down decision making by encouraging fuller exploration of issues. Another thought that critical reflection would prompt her to continually seek to make links between the community members individually and collectively, and broader structural issues. Another thought it would be useful to remember to check such questions as 'Whose voice is not being heard here?' and ask 'What do we do about that?'

Using journals or other tools for critical reflection

Community workers might use a journal for their own reflection. Given that many community workers work in isolation rather than as part of a team, using a critical reflection journal can provide a safe space for exploring an issue more fully.

In a community, individuals might be asked to write up an experience of their own, something that has been significant in how they perceive their role in the community. Such writings could be put together and published to give a variety of perspectives on the community's history and diversity. For communities experiencing conflict, critically reflective journalling could be used to encourage people to write initially from their own perspective, then from the perspective of someone they disagree with.

Many communities use art as a form of expression of community life (Delgado 2000). Community work practitioners could help take this further by having a critical reflection on what this means and why it is important to the community.

Asking critically reflective questions

For community workers another way to generate an atmosphere of critical reflection is to have a set of questions to consider individually or as a regular part of meetings or in developing projects. These questions can be adapted to suit the particular context and reflect the theories of critical reflection.

Community work and critical reflection: suggested questions

What is happening here?

What are the different perspectives about this incident/issue?

Whose voices are not being heard?

Where are people coming from? What are the assumptions and values being expressed?

How do the community's perceptions reflect those of the broader social structure? How are dominant discourses being expressed?

What are the variety of views about how to move forward?

Jo is based at a community health centre in a small rural community. For six months, she had been working with a small community group interested in developing more activities for young people in the community. The group seemed to be stuck; they could not agree about what to do or how to work. She suggested reviewing where they were up to using a set of critical reflection questions (see the preceding box). When the group asked themselves whether there were missing perspectives, it quickly became clear that several group members were speaking on behalf of young people in the community rather than involving them directly. The group quickly became energized as they moved to consulting more widely and directly with the young people themselves.

Critical reflection and working with individuals and/or families

What can critical reflection bring to the hugely varied field of work with individuals and families? The potential range of theories and methods for working with individuals is enormous (Compton and Galaway 1999; Payne 2005), although some theories are clearly more compatible with critical reflection than others. Participants who have trained using narrative approaches, for example, often talk about the related use of postmodern thinking (White and Denborough 1998; Morgan 2000). However, participants also connect aspects of psychoanalytic approaches (Nathan 2002) or systems theory. Others would talk about professional (Higgs and Titchen 2001) or clinical practice in general (Bond and Holland 1998) or a patient-centred approach to clinical practice (Binnie and Titchen 1999), then connect these to critical reflection.

In general, participants in critical reflection workshops generally assert that they can apply critical reflection theory and processes across the other theories and approaches they use. Such participants come from such diverse fields as:

- working with children at risk
- mental illness
- chronic and acute illness
- families with a child with disabilities
- rehabilitation for all age groups
- student counselling
- relationship issues
- loss and grief, and palliative care.

What critical reflection seems to provide is a way of understanding what is happening from a different perspective, enabling participants to stand back from their experience and see it with a new vision (Johns and Freshwater 2005). This often includes seeing the connections between individual and community issues – for example, the influence of social and geographical context on children at risk (Garbarino and Eckenrode 1997) or understanding how cultural meaning is embedded in language (Taylor and White 2000), including in other practice theories, and how this affects their practice.

More specifically, workers with individuals and families can use the following approaches.

Critical incidents

This can be a way of working with individuals and families that complements other approaches. A physiotherapist might ask a patient to tell a story about when he/she has chosen not to use an aid. In exploring the assumptions the patient has made about how and when the tool has been used it might become clear that the patient had made assumptions about the value of the tool and the need to not overuse it that reflected his underlying views about money and worth.

A family worker might ask all family members to give their perspective about a particular incident important to the family. This could quickly demonstrate that each family member has a different view about the incident that needs to be taken into account; the family might identify that they have some similar assumptions about what is important, but others that are quite different. Reflecting on this might lead to an awareness of where those assumptions have come from – past family, the community, what is socially acceptable and readiness to explore what could be different.

Depending on the situation, the worker might also contribute to such a discussion, presenting their perspective as the worker – possibly representing another, institutional view that needs to be taken into account. The assumptions and values underlying the worker's – and possibly their organization's – views are then important knowledge for the clients to use in their understanding of the situation.

Informal/implicit use of critical reflection

Some participants have talked about critical reflection becoming part of how they operate so that they are more likely to explore issues with individuals and families in a critically reflective way. What this means will vary depending on the worker and the situation. Some talk about being more aware of slowing down conversations, being more inclined to explore complexity rather than seeking quick resolution of issues. Part of this is to do with feeling more comfortable about sitting with uncertainty, waiting for individual clients to be ready to make decisions. Having an awareness of core values and a social justice perspective enables workers to resist organizational pressure to work to agreed outcomes instead of what is more fitting for a client.

Using journals or other tools for critical reflection

Not all clients find talking the most helpful way to explore issues and dilemmas. Some prefer, at least part of the time, to write, draw or use other creative means. Again these can be used with critical reflection. Individuals or families might choose to keep a journal about what new perspectives they see themselves or their family using – how able they are as a family to work on new assumptions identified with a worker.

Rather than a written journal some individuals or families might choose to explore their experience or document change in less verbal ways, as mentioned above – drawing, painting, sculpture, acting something out (Schuck and Wood 2006).

Critical reflection questions

Some possible questions that can be used when working with individuals and families are presented in the box below. Workers will need to develop questions that suit both themselves and the particular context and individuals they are working with.

Questions to aid using critical reflection with individuals and families

What happened?

What did you do?

Where were you coming from?

- What were you thinking would happen? What made you think that?
- What did you take for granted?

How did you react? What were you feeling? What were you thinking?

How did other people react?

How else could you have reacted?

How else could the other people involved react? Where might they have been coming from?

What did it mean for you? What was important to you about this?

Where are you now? What is important for you now?

Where might you go with this?

Critical reflection and policy development and implementation

This is less often thought about as an area of direct practice, but we have chosen to include it here because policy does have a clear impact on people and communities (McClelland and Smyth 2006). Policy workers often engage in processes of consultation or some kind of dialogue to see how policy might develop in relation to particular issues (Darling 2000). They may also be actively seeking change in the systems in which they work (Healy 2000). Critical reflection can or could be useful in these settings.

Some writers about policy also use critical reflection theory to explore the meaning of policy. Bacchi (1999), for example, points out that policy is generally written about as if there is only one way to look at a particular issue. By asking the question 'What is the problem represented to be?' she makes explicit that policy can be seen in many ways, and that each policy has its own implicit assumptions and values. Writers such as Ferguson *et al.* (2002) suggest that policy development needs a critical perspective: combining postmodernism with recognition of structural issues in order to develop more socially just policy.

Participants who are policy workers do value similar aspects of critical reflection to other direct service workers. They suggest that using critical reflection helps them to be conscious of how their own and cultural values are implicit in policies, and the implications of making these more explicit.

How, then, can policy workers use critical reflection?

Using critical incidents

A policy worker might ask a group he/she is interested in consulting with about a specific issue, to come to a consultation meeting with an example that they think illustrates that issue. The examples could then be deconstructed by the group to articulate and clarify what needs to be addressed by the new policy.

For example, a policy worker has been asked to assess the needs of families with children with autism in rural communities. As well as surveying families and checking health service data, she might ask a small group of families to meet with her, each bringing an incident about their experience of seeking resources for their child. The data from this are likely to produce a wealth of knowledge about accessing services, desirability of service provision, and values about how services should be provided that can strengthen the development of the policy. Alternatively, a worker might ask clients for an incident that illustrates their experience of a policy – this might in turn lead to a revision of the policy so that it is more attuned to client needs.

Informal/implicit critical reflection

Practitioners who are policy workers also say that they use the theory and processes of critical reflection so that they become an integral part of their work. What this means varies depending on the individual's approach to their work; for one it meant always asking 'What else is happening here?' What she meant by this was that she should be checking the multiple perspectives there might be on any policy, particularly ensuring that the least powerful views were also heard. Another became more conscious of thinking about how policies could be developed so that they were more likely to work in practice, partly because of her own experience of the limited value of family-friendly policies in the workplace. For her this was about making connections between individual change and structural change: the need to change culture as well as write policy.

Using journals for critical reflection

A policy worker could use a journal to critically reflect on their own practice – as a check, for example, that they were continuing to hear from a variety of perspectives about any issue. Using biographies is a powerful way to influence policy development; participants whose experience is particularly illuminating are asked to write about it using a critical reflection theory base (Chamberlyne *et al.* 2004).

Critical reflection journals might also be used to document the impact of a new or existing policy. A group of people representing different interests could be asked to note any significant incidents that relate to the policy over a period of time. Each would also document their reactions and their thoughts about underlying assumptions and values, using a critical reflection framework. This would then provide a rich source of information for policy review.

Using critically reflective questions

Again, critically reflective questions, such as those used for community work, could be used in various settings to prompt deeper understanding of policy issues. At a consultation, for example, people could be divided into small groups and presented with a scenario to consider using critical reflection questions. Alternatively, people could be asked to bring their own incident to use with these questions.

Chapter summary

This chapter has explored how to apply critical reflection to direct practice, which we have described as practice in three areas: with communities, individuals and/or families, and in policy development and implementation. We began by looking at what direct practice across these areas had in common including, for example, prompting the articulation of underlying assumptions and values, reinforcing a socially just approach to practice and seeing practice in new ways. Four ways of using critical reflection were then identified:

1. using critical incidents to encourage critical reflection with a community or family
2. using critical reflection in an informal way as part of interactions
3. using journals or other tools for critical reflection
4. using sets of critical reflection questions.

These were then applied to each area with specific examples relating to community work, work with individuals and families, and policy development.

12 Ongoing issues

What is the experience of working with critical reflection like for us as facilitators, learners, educators, professionals and, above all, as people? While this book has been primarily about our use of critical reflection as educators, we hope that our experience of the value of critical reflection for learning, and in the broader concern of being human, has infused our discussion. In this chapter, however, we focus on some of the ongoing issues that are raised, and that invite continual dialogue and reflection. Specifically we cover: issues of balancing safety and challenge; questions about the inclusivity of the process; participants who don't participate fully; balancing between the focus on self and the focus on others; the differences between critical reflection and critical practice; and the differences between critical reflection and therapy. We finish by considering briefly what critical reflection means to us as professionals and as people.

Balancing safety and challenge

This has been one of the recurring themes in our discussions of how to facilitate critical reflection, and also regarding the most conducive climate for learning. There is always a question in educational circles as to whether, and how much, anxiety actually assists learning, and at what point the balance tips (Mezirow 1991; Duke and Copp 1994). Yet critical reflection by its nature must be a challenging process: participants are being asked to confront assumptions and values they have been taking for granted. For some people, just the idea that they have not been conscious of their own assumptions and values is challenging in itself. What is challenging for a particular person varies; participants often say that they are surprised by what has challenged them in the process. What they thought would be hard is not necessarily what they find difficult in practice. For example, many participants who are used to regarding themselves as 'academic' or 'intellectual' (for instance, who were used to getting good grades in formal study programmes) are often shocked when they find reflection difficult. They are used to dealing with issues purely intellectually or through recourse to research literature or theory, and a focus on their own ideas or constructions or experience can be very challenging. For others the experience of unearthing values or assumptions that are contrary to their espoused views can be challenging. For some it is the vulnerability of sharing an incident they felt they handled badly. Others are challenged by new theoretical ideas, and others still by their reactions to being questioned. Occasionally a participant will feel particularly challenged by their reaction to someone else's example.

As emerged clearly from our evaluations of workshops, what participants do agree on is that to be able to work with these challenges, they need to be in what they regard as a 'safe' environment. One of the appealing aspects of this model of critical reflection is that participants can recognize their need to be challenged in the way they are, and this includes being challenged in a way that allows them to preserve their own sense of dignity and integrity. Because critical reflection potentially challenges people's deeper senses of themselves, participants may often feel quite vulnerable. Therefore treading the fine line between protecting the vulnerability, but allowing openness to change, is a constant and delicate balancing act.

This balancing act may be easier to deal with depending on whether the critical reflection is happening in a group or one-to-one situation, over the shorter or longer term. In a critical friendship or supervisory relationship, how to work with this develops over time – although it may need some direct and open discussion about how each participant likes to work. It is generally more of an issue in a group, especially a short-term group, where participants may have different perceptions of what is enough safety or enough challenge. What is crucial (as we have discussed extensively in Chapter 5) is establishing a climate of critical reflection before you start the process; exploring what respect means in this context, what the aim of the process is. Sometimes it is helpful to stop and talk as a group about how the process is going, how participants are feeling about the climate, what is working well and what they would like to be different. Ideally, anyone in the critical reflection process can suggest this. Asking the participant who is presenting something for discussion how they are feeling about the process in terms of safety and challenge can be useful. This reinforces a critically reflective approach – it names the issue and says that we can examine our assumptions about it specifically, as well as about how groups work. This becomes a way of reinforcing that people will have different perceptions of the same experience, and that such differences are valid and can be worked with, reflecting the theory on which critical reflection is based.

This issue is discussed more extensively in Fook and Askeland (in press).

Inclusivity

Is this type of critical reflection training appropriate for every type of learner? Do individual or social or cultural differences perhaps preclude some people from significant learning through critical reflection? Are these even appropriate questions to ask?

There are no clear and simple answers to these questions. Much writing about critical reflection seems to assume that anyone can take part in critical reflection training. Many professional courses assume that all students will be able to participate in some kind of critical reflection across many disparate fields, including teaching (Brookfield 1995), nursing (Taylor 2000), management (Reynolds and Vince 2004), and economics (Fisher 2003). Indeed it may be regarded as a mandatory part of training for some professions, like social work.

Some writers suggest the need for a scale of readiness or ability to reflect critically (Burns 1994, cited in Palmer *et al.* 1994). This assumes a certain level of self-awareness and ability to analyse your own reactions (Todd 2005). Mezirow (2000: 11) acknowledges the need for a type of personal or emotional maturity in order to engage in critical reflection. As educators we perhaps need to understand more about the role of difference in learning from critical reflection. Cranton (2000) provides some helpful discussion on the implications of different learning and cognitive styles for critical reflection. In addition, it may be that some cultural groups or genders are more comfortable with technical rationality (Sung and Leung 2006) so more time may need to be taken in preparing the educational culture for such groups. History – both personal and societal – may also affect individuals. We may need to consider the different emotional experiences of individual participants, and perhaps accept that some may experience critical reflection as potentially damaging.

One of the difficulties of this question is that those who are not interested in or able to carry out critical reflection may simply select themselves out of voluntary training programmes. With our voluntary continuing education programmes, the idea of having a briefing session and aiming for informed consent means that people can self-select (provided their organization allows them to). Some potential participants decide not to continue either after a briefing session or a beginning presentation. Unfortunately we do not have much feedback about why people choose not to participate; certainly some say 'This is not for me' – often they seem doubtful about the experiential nature of the training, uncomfortable about the range and depth of questions that might be asked, concerned about what they might have to reveal about themselves and their practice, particularly if they do not perceive their work environment to be 'safe'. We have even had some people withdraw from a programme when they discovered the identities of some of the other participants.

In many cases these doubts are overcome when participants are required to participate by their organization. (We discussed how to handle such situations in Chapter 5.) They may discover that trust builds in the group (even when they did not expect it to) and that they can establish different relationships with colleagues from within the confines of a safe microclimate. They also have some freedom to try out the process at a level of disclosure that feels comfortable for them and, in trying it out, they usually become more comfortable with further levels of disclosure.

There do, however, seem to be some people who have more difficulty 'getting it', grasping the process. In some cases, what is behind this is feeling such a strong need to present as a competent worker that they cannot acknowledge or seek new learning: they come with a closed mind. They may be interested in the process on a theoretical or intellectual level, but they are not sufficiently open to it for it to work on an experiential level with colleagues. Sometimes this comes across as being intellectually interested but not emotionally open. This limits how much they can really engage with the process. Alternatively, there are some participants who struggle to be more aware, to be able to articulate and analyse their own thoughts and feelings. It isn't that they aren't willing, but more that they have not developed, or cannot develop, the ability. It may be that these participants need more time and work to develop a capacity for reflection and self-awareness.

A related question is about the interaction between personality and critical reflection: are some personalities better suited to critical reflection or is it a matter of adapting processes to suit personalities? Cranton (2000: 190) suggests that:

> people, due to their psychological makeup, vary in how they experience the process of transformation. Our psychological preferences are a habit of mind. They filter how we see the world, make meaning out of our experiences, and determine how we reconstruct our interpretations.

She uses the Myers Briggs Type Indicator to explore how personality can affect how critical reflection is experienced.

This suggests – and is confirmed by our experience – that we need to consider the interaction between individual personality and critical reflection training. For example, the process is often quite extroverted, using a group process. This is likely to work better for extroverts who become clearer about what they think by talking than introverts who need time on their own to process. Participants need to be able to stand back from specific issues or incidents to link these with broader theory and context, and this may be easier for some personality types to do. Other formulations (Kolb 1974) suggest that there are different learning styles. Some of these learn better through reflection on experience, as opposed to more active or intellectual styles.

One of the benefits of using a group for critical reflection training is that there is likely to be a wider range of personalities that can complement each other. Indeed the participatory and group nature of the learning experience was commonly identified by our participants as being one of the key features that assisted their learning. Having a range of diverse perspectives can contribute to the group process with benefits for both individual and group learning as a whole (Kasl and Elas, cited in Mezirow 2000). One participant may articulate more clearly what another has felt, or one may be better able to connect the detail to the broader picture. It can help to articulate this as part of the process in the group; this also reinforces the valuing of diversity and multiple perspectives seen as part of the theoretical approach to critical reflection.

Participants who don't participate fully

Most participants in critical reflection training treat the process with respect: they arrive on time, engage in the process and seriously try to enact the expectations of a critically reflective climate. However, occasionally there are participants who don't, creating issues such as those described below.

People who only attend partial sessions

This has a major impact on the sense of continuity in a group. Participants usually see this as very disruptive to the critical reflection process. Critical reflection works best in a reasonably stable setting where trust can be built over time, and where there is clear commitment to the full process. Participants generally value the expectation that everyone must participate and so expect that everyone will be present for each other's presentation. This means that having people who arrive late and/or leave early, or disappear for a while in the middle, is very disruptive to the process, and communicates a disrespect or devaluing of other people's experiences.

We usually take the view that it is unacceptable to only partially attend (unless of course because of unforeseen circumstances), and we make the point that this training is unlike more conventional training, which may be offered in content sections that are relatively independent of each other. We explain that the training offered is the whole process, and the process is an integral part of the training. Our preference would normally be that if people feel they cannot commit to the whole process beforehand, they not undertake the training programme.

People who don't attend the introductory session

If a participant does not attend the introductory session should they still be able to participate in the remainder of the programme? Is it realistic to think that someone else could help them catch up? Participants vary in what they think about this: sometimes if a team is undertaking training together they will really want everyone to be involved and will find a way to make this work. At other times, participants will say at the end of the introductory session that they feel the group has already started to form and wouldn't be comfortable about someone else joining. If you have had to limit group numbers and then some people don't arrive, it is obviously frustrating because other participants could have joined the group.

It helps to have clear expectations about this, which fit the particular context. Usually we take the view that the introductory session is the most vital to the programme, as it sets out the culture and theory of the process. Indeed it is very difficult for participants to follow what is happening in subsequent sessions without this, and in our experience they often pull a group off-track because they do not understand what is involved, and the tendency is to assume it is like a case conference.

If the programme is providing initial critical reflection training, a person who does not attend the introductory session may need to wait and participate in a later programme. Certainly, this reinforces the message that the process is important. If a potential participant in something like a supervision group or critical friendship consistently doesn't arrive, again it can help to look at process issues: what is happening that means this person is not coming? Sometimes there may need to be group decisions made about how/whether a non-attending person continues in the group. If the decision is made that they are included, the group may identify ways in which they can be 'brought up to speed' with where the group is at.

Balancing the focus on self and on others

In some ways this issue will arise in any group: how to make sure each participant is heard. In critical reflection training it emerges as an issue when participants are not able to maintain a balance between their own views and reactions and paying attention to those of other participants. The incidents used are often familiar to participants – issues of power and its misuse, difficulties with supervision, conflict about clients and priorities – and can evoke strong reactions. Some participants say that they find it almost impossible not to assume that the other participants' reactions will be the same as theirs. Assertive facilitation can help – for example, stopping the process and asking participants to look at what is happening, reminding participants that the focus is on what the incident means to the participant and that there are many possible meanings. Participants say that the process often helps them get better at this balance: seeing that the participant with the incident has a different reaction to it reinforces the need to set aside their own reactions and concentrate on the other.

Critical reflection and critical practice

One of the questions we are often asked is how critical reflection and critical practice differ? In particular, because of our professional backgrounds, we are often asked what is the difference between critical reflection and critical social work. This conflation of the two seems to reflect a common misunderstanding, so it is relevant to discuss this issue here.

Both critical reflection (in our approach) and critical social work (as outlined by Fook 2002) are based on similar understandings of critical theory, namely the recognition of how socially dominant views may be internalized by individuals, who then may act against their own interests. Critical reflection, however, is primarily a method or process for unearthing the hidden operation of these views, and for enabling practice that is less socially restrictive because it does not simply pander to dominant interests. Critical reflection should be an integral part of critical social work practice, in that all critical practitioners will need to be aware of how their own practice may unwittingly support established power arrangements. While we would hope that critical reflection will automatically lead to critical practices, it is most likely that being able to act as a critical social worker involves other skills and conditions, such as political skills to mobilize resources, or skills in argument to convince funding bodies. In this sense, critical reflection is a starting point and a basis for critical practice, but it is not a substitute for the totality of activities that may be needed to bring about the desired social changes. The concept of criticality as developed by Barnett (1997) and Ford et al. (2005) is useful in conceptualizing the broader totality of mindsets and abilities that are involved in being critical and practising critically.

Critical reflection, in our approach, is essentially a process for learning about and developing professional practice. It is not a total model for practising within the many different environments of professional practitioners today. Nevertheless, without critical reflective abilities, it is hard to see how today's professionals will be able to be flexible enough to transfer and adapt relevant knowledge across changing and unpredictable environments. Critical reflection and critical practice are soulmates, not substitutes for each other.

Critical reflection and evidence-based practice

We discussed evidence-based practice and its relationship to critical reflection a little in Chapter 10. There are ongoing questions, however, about how the two approaches sit together, and whether they are mutually exclusive orientations. In our view, this question involves a limited view of both approaches. Even though it might be argued that both come from radically different epistemological bases, at heart both are concerned with accountability. The methods, of course, for enacting this, and even what constitutes accountability, may be divergent.

On a more pragmatic level, however, we would argue that they need not be mutually exclusive activities. It is possible to use critical reflection to complement aspects of evidence-based practice. This may occur in several main ways:

- using critical reflection to make the assumptions behind practice explicit, then examining the 'evidence' for these
- using critical reflection to make explicit the uncertainties of practice, in a way that allows further systematic examination
- using critical reflection to separate which assumptions are 'researchable' and therefore require evidence, and those that are based on less researchable foundations, such as fundamental value positions
- using critical reflection to distinguish between which aspects of practice are more certain, and which less so
- using critical reflection to examine the bases of research designs, methods and practices, in order to ensure relevance, and that the practice of research matches the stated intentions.

We are in fact arguing that critical reflection is an essential component of good evidence-based practice and that, put to good use, critical reflection may help ensure that research activities, designed to elicit the evidence base:

- are better focused
- do not overstep what they are able to identify
- are not substituted for other forms of thinking and information that are needed for decision making.

For further discussion of the types of evidence-based practice that we believe accord with our view, please see Webb (2001) and Fook (2004c).

Differentiating critical reflection and therapy

This is a very common issue, raised by both participants and educators. The experience of critical reflection may feel very much like therapy (partly because of its initial focus on personal experience, and often the emotional aspects of this). While, on one level, the therapeutic benefits of critical reflection are of course desirable, it is important that the two not be conflated, for several reasons.

First, some participants may feel they have been lured into critical reflection training under false pretences, and while benefiting from dealing with emotional issues, might not have chosen to participate if they had been aware that this might happen. This potentially undermines our principle of informed choice.

Second, conflating the two may mean that some vital aspects of critical reflection are misunderstood, particularly the emphasis on professional learning and knowledge-making, and the theoretical focus on the connections between the individual and their social context. If these aspects are misunderstood, the learning potential of critical reflection is very much weakened.

Third, critical reflection sessions are not primarily set up to cope with therapeutic problems. There is potential to do emotional harm without significant learning gain if the boundaries between critical reflection and therapy are not understood. So what then are the differences and similarities?

Probably the most common elements are the type of 'safe' environment that is crucial to maximize the learning from each. And of course there is great similarity between many of the skills used, particularly questioning and empathic skills.

In addition, many of the outcomes experienced may be similar, as indicated by a number of our participants. For instance, there were repeated statements by participants that indicated the following 'therapeutic' effects of participating in our critical reflection workshops:

- recognition of and support for the emotional aspects of work
- a debriefing function
- a sense of 'healing', easing trauma, and providing comfort and reassurance
- a greater sense of self-acceptance and acceptance of uncertainties
- assistance in dealing with emotional 'blocks', and helping to resolve dilemmas (either internal or in the workplace between colleagues)
- assistance in helping to incorporate and use emotions constructively in work
- restoring a sense of integrity
- as a tool for self-care in the workplace.

For an in-depth discussion of this, please refer to the full analysis of evaluation forms from our workshops, included in the online resource materials at www.openup.co.uk/fook&gardner.

Clearly, there is some commonality in some of the material focused on. Both therapy and critical reflection may use personal experience as a trigger to examine further issues. Both of course, respectively, may draw on a wealth of different material as well. For instance, critical reflection can be conducted on more 'objective' material, such as policy documents, but may still elicit personally held beliefs.

Perhaps the greatest differences lie in the respective primary aims of each. While therapy aims, presumably, to assist with perceived personally experienced problems, critical reflection starts from no such premise. Its main aim is to develop professional learning, so it may have numerous starting points. (It can be argued, of course, that reflection is more naturally triggered by experience that is perceived as discrepant (Boud *et al.* 1985).) Presumably therapy may deal with people who are emotionally fragile or in periods of personal crisis; in critical reflection, it is assumed that participants are reasonably robust and, if they are not, the focus is nonetheless on their learning, not on working through personal problems or issues. Of course this may not be as clear-cut as it sounds, as naturally some learning may involve working through problems. However, working through problems is not the main focus of critical reflection – problems are worked through only in so far as they provide learning about professional practice.

The distinction perhaps becomes clearer if we discuss it in relation to how the emotions are used.

We have discussed the role of emotions in critical reflection earlier in the book. For instance, they may be used as a trigger for learning, or as a flag to indicate what may need to be focused upon. In this sense they are used as a guide to fundamental assumptions. They are not, however, the object of the critical reflection process. This is perhaps best illustrated by an example.

In one of my more recent workshops, I [Jan] presented an incident in which I felt some anger. This feels quite normal for me, and is not something that particularly concerns me – that is, I accept that feeling angry is part of the normal workplace experience, and I did not feel that this was a remarkable aspect of my experience. This partly explains, I think, my anger (!) when one participant asked (in what I perceived to be a very patronizing 'therapeutic' type of tone) what I was going to do with the anger. Leaving aside what my assumptions about anger were/are, what made this significant for me was that I realized that her question raised for me the clear distinctions between what I believed to be therapy, and what I believed to be critical reflection. In therapy, I would have felt it legitimate to ask about the anger for its own sake, to perhaps treat it as a problematic emotion that needed to be worked on in some way. In critical reflection, I would have felt it more appropriate to focus on what my assumptions were about anger. A more appropriate question to ask would have been: 'What does anger at work mean to you?' The distinctions may seem slight, but they do potentially lead in quite disparate directions.

The meaning of critical reflection

Most of this book has been written from our perspective as educators. But what has critical reflection meant to us as human beings, as people concerned with the business of living, working, and trying to make a social contribution?

Using critical reflection has, for me (Fiona), been an enriching and humbling experience. People in workshops are constantly inspiring: being prepared to share at a deep level the frustrations and challenges of their work, as well as demonstrating their commitment to a vision based on holistic and compassionate practice. On a personal level, the process gently – or sometimes not so gently – but firmly illuminates what I need to work on in my own practice, and how often I need to hear the message to truly understand and act on it. It encourages openness and depth, an attitude of mind that stresses connectedness – between the internal and external and across our experiences as human beings sharing the dilemmas of life and practice. I particularly value seeing for myself and others the links between the personal and professional, the sense of wholeness in who we are and what we do. Critical reflection for me is both challenging and affirming, reminds me of the vision as well as the processes to achieve it.

Critical reflection has been a dominant force in my (Jan's) professional life now for about 15 years. I have designed several professional degree programs based on it as both a whole approach to learning, as well as teaching about it in its own right. First discovering the approach was exciting, what felt like a real alternative to more established approaches to education. It provided the basis for what I felt were much more innovative teaching methods. I liked the challenge of questioning my most cherished ideas about teaching, and experimenting with turning them inside out to find new ways of working. Critically reflecting with students led to much more interesting experiences as an educator. I found it both fascinating and intriguing, first on an intellectual level, and then on emotional levels as well. I have rediscovered professional practice as a source of wonderment and mystery, and am excited by the greatness buried in the mundane. I revel in the process of uncovering the grand themes of life, in its small daily incidents. Most of all perhaps I have found that the social and personal distances between me as an educator, and my students as learners, slowly disintegrate. What divides us becomes insignificant as we jointly refind the common values which put us here in the first place. And it is this reminder, of the big picture, where we fit, and of what is fundamentally important, which also allows me to constantly reconnect with what I hope is my social contribution.

References

Adams, R. (2002) Developing critical practice in social work, in R. Adams, L.A. Dominelli and M. Payne (eds) *Critical Practice in Social Work*. Houndmills, Hampshire/New York: Palgrave.

Agger, B. (1998) *Critical Social Theories*. Boulder/Oxford: Westview Press.

Argyris, C.A. and Schon, D.A. (1974) *Theory in Practice: Increasing Professional Effectiveness*. San Francisco: Jossey-Bass.

Argyris, C.A. and Schon, D.A. (1996) *Organizational Learning 11: Theory, Method and Practice*. Reading, Mass.: Addison-Wesley.

Askeland, G.A. (2003) Facilitator in Focus. Paper presented at the Joint Seminar of the International Association of Schools of Social Work Board and the Association for Social Work Education, New Zealand.

Bacchi, C. (1999) *Women, Policy and Politics; the Construction of Policy Problems*. London/Thousand Oaks, California: Sage.

Banks, S. (2001) *Ethics and Values in Social Work*. Basingstoke: Palgrave.

Banks, S. (2002) Professional values and accountabilities, in R. Adams, L.A. Dominelli and M. Payne (eds) *Critical Practice in Social Work*. Houndmills, Hampshire/New York: Palgrave.

Barnett, R. (1997) *Higher Education: A Critical Business*. Buckingham: Open University Press.

Barnett, R. (1999) Learning to work and working to learn, in D. Boud and J. Garrick (eds) *Understanding Learning at Work*. London: Routledge.

Beck, U. (1992) *Risk Society: Towards a New Modernity*. London: Sage.

Berlin, S. (1990) Dichotomous and complex thinking, *Social Service Review*, March: 46–59.

Bilson, A. (2006) Rationalities, reflection and research, in S. White, J. Fook and F. Gardner (eds) *Critical Reflection in Health and Social Care*. London: Open University Press.

Binnie, A.A. and Titchen, A. (1999) *Freedom to Practise the Development of Patient-centred Nursing*. Oxford, UK: Butterworth Heinemann.

Bishop, V. (1998) *Clinical Supervision in Practice*. Houndmills: Macmillan Press.

Bolton, G. (2001) *Reflective Practice Writing and Professional Development*. London/Thousand Oaks: Paul Chapman Publishing Ltd/Sage.

Bond, M.A. and Holland, S. (1998) *Skills of Clinical Supervision for Nurses*. Buckingham/Philadelphia: Open University Press.

Boud, D.A. and Garrick, J. (eds) (1999) *Understanding Learning at Work*. London: Routledge.

Boud, D., Cressey, P.A. and Docherty, P. (2006) *Productive Reflection at Work*. London/New York: Routledge.

Boud, D., Keogh, R. and Walker, D. (1985) *Reflection: Turning Experience into Learning*. London: Kogan Page Ltd.

Braye, S. (2000) *Participation and Involvement in Social Care*. London: Jessica Kingsley.

Brechin, A. and Sidell, M. (2000) Ways of knowing, in R. Gomm and C. Davies (eds) *Using Evidence in Health and Social Care*. London: Sage.

Brookfield, S. (1994) Tales from the dark side: a phenomenography of adult critical reflection. *International Journal of Lifelong Education*, 13: 203–16.

Brookfield, S.D. (1995) *Becoming a Critically Reflective Teacher*. San Francisco: Jossey-Bass Publishers.

Brookfield, S.D. (2000) Transformative learning as ideology critique, in J. Mezirow and associates (eds) *Learning as Transformation*. San Francisco: Jossey-Bass.

Brookfield, S.D. (2001) Unmasking power: Foucault and adult learning, *Canadian Journal for the Study of Adult Education*, 15(1): 1–23.

Brookfield, S.D. (2005) *The Power of Critical Theory: Liberating Adult Teaching and Learning*. San Francisco: Jossey-Bass (A Wiley Imprint).

Brown, A. (1994) *Groupwork*. Aldershot, UK: Arena.

Brown, A. and Bourne, I. (1995) *The Social Work Supervisor: Supervision in Community, Day Care and Residential Settings*. Buckingham/Philadelphia: Open University Press.

Burns, S. (1994) Assessing reflective learning, in A. Palmer, S.A. Burns and C. Bulman (eds) *Reflective Practice in Nursing: the Growth of the Professional Practitioner*. Oxford: Blackwell Scientific Publications.

Chamberlyne, P., Barnat, J.A. and Apitzsch, U. (2004) *Biographical Methods and Professional Practice*. Bristol, UK: The Policy Press.

Cheetham, J., Fuller, R., McIvor, G.A. and Petch, A. (1992) *Evaluating Social Work Effectiveness*. Buckingham/Philadelphia: Open University Press.

Cherry, N. (1999) *Action Research A Pathway to Action, Knowledge and Learning*. Melbourne: RMIT Publishing.

Compton, B. and Galaway, B. (1999) *Social Work Processes*. Pacific Grove, California: Brooks/Cole Publishing Co.

Cooper, A. and Darlington, Y. (2004) The discovery and loss of a compelling space: a case study in adapting to a new organizational order, in C. Huffington, D. Armstrong, W. Halton, L. Hoyle and J. Pooley (eds) *Working Below the Surface: The Emotional Life of Contemporary Organizations*. London: Karnac.

Coulshed, V. and Mullender, A. (2001) *Management in Social Work*. Houndmills, UK: Palgrave.

Cousins, J.B. and Earl, L.M. (1992) The case for participatory evaluation, *Educational Evaluation and Policy Analysis*, 14(4): 397–418.

Cranton, P. (1996) *Professional Development as Transformative Learning: New Perspectives for Teachers of Adults*. San Francisco: Jossey-Bass Publishers.

Cranton, P. (2000) Individual differences and transformative learning, in J. Mezirow and associates (eds) *Learning as Transformation*. San Francisco: Jossey Bass.

Crawford, F. (2006) Research for and as practice: educating practitioners in inquiry skills for changing cultural contexts, in S. White, J. Fook, and F. Gardner (eds) *Critical Reflection in Health and Social Care*. London: Open University Press.

Cressey, P. (2006) Collective reflection and learning, in D. Boud, B. Cressey and P. Docherty (eds) *Productive Reflection at Work*. London/New York: Routledge.

Dadds, M.A. and Hart, S. (2001) *Doing Practitioner Research Differently*. London/New York: Routledge Palmer.

Darling, R.B. (2000) *The Partnership Model in Human Services: Sociological Foundations and Practices*. New York/Boston/Dordrecht/London/Moscow: Kluwer Academic/Plenum Publishers.

Darlington, Y. and Scott, D. (2002) *Qualitative Research in Practice: Stories from the Field*. Sydney: Allen & Unwin.

D'Cruz, H., Gillingham, P. and Melendez, S. (2007) Reflexivity, its meanings and relevance for social work: a critical review of the literature, *British Journal of Social Work*, 37: 73–90.

Delgado, M. (2000) *Community Social Work Practice in an Urban Environment*. New York/Oxford: Oxford University Press.

Dewey, J. (1933) *How we Think: A Restatement of the Relation of Reflective Thinking to the Educative Process*. Boston: D.C. Heath.

Driscoll, J. (2000) *Practising Clinical Supervision*. London: Bailliere Tindall, Harcourt Publishers.

Duke, S. and Appleton, J. (2000) The use of reflection in a palliative care programme: a quantitative study of the development of reflective skills over an academic year, *Journal of Advanced Nursing*, 32(6): 1557–69.

Duke, S. and Copp, G. (1994) The personal side of reflection, in A. Palmer, S.A. Burns and C. Bulman (eds) *Reflective Practice in Nursing: The Growth of the Professional Practitioner*. Oxford: Blackwell Scientific Publications.

Ellerman, A. (1998) Can discourse analysis enable reflective social work practice? *Social Work Education*, 17(1): 35–44.

Everitt, A. and Hardiker, P. (1996) *Evaluating for Good Practice*. London: Macmillan.

Ferguson, H. (2001) Social work, individualization and life politics, *British Journal of Social Work*, 31: 41–55.

Ferguson, I., Lavalette, M.A. and Mooney, G. (2002) *Rethinking Welfare: A Critical Perspective*. London: Sage.

Fetterman, D.M. (2000) *Foundations of Empowerment Evaluation*. Thousand Oaks, California: Sage.

Finlay, L.A. and Gough, B. (2003) *Reflexivity: A Practical Guide for Researchers in Health and Social Sciences*. Aylesbury, UK: Blackwell Publishing.

Firth, R. (2005) Meeting the needs of the social care and health care workforce: can a duck sleep with a hippopotamus? *Social Work Education*, 24(8): 903–11.

Fisher, K. (2003) Demystifying critical reflection: defining criteria for assessment, *Higher Education Research and Development*, 22(3): 313–25.

Fook, J. (1993) *Radical Casework: A Theory of Practice*. Sydney: Allen & Unwin.

Fook, J. (ed.) (1996) *The reflective researcher: social workers' theories of practice research*. Sydney: Allen & Unwin.

Fook, J. (1999a) Critical reflectivity in education and practice, in B. Pease and J. Fook (eds) *Transforming Social Work Practice*. Sydney: Allen & Unwin, 195–208.

Fook, J. (1999b) Reflexivity as method, in J. Daly, A. Kellehear and E. Willis (eds) *Annual Review of Health Social Sciences*, 9: 11–20.

Fook, J. (2000) The lone crusader: constructing enemies and allies in the workplace, in L. Napier and J. Fook (eds) *Breakthroughs in Practice: Social Workers Theorise Critical Moments*. London: Whiting & Birch.

Fook, J. (2001) *Identifying Expert Social Work: Qualitative Practitioner Research*. London: Sage.

Fook, J. (2002) *Social Work Critical Theory and Practice*. London: Sage.

Fook, J. (2004a) Some considerations on the potential contributions of inter-cultural social work, *Social Work and Society* (Europe), 2(1): 83–6, http: // www.socwork.de.

Fook, J. (2004b) Towards inclusive futures, keynote address delivered at the Inclusive Futures Conference, Bendigo, April.

Fook, J. (2004c) What professionals need from research, in D. Smith (ed.) *Evidence-based Practice*. London: Jessica Kingsley, 29–46.

Fook, J. (2004d) The transformative possibilities of critical reflection, in L. Davies and P. Leonard (eds) *Scepticism/Emancipation: Social Work in a Corporate Era*. Avebury: Ashgate, 16–30.

Fook, J. (2004e) Critical reflection and organizational learning and change, in N. Gould and M. Baldwin (eds) *Social Work, Critical Reflection and the Learning Organization*. Aldershot: Ashgate.

Fook, J. (2007) Uncertainty: the defining characteristic of social work?, in K. Postle and M. Lymbery (eds) *Social Work: A Companion for Learning*. London: Sage.

Fook, J. and Askeland, G.A. (in press) Challenges of critical reflection: 'Nothing ventured, nothing gained', *Social Work Education*.

Fook, J. and Napier, L. (2000) From dilemma to breakthrough: retheorising social work, in L. Napier and J. Fook (eds) *Breakthroughs in Practice: Social Workers Theorise Critical Moments*. London: Whiting & Birch, 212–22.

Fook, J., Ryan, M. and Hawkins, L. (2000) *Professional Expertise: Practice, Theory and Education for Working in Uncertainty*. London: Whiting & Birch.

Fook, J., White, S.A. and Gardner, F. (2006) Critical reflection: a review of con-temporary literature and understandings, in S. White, J. Fook and F. Gardner (eds) *Critical Reflection in Health and Social Care*. London: Open University Press.

Ford, P., Johnson, B., Brumfit, C., Mitchell, R. and Myles, F. (2005) Practice learning and the development of students as critical practitioners. *Social Work Education*, 24(4): 391–407.

Frances, R. (1997) *Another Way of Knowing Another Way of Living: Participatory Evaluation in a Community Setting*. Melbourne: Preston Creative Living Centre.

Froggett, L. (2006) Thinking with the body: artistic perception and critical reflection, in S. White, J. Fook and F. Gardner (eds) *Critical Reflection in Health and Social Care*. London: Open University Press.

Garbarino, J. and Eckenrode, J. (1997) *Understanding Abusive Families: An Ecological Approach to Theory and Practice*. San Francisco: Jossey-Bass Publishers.

Gardner, F. (2003) Critical reflection in community-based evaluation, *Qualitative Social Work*, 2: 197–212.

Gardner, F. (2006) *Working with Human Service Organisations: Creating Connections for Practice*. Melbourne, Australia: Oxford University Press.

Gardner, F. and Nunan, C. (forthcoming) How to develop a research culture in a human services organisation: integrating research and practice with service and policy development, *Qualitative Social Work*.

Ghaye, T.A. and Lilyman, S. (2000) *Reflection: Principles and Practice for Healthcare Professionals*. Wiltshire: Mark Allen Publishing Ltd.

Gibbs, A. (2001) Social work and empowerment-based research: possibilities, process and questions, *Australian Social Work*, 54(1): 29–40.

Gibbs, J. (2002) Sink or swim: changing the story of child protection: a study of the crisis in recruitment and retention of staff in rural Victoria. PhD thesis, La Trobe University School of Social Work and Social Policy.

Giddens, A. (1991) *Modernity and Self-Identity*. Cambridge: Polity.

Giddens, A. (1992) *The Transformation of Intimacy*. Cambridge: Polity.

Gould, N. (2000) Becoming a learning organisation: a social work example, *Social Work Education*, 19: 585–96.

Gould, N. (2004) The learning organization and reflective practice – the emergence of a concept, in N.A. Gould and M. Baldwin (eds) *The Learning Organization and Reflective Practice*. Aldershot, UK: Ashgate.

Gould, N. and Baldwin, M. (eds) (2004) *The Learning Organization and Reflective Practice*. Aldershot, UK: Ashgate.

Grant, P. (2001) The power of uncertainty: reflections of pre-service literacy teachers, *Reflective Practice*, 2(1): 237–48.

Greenman, N.P. and Dieckmann, J.A. (2004) Considering criticality and culture as pivotal in transformative teacher education, *Journal of Teacher Education*, 55(3): 240–55.

Griffin, M. (2003) Using critical incidents to promote and assess reflective thinking in pre-service teachers, *Reflective Practice*, 4(2): 207–20.

Habermas, J. (1984) *The Theory of Communicative Action, Vol. 1*. Boston: Beacon Press.

Habermas, J. (1987) *The Theory of Communicative Action, Vol. 2*. Boston: Beacon Press.

Hamlin, K.D. (2004) Beginning the journey: supporting reflection in early field experiences, *Reflective Practice*, 5(2): 167–79.

Hargreaves, J. (2004) So how do you feel about that? Assessing reflective practice, *Nurse Education Today*, 24: 196–201.

Hatton, N. and Smith, P. (1995) Reflection in teacher education: toward definition and implementation, *Teaching and Teacher Education*, 11: 33–49.

Hawken, D. and Worrall, J.W. (2002) Reciprocal mentoring supervision. Partners in learning: a personal perspective, in M.A. McMahon and W. Patton (eds) *Supervision in the Helping Professions*. Frenchs Forest: Prentice Hall/Pearson Education.

Hawkins, P. and Shohet, R. (1989) *Supervision in the Helping Professions*. Milton Keynes: Open University Press.

Hawkins, P. and Shohet, R. (2000) *Supervision in the Helping Professions*. New York: Open University Press.

Healy, K. (2000) *Social Work Practices: Contemporary Perspectives on Change*. London: Sage.

Heron, J. (1996) *Co-operative Inquiry Research into the Human Condition*. London: Sage.

Hertz, R. (ed.) (1997) *Reflexivity and Voice*. Thousand Oaks, California: Sage Publications.

Higgs, J. and Titchen, A. (eds) (2001) *Professional Practice in Health, Education and the Creative Arts*. Oxford: Blackwell Science.

Ife, J. (2002) *Community Development*. French's Forest, NSW: Longman.

Issit, M. (1999) Towards the development of anti-oppressive reflective practice: the challenge for multi-disciplinary working, *Journal of Practice Teaching*, 2(2): 21–36.

Issit, M. (2000) Critical professionals and reflective practice, in J. Batsleer and B. Humphries (eds) *Welfare, Exclusion and Political Agency*. London/New York: Routledge.

Ixer, G. (1999) There's no such thing as reflection, *British Journal of Social Work*, 29: 513–27.

Ixer, G. (2000) Assessing reflective practice: new research findings, *Journal of Practice Teaching in Health and Social Work*, 23(3): 19–27.

Johns, C. (2002) *Guided Reflection*. Oxford: Blackwell Science.

Johns, C. (2005) Balancing the minds, *Reflective Practice*, 6(1), February: 67–84.

Johns, C.A. and Freshwater, D. (2005) *Transforming Nursing Through Reflective Practice*. Oxford: Blackwell Publishing.

Jones, C. (2001) Voices from the front line: state social workers and New Labour, *British Journal of Social Work*, 31: 547–62.

Jones, M. (2001) Hope and despair on the front line: observations on integrity and change in the human services, *International Social Work*, 43(3): 365–80.

Kadushin, A. (1985) *Supervision in Social Work*. New York: Columbia University Press.

Kellehear, A. (2005) *Compassionate Cities: Public Health and End-of-life Care*. London/New York: Routledge Taylor & Francis Group.

Kemmis, S. (2001) Exploring the relevance of critical theory for action research: emancipatory action research in the footsteps of Jurgen Habermas, in P.A. Reason and H. Bradbury (eds) *Handbook of Action Research: Participative Inquiry and Practice*. London/Thousand Oaks/New Delhi: Sage.

Knights, S. (1985) Reflection and learning: the importance of a listener, in D. Boud, R. Keogh and D. Walker (eds) *Reflection: Turning Experience into Learning*. London: Kogan Page Ltd.

Kolb, D.A. (1974) *Experiential Learning*. Englewood Cliffs, NJ: Prentice-Hall.

Kondrat, M.E. (1999) Who is the self in self-aware: professional self-awareness from a critical theory perspective, *Social Service Review*, 3: 451–77.

Lahad, M. (2000) *Creative Supervision*. London: Jessica Kingsley.

Lane, M.A. (1999) Community development and a postmodernism of resistance, in B. Pease and J. Fook Transforming Social Work Practice. St Leonards, Australia: Allen & Unwin.

Lane, M.A. and Henry, K. (2001) Community development, crime and violence: a case study, *Community Development Journal*, Oxford University Press.

Ledwith, M. (2001) Community work as critical pedagogy: re-envisioning Freire and Gramsci, *Community Development Journal*, Oxford University Press.

Lee, S.K.F. and Loughran, J. (2000) Facilitating pre-service teacher's reflection through a school based teaching program, *Reflective Practice*, 1(1): 69–89.

Lehmann, J. (2003) *The Harveys and Other Stories*. Bendigo: St Lukes Innovative Resources.

Lehmann, J. (2006) Telling stories . . . and the pursuit of critical reflection, in S. White, J. Fook and F. Gardner (eds) *Critical Reflection in Health and Social Care*. London: Oxford University Press.

Lowe, P. and Kerr, C. (1998) Learning by reflection: the effect on educational outcomes, *Journal of Advanced Nursing*, 27(5): 1030–3.

Maich, N.M., Brown, B. and Royle, J. (2000) 'Becoming' through reflection and professional portfolios: the voice of growth in nurses, *Reflective Practice*, 1(3): 309–24.

Marcus, G.E. (1994) What comes just after 'post'? The case of ethnography, in M. Denzin and Y. Lincoln (eds) *Handbook of Qualitative Research*. London: Sage.

Mason, J. (2002) *Researching Your Own Practice: The Discipline of Noticing*. London: Routledge/Faber.

McClelland, A. and Smyth, P. (2006) *Social Policy in Australia: Understanding for Action*. Melbourne: Oxford University Press.

McDrury, J.A. and Alterio, M. (2002) *Learning Through Storytelling*. Palmerston North, New Zealand: Dunmore Press.

McKee, M. (2003) Excavating our frames of mind, *Social Work*, 48(3): 401–8.

McMahon, L. and Ward, A. (2001) *Helping Families in Family Centres: Working at Therapeutic Practice*. London/Philadelphia: Jessica Kingsley.

Mezirow, J. (1991) *Transformative Dimensions of Adult Learning*. San Francisco: Jossey-Bass Publishers.

Mezirow, J. and associates (1990) *Fostering Critical Reflection in Adulthood*. San Francisco: Jossey-Bass.

Mezirow, J. and associates (2000) *Learning as Transformation: Critical Perspectives on a Theory in Progress*. San Francisco: Jossey-Bass.

Moon, J. (1999) *Reflection in Learning and Professional Development: Theory and Practice*. London: Kogan Page.

Moon, J. (2004) *A Handbook of Reflective and Experiential Learning: Theory and Practice*. London/New York: Routledge Falmer.

Morgan, S. (2000) *What is Narrative Therapy?* Adelaide, Australia: Dulwich Centre Publications.

Napier, L. and Fook, J. (eds) (2000) *Breakthroughs in Practice: Theorising Critical Moments in Social Work*. London: Whiting & Birch.

Nathan, J. (2002) Psychoanalytic Theory, in M. Davies (ed.) *The Blackwell Companion to Social Work*, 2nd edn. Oxford: Blackwell Publishing.

Northen, H. and Kurland, R. (2001) *Social Work with Groups*, 3rd edn. New York: Columbia University Press.

O'Looney, J. (1998) Mapping communities: place-based stories and participatory planning, *Journal of the Community: Development Society*, 29(2): 201–36.

Ooijen, E.V. (2000) *Clinical Supervision: A Practical Approach*. Edinburgh/London/ Sydney: Churchill Livingstone.

Owen, J.M.A. and Rogers, P.J. (1999) *Program Evaluation Forms and Approaches*. Sydney: Allen & Unwin.

Page, S. and Wosket, V. (2001) *Supervising the Counsellor*. East Sussex: Brunner Routledge/Taylor & Francis.

Palmer, A., Burns, S.A. and Bulman, C. (eds) (1994) *Reflective Practice in Nursing: The Growth of the Professional Practitioner*. Oxford: Blackwell Scientific Publications.

Parton, N. (1994) Problematics of government, (post)modernity and social work, *British Journal of Social Work*, 24: 9–32.

Payne, M. (1997) *Modern Social Work Theory*, 1st edn. London: Palgrave.

Payne, M. (2000) *Narrative Therapy: An Introduction for Counsellors*. London: Sage.

Payne, M. (2005) *Modern Social Work Theory*, 2nd edn. Houndmills, Basingstoke/ London: Macmillan.

Pease, B. and Fook, J. (eds) (1999) *Transforming Social Work Practice*. Sydney: Allen & Unwin/London: Routledge.

Pedro, J. (2005) Reflection in teacher education: exploring pre-service teachers' meanings of reflective practice, *Reflective Practice*, 6(1): 49–66.

Pellizoni, L. (2003) Knowledge, uncertainty and the transformation of the public sphere, *European Journal of Social Theory*, 6: 327–55.

Platzer, H., Blake, D. and Ashford, D. (2000) Barriers to learning from reflection: a study of the use of groupwork with post registration nurses, *Journal of Advanced Nursing*, 31(5): 1001–8.

Preskill, H. and Torres, R. (1999) Building capacity for organizational learning through evaluative inquiry, *Evaluation*, 5(1), 42–60.

Reason, P.A. and Bradbury, H. (2001) *Handbook of Action Research: Participative Inquiry and Practice*. London/Thousand Oaks/New Delhi: Sage.

Redmond, B. (2004) *Reflection in Action*. Aldershot, UK: Ashgate.

Reynolds, M.A. and Vince, R. (eds) (2004) *Organizing Reflection*. Aldershot, UK: Ashgate.

Riemann, G. (2006) Ethnographers of their own affairs, in S. White, J. Fook and F. Gardner (eds) *Critical Reflection and Professional Practice*. London: Open University Press.

Rolfe, G. (2000) *Research, Truth and Authority: Postmodern Perspectives on Nursing*. Houndmills, Basingstoke: Macmillan Press.

Rolfe, G. (2005) Evidence, memory and truth: towards a deconstructive validation of reflective practice, in C. Johns and D. Freshwater (eds) *Transforming Nursing Through Reflective Practice*. Oxford: Blackwell Publishing.

Rolfe, G., Freshwater, D.A. and Jasper, M. (2001) *Critical Reflection for Nursing and the Helping Professions: A User's Guide*. Basingstoke: Palgrave.

Rosaldo, R. (1993) *Culture and Truth*. London: Beacon Press.

Rose, M. and Best, D. (eds) (2005) *Transforming Practice Through Clinical Education, Professional Supervision, and Mentoring*. Edinburgh/New York: Churchill Livingstone/Elsevier.

Rossiter, A. (2005) Discourse analysis in critical social work: from apology to question, *Critical Social Work*, 6(1).

Royse, D., Thyer, Br., Padgett, D. and Logan, T. (2006) *Program Evaluation: An Introduction* 3rd edn. Belmont, CA: Brooks/Cole.

Ruch, G. (2002) From triangle to spiral: reflective practice in social work education, practice and research, *Social Work Education*, 21(2): 199–216.

Schon, D.A. (1983) *The Reflective Practitioner: How Professionals Think in Action*. USA: Basic Books.

Schon, D.A. (1987) *Educating the Critically Reflective Practitioner: Toward a New Design for Teaching and Learning in the Professions*. San Francisco: Jossey-Bass.

Schon, D.A. (1995) Reflective inquiry in social work practice, in P.M. Hess and E.J. Mullen (eds) *Practitioner–Researcher Relationships*. Washington, DC: NASW Press.

Schuck, C. and Wood, J. (2006) Playing, reflecting, and reality, *Journal of Holistic Healthcare*, British Holistic Medical Association.

Senge, P.M. (1990) *The Fifth Discipline: The Art and Practice of the Learning Organization*. New York: Doubleday Currency.

Shaw, I. (2004) Evaluation for a learning organization?, in N. Gould and M. Baldwin (eds) *The Learning Organization and Reflective Practice*. Aldershot, UK: Ashgate.

Smale, G., Tuson, G.A. and Statham, D. (2000) *Social Work and Social Problems – working towards social inclusion and social change*. Houndmills, Basingstoke: Palgrave.

Steier, F. (ed.) (1991) *Research and Reflexivity*. London: Sage.

Stringer, E. and Dwyer, R. (2005) *Action Research in Human Services*. Upper Saddle River, New Jersey: Pearson Merill Prentice-Hall.

Stuart, C. and Whitmore, E. (2006) Using reflexivity in a research methods course: bridging the gap between research and practice, in S. White, J. Fook. and F. Gardner (eds) *Critical Reflection in Health and Social Care*. London: Open University Press.

Sung, P. and Leung, A. (2006) Reflections on building a reflective practice community in China, in S. White, J. Fook and F. Gardner (eds) *Critical Reflection in Health and Social Care*. Maidenhead: Open University Press.

Tannen, D. (1998) *The Argument Culture*. New York: Random House.

Taylor, B.J. (2000) *Reflective Practice: A Guide for Nurses and Midwives*. Sydney: Allen & Unwin.

Taylor, C.A. and White, S. (2000) *Practising Reflexivity in Health and Welfare: Making Knowledge*. Buckingham/Philadelphia: Open University Press.

Taylor, I. (1997) *Developing Learning in Professional Education: Partnerships for Practice*. Buckingham: SRHE and Open University Press.

Thorpe, K. (2004) Reflective learning journals: from concept to practice, *Reflective Practice*, 5(3): 327–43.

Todd, G. (2005) Reflective practice and Socratic dialogue, in C. Johns and D. Freshwater (eds) *Transforming Nursing Through Reflective Practice*. Oxford: Blackwell Publishing.

Tosey, P. (2003) The learning organisation, in P. Jarvis, J. Holford and C. Griffin (eds) *The Theory and Practice of Learning*. London and Stirling: Kogan Page.

Tsang, A.K.T. (2000) Bridging the gap between clinical practice and research: an integrated practice-oriented model, *Journal of Social Service Research*, 26(4): 69–90.

Tsang, A.K.T. (2003) Journaling from internship to practice teaching, *Reflective Practice*, 4(2): 221–40.

Van Woerkem, M. (2004) The concept of critical reflection and its implications for human resource development, *Advances in Developing Human Resources*, 6(2): 178–92.

Van Woerkem, M., Nijhof, W.J. and Neuwenhuls, L.F.M. (2002) Critical reflective working behaviour: a survey research, *Journal of European Industrial Thinking*, 26(8/9): 375–83.

Wadsworth, Y. (1998) 'Coming to the table': some conditions for achieving consumer-focused evaluation of human services by service providers and service users, *Evaluation Journal of Australasia*, 10: 11–29.

Webb, S. (2001) Some considerations on the validity of evidence-based practice in social work, *British Journal of Social Work*, 31(1): 57–79.

Webster, J.A. and Osborne, S. (2005) *Using the Right Type of Evidence to Answer Clinical Questions: Evidence for Nursing Practice*. Marrickville, NSW: Churchill Livingstone.

Weedon, C. (1987) *Feminist Practice and Poststructuralist Theory*. Oxford: Basil Blackwell.

Whipp, J. (2003) Scaffolding critical reflection in online discussions, *Journal of Teacher Education*, 54(4): 321–33.

White, C.A. and Denborough, D. (1998) *Introducing Narrative Therapy*. Adelaide: Dulwich Centre Publications.

White, S. (2002) Accomplishing the case in paediatrics and child health: medicine and morality in inter-professional talk, *Sociology of Health and Illness*, 24(4): 409–35.

White, S. (2006) Unsettling reflections: the reflexive practitioner as 'trickster' in interprofessional work, in S. White, J. Fook and F. Gardner (eds) *Critical Reflection in Health and Social Care*. Maidenhead: Open University Press.

White, S.A. and Stancombe, J. (2003) *Clinical Judgement in the Health and Welfare Professions: Extending the Evidence Base*. Maidenhead: Open University Press.

Winstanley, J.A. and White, E. (2002) *Clinical Supervision: Models, Measures and Best Practice*. Greenacres, South Australia: Australian and New Zealand College of Mental Health Nurses Inc.

Winter, R. (1987) *Action-Research and the Nature of Social Inquiry: Professional Innovation and Educational Work*. Aldershot: Avebury Gower Publishing Company.

Winter, R. and Munn-Giddings, C. (2001) *A Handbook for Action Research in Health and Social Care*. London/New York: Routledge.

Wong, M., Kember, D., Wong, F. and Loke, A. (2001) The affective dimension of reflection, in D. Kember (ed.) *Reflective Teaching and Learning in the Health Professions*. Oxford: Blackwell Science.

Wood, J. (2003) Creative supervision, *The Homoeopath*, 91, November: 28–30.

Yip, K.S. (2006) Reflectivity in social work practice with clients in mental health-illness, *International Social Work*, 49(3): 245–55.

Index